A Practical Workbook for the D<u>e</u>press<u>e</u>d Christian

A Practical Workbook

for the
Depressed
Christian

Dr. John Lockley

WORD BOOKS

WORD PUBLISHING
Milton Keynes, England

WORD AUSTRALIA
Nunawading, Victoria, Australia

WORD ENTERAINMENT LTD
Vancouver, B.C., Canada

STRUIK CHRISTIAN BOOKS (PTY) LTD
Cape Town, South Africa

CAMPUS CRUSADE BOOK (ASIA) LTD
Singapore

CHRISTIAN MARKETING NEW ZEALAND LTD
Hastings, New Zealand

JENSCO LTD
Hong Kong

SALVATION BOOK CENTRE
Malaysia

1991

A PRACTICAL WORKBOOK FOR THE
DEPRESSED CHRISTIAN

© 1991 Dr John Lockley

Published by Word Publishing, 1991 a division of Word
Entertainment Ltd

ISBN 0-85009-237-X (Australia 1-86258-128-2)

Typesetting by Dataserve Associates, Milton Keynes.
Reproduced, printed and bound in Great Britain for Word Pubishing Lt
by Cox & Wyman Ltd, Reading, Berkshire

94 / 10 9 8 7 6 5 4

ACKNOWLEDGEMENTS

To Rev. Stephen Hough, Nurse Tutor Trish Lancaster, Sister Hilary Maunders, Mr. Bernard Palmer and Rev. Ryder Rogers for their comments, help and constructive criticisms during the preparation of this book.

To Tricia Massey, my secretary, for whom it was written in the first place, and who has loyally put up with rewriting each chapter ten times at least . . .

To all those who helped me through my own depression. Without it, and without them, this book could not have been written.

And to God, who puts up with me . . . all the time!

Note

I do wish there were a single word in the English language that meant 'either he or she' — its absence makes concise writing difficult! I've tried to use 'he' and 'she' equally throughout the book — they are intended to be interchangeable.

CONTENTS

Part 4   Helping and Healing

HOW TO USE THIS BOOK

This is a book that you can use in several ways. It's quite long, because there's a lot to discuss. However, not everyone has the same type of depression, so you may find it helpful to pick and choose which chapters you read. I've tried to make each chapter self-contained, at the expense of a certain amount of repetition over the book as a whole.

1. **If you're a depressed Christian** – start by reading the first four chapters, to give you a rough idea of what depression is. Then read any other chapters whose titles seem relevant to you. Do look particularly at those on Mental Energy, The Spiritual Gymnasium and Guilt, because these form the core of this book.

   Most of the chapters have an exercise at the end: even if you don't read the chapter itself, you'll find it helpful to do the exercises. However, if you take an exercise in isolation, it may seem a bit strange, and you may need to read the chapter it relates to, in order to understand what the exercise is trying to achieve.

2. **When you're depressed it isn't easy to concentrate.** If you have problems like this, it may be a help to get someone else to read the book, chapter by chapter, and then talk with you about those bits that seem relevant.

3. **If you are reading it as a textbook for Christian leaders and counsellors:** start at the front and read through to the end!

PART 1

SOME BASICS

1

INTRODUCTION

Some years ago, one of my friends who is a Christian doctor observed that Mrs. X would have greater problems in dealing with her depression *just because she was a Christian*. Her faith, instead of being a help, would become a hindrance.

He was right. But why should this happen? With an all-powerful loving God to help us, why should Christians find anxiety and depression such a problem?

Christians often cope very badly with depression. Some of this is due to guilt – the feeling that "real Christians don't get depressed". Sometimes it's fear of the truth about ourselves – we feel that we are unacceptable as we are, even as Christians. And our Christian friends may inadvertently make things worse through what they do and say.

So where is God in all this? Why should Christians get depressed? Why do they find depression so difficult to deal with when they have a loving God on their side? And why does the church so often cause extra problems?

I hope that some of the answers will be found in this book. It has been written specifically to give practical advice to the depressed Christian. If you work through the book *slowly,* carrying out the exercises at the end of each chapter, you will learn at first hand some of the principles involved in getting rid of anxiety and depression.

Be warned! Some of the exercises are rather strange. They are all recommended for very good Christian reasons, but don't worry if some of them seem odd – all will be explained eventually! Equally, don't expect to get better by carrying out each exercise just the once – they aren't like that. Each exercise contains a principle to be carried through repeatedly into your normal life. In any case depression doesn't go away in just a day or two – it may take many weeks or months to lift.

A word about the function of the church in all this. Some churches are wonderfully supportive in dealing with depression. Others are not – and as a result can make life much worse for the depressed Christian. I've tried to indicate what can go wrong and why. Please don't assume that, because things can (and do) go wrong, the church is useless – far from it. The church, *working correctly,* provides the best possible support for *anyone* with depression. Unfortunately, many churches don't understand the real nature of depression and as a result can make life harder, not easier, for the sufferer.

Finally, I hope this book will be of help to three quite different types of people – depressed Christians; their families and friends; and fellow church members.   The more that Christians understand depression, the more effective they will be in helping themselves – and others – who may be suffering from it.

★   ★   ★

Being depressed is bad enough in itself, but being a depressed Christian is worse. And being a depressed Christian in a church full of people who do not understand depression is like a little taste of hell.

A depressed Christian has a double burden.   Not only is he depressed but he also feels guilty because, as a Christian, he feels he is supposed to be full of joy. Joy is one of the fruits of the Spirit. So what's wrong with your spiritual life if there's no joy?

Not only are you facing your own problems, but you also have to deal with criticism from your Christian and non-Christian friends. Your non-Christian friends will be saying (probably out loud), "I thought you were supposed to lose your worries when you became a Christian." Your Christian friends will be muttering things about unconfessed sin, are you truly a Christian, they can't put their trust in you because of your mental state, and what sort of a witness are you giving anyway?

 The sad thing is that the guilt that you feel is totally undeserved. Yet this guilty feeling is probably harder to deal with than the depression itself: for a start, it makes you doubt the validity of your Christian life and experience. Then you start asking yourself whether you really were a Christian in the first place. Maybe you weren't, (you think) and God is angry with you. On this basis, the treatment ought to be to pray harder, read the Bible more, confess more, be *really* penitent for your sins.

So you try it – and it doesn't work. You try harder – and it's like banging your head on a brick wall – nice when you stop. So you feel even worse. Maybe God is really angry with you for being so stupid as not to get things right. Or maybe your name isn't on the list of those who are predestined to be Christians, so no matter how hard you try you can *never* be a Christian, no matter what you confess, do or say.

Alternatively, maybe you think you've committed the unforgivable sin.

Whatever it is you are feeling, *stop*. None of it is correct, and you're trying to change the wrong things. Part of the problem is that you are exhausting yourself trying to change things that seem to be immutable: and they seem immutable mainly because you are attacking them from the wrong direction.

Do stop *trying* – for a bit, anyway. Read to the end of this chapter, then go away and think about it. Don't do anything more. Don't *try* to get better. The harder you try, the worse it is likely to get.

★   ★   ★

Man has physical, mental and spiritual aspects. Don't make the mistake of lumping together the spiritual and the mental and thinking they are the same thing, because they are not identical. Most depressions have physical or mental causes – it is seldom that a spiritual cause is the problem. Yet many Christians assume that depression is entirely spiritual in nature, and try to treat it by spiritual means alone. It doesn't work – it *can't* work, because it's addressing the problem from the wrong angle. Do you think a Christian is spiritually at fault if he goes down with mumps?   Nor should you assume that depression only has a spiritual cause. In fact muddling up the spiritual and the mental creates a lot of unnecessary problems for Christians when thinking about depression.

For most depressed Christians, the depression is not caused by their spiritual state. On the other hand, depression will certainly have a knock-on effect on your spiritual life. (Get it right – there is often an effect *from* the depression *onto* the spiritual, seldom the other way round.) So stop feeling guilty: it's almost certainly not your spiritual life that's the cause.   On the other hand, your spiritual life will be taking a bashing from the depression, so I want to start by addressing your spiritual state, not because it's bad, but because it's needy.

Relax! You are a Christian. You therefore have the kindest, most loving, most caring, most sensitive, most trustworthy Friend on your side. He really is there – and He's not going to let go of you! I don't usually like quoting *isolated* verses of Scripture to depressed people. I'd rather quote the overall meaning of a passage instead.[1] But there is one verse that should be engraved upon the heart of every depressed Christian: "Christ died for us while we were still sinners."

Look at it again. "While we were still sinners . . ." – *you* were once in that situation as an unbeliever and Jesus was quite prepared to die for you, because He loved you *as you were* at that time – an unbelieving sinner. Now you are a Christian. Do you think God loves you any the less because of your depression?   Do you think that you are

---

[1] It's all too easy for depressed Christians, *as a symptom of their disease*, to read into Bible passages things that are not there, or get parts of verses totally out of proportion; and because it's Scripture they think it *must* be true for them. So I'd rather just quote the underlying principle, to give the depressed reader an overview of what the passage says without getting bogged down in details. Hence, most times I have quoted from the Bible I have deliberately used paraphrases to give the meaning without the complications. If you want to know more about why this is helpful, read Chapters 22 and 26.

somehow *worse* than your original non-Christian state because of the way you feel? If Jesus was prepared to go to the lengths He did to save people who hated Him, then how much more can you trust Him now that you are on His side and He on yours?

God loves you *now,* as you are. He does *not* love you for what you could become, nor for what you might have been, but *as you are, now*. He loves you unconditionally – He does not insist upon your prayers, your praise, your time, your money, your attention, your Bible study, or even your thoughts as a prior condition before He is prepared to love you. He loves you *as you are*.

Yes, of course He looks forward to the day when you will be happier, when you will feel closer to Him, when you will feel that your prayers are 'getting through', when you *want* to pray, read your Bible or do any of the myriad things in which Christians usually take part. But that day may well be some time yet, and God has His own good reasons for allowing your depression. Meanwhile He loves you unconditionally, *whether you are aware of it or not*.

In later chapters we will see how depression can be a gymnasium where you can learn to exercise your spiritual muscles. Depression is often God's training ground in sensitivity, so don't think that you are in some way inferior to other Christians if He is allowing a depression to happen to you, any more than a man who has spent three hours weight-training should feel that he is weaker than his fellow men simply because he has no energy left at all after his workout! If God is allowing a depression to happen to you then *you may well need to go through this phase before He can use you as He wants to*. (You do *want* to be of use to Him, don't you?..... I thought so....) If He had said, "Go out and preach....", you'd have gone. If He'd said, "I want you to be a missionary", you'd have gone (possibly reluctantly, depending upon your own hopes and desires!). But because He has said, "Sit there and be depressed for a bit, it will teach you some important lessons", you don't feel that it is God calling you at all... *do you?*

Do you remember Naaman, who wanted to be cured of his leprosy? (See 2 Kings 5.) If he had been asked to do something glorious he would have been happy. Because he was asked to bathe in the murky old Jordan he wasn't so keen – yet this was God's plan for him, and it cured him. God has better plans for us than we have for ourselves – unfortunately, as we can't see into the future, we don't always appreciate just *why* God's plans are better. With hindsight it's somewhat easier!

However strange it may seem to you, *God wants you to go through this depression* – so look at it positively, not negatively. What does He want you to learn from it? What can you gain from going through it?

When you begin to think in this fashion your guilt feelings start to drop away. You can begin to understand that what is happening is part of God's plan for you – and *so your depression is not a punishment from God*. You are actually where God wants you to be, even if it is emotionally painful. To put it another way, if God wants you to go through this it would be wrong for you to avoid it, wouldn't it?

At this stage it is not wise to start asking, "Why should God want me to go through this?" For a start, you haven't necessarily got the emotional strength nor stability to see the answer; and in any case, it's often only on looking back after a number of years that you can begin to see the reason why. Those who do best out of a troublesome time are the ones who say, "OK, Lord, what do you want me to do with it?", whereas those who say, "Why, Lord? Why *me?*" tend not to progress as well, presumably because they are more self-orientated, thinking why should it happen to good old *them*. On the other hand, those who accepted the situation were accepting the sovereignty of God, acknowledging that He knew what was going to be the best for them.

So cut out the whys and the wherefores and the doubts about whether God is actually there because He doesn't seem to be answering your prayers. Stop the continual re-reviewing of your own personal failings. You may have done things that have contributed towards your depression, but don't think of your depression as a punishment from God. Forget the questions: we will sort out the answers later. Just concentrate on this – God loves *you, now, as you are, unconditionally*. You do not have to earn His love, *and your depression is not the result of His love being taken away from you*.

God loves you as you are, unconditionally. He loved you when you were a sinner, in rebellion against Him. *How can He possibly love you less now that you are a Christian, however shallow you feel your faith to be at the moment?*

So relax. You are where God wants you to be. You have some lessons to learn – about yourself, about others, about God. The lesson you need to learn right now is:

> *God loves you, as you are, **unconditionally**.*

When you are tempted to despair go back to this chapter and read it again.

EXERCISE

Some people use their quiet time and their prayers as a sort of Christian talisman, with the idea that if they don't do them things will go wrong.

God doesn't work like this. He will always be with you, whatever happens, whether you are thinking of Him or not. Even if you forget about Him, He will *never* forget about you.

Unfortunately, Christians who are depressed often get obsessional and fearful, frightening themselves into thinking that if they stop being 'good' Christians, God will take it out on them.

So let's start off with a bit of trusting, shall we? Don't read your Bible tonight, or pray, unless you *really* want to.   You don't 'need the points'.   Your relationship with God doesn't depend upon your being 'good', but upon Him *always* being gracious. So relax into bed and remind yourself that God loves you *as you are*.

Goodnight!

DEPRESSED *CHRISTIANS?*

2

Some people think, quite wrongly, that if you are a Christian you shouldn't be depressed. Others go even further and say categorically that for a Christian to be depressed is a denial of his beliefs. But they are *wrong*. Being a Christian does not guarantee immunity from depression, and being depressed certainly doesn't mean that your beliefs are rendered invalid.

However, it is an easy mistake to make, and when you're depressed and oversensitive it is easy to accept the criticism and feel that to be depressed is sinful and a denial of your beliefs.

I will say it again – people who think like this are *wrong*. If they were correct then what was the point of Jesus' words in the Sermon on the Mount?

"Blessings on those who know that they are spiritually poor – the Kingdom of Heaven belongs to them".

"Blessings on those who mourn – God will comfort them."

Now the Sermon on the Mount was spoken *to Jesus' followers* – not to the world generally. You don't say things like these to happy Christians who haven't a care in the world! These are words for the broken, for the cut-up, for those who are crying inside (if not outwardly). Jesus is saying to the Christian, "No matter how poor you feel yourself to be, no matter how wretched and dejected and depressed you are, don't feel alienated from Me – I will bless you through it all."

There are no conditions attached. He doesn't say, "Go away and do better – exert more faith, believe more, trust more." Instead His response is, "I love you and bless you *now*."

It is very easy to think that because somebody is low emotionally, their faith is in some way at fault. Sometimes it is – but it doesn't have to be, as we will see in later chapters. You need to understand that God is on your side, and loves you dearly whatever you think about yourself – whoever you are, whatever you've done, or whatever you've failed to do: you are the apple of His eye whether you realise it or not.

But shouldn't being in contact with the omnipotent God who made the universe free you from emotional problems, and fill you with an overwhelming and overflowing joy in the happiness of your position? After all, there's the promise of everlasting life, and the knowledge of His power and guidance to assist you in your earthly life. Shouldn't you expect to be free of emotional problems? Won't God make sure you're freed from all your worries?

Well actually, no, He won't. And a little thought will enable you to realise why. Firstly, if becoming a Christian guaranteed instant happiness and freedom from problems and pain, then nobody would need to live by faith, because there would be proof around for all to see. Everybody would want to become a Christian for all the wrong reasons – selfish ones!

Secondly, God is interested in sorting you out *permanently*! If you think of your depression as being a carry-over of problems from the past, you will have quite a good appreciation of what is going on. Think of it, if you will, as being unwanted luggage that you have to carry around – a legacy from the past which is weighing you down, and which hasn't yet been shed. It's rather like the problems which may face someone who has sprained his ankle particularly badly – so much so that the slightest tweak or slip on a cobbled street and the ankle gives way again. The legacy from the past of the injured ankle may well affect what happens in the future, rendering him vulnerable to injuries that would hardly trouble anyone else.

Exactly the same is true of depression. We may be saved to everlasting spiritual life, but we still have the same genetic make-up, and we still carry with us memories and upsets from the whole of our past life. Conversion does not change our genes, nor alter what has gone before. After conversion we can begin to change our reactions to what has happened in the past, and alter the way we react to things in the present, but it doesn't all happen at once. There may be a lot to undo and rework, and it may well be too difficult and/or emotionally painful to do it all at once.

Christians have to seek out, understand, and work through their own baggage. For example, what effect do you think it will have on a new Christian's idea of God as Father when her own father abused her? How does a Christian view God when his earthly father never praised him no matter how hard he tried? How do you teach a woman about the love of God when she was abandoned by her parents and grew up in an orphanage?

In other words, how far does your own personal baggage, which you have seen with your own eyes, and experienced in your own life, affect the way in which you view God, whom you have not seen? Any problems that you have in your earthly relationships will be reflected in your relationship with God. If a person has difficulty forming stable and secure relationships on earth, how can we possibly expect him to form stable and secure relationships of faith with God?

This baggage we carry from our earlier lives is often the source of our depressions. Not only can it act as a direct and obvious hangover from the past, but it can also be silently ticking away like a timebomb, programmed to go off some time in the future. If all your family have died in their mid-fifties from coronaries or strokes, small wonder if you develop a depression around your fiftieth birthday. You may not be consciously aware of the reason, but your subconscious may be hammering away at you!

For some of us, past memories are nice, generally speaking. But for others their experiences, particularly in the formative years, can greatly hinder their ability to develop into positive Christians. There is no shame in this – but we have to recognise that each person can only develop at his or her own rate. The process of "going on as a Christian", particularly when supported and guided by wise, older Christians, can help to undo those memories, unlock the hurt that they contain, and change a life that was once disorganised and disheartened (and perhaps downright sinful), into one that more closely approximates that which Jesus would have us be. But there will still be a large amount of baggage and a lot of memories that need to be dealt with in the process.

Therefore for the Christian, dealing with depression is not a matter of saying, "You shouldn't have it – think joyful" (which doesn't help a bit). Instead, be aware of those physical, mental, emotional and spiritual traumas that have shaped and moulded that person, injuring him so that he does not react as he would like to, nor perhaps as others would like.

The Christian life is ongoing. You don't stop changing and growing until you die, to be translated to be with Jesus permanently. At conversion you don't suddenly become a perfect, wonderfully mature Christian. Just as children have to mature, so each Christian has to undergo continuing spiritual maturation. And just as a child who is learning to walk has to learn through experience (by falling over a lot), so Christians have to take risks and learn by their mistakes. We all know from adolescence that maturing can be an emotionally painful process. But if you don't grow, you stand still. Unfortunately it is often less painful to go back than to go on – which is why I want to encourage you to be brave and look at your depression as something which you have to grow through. It is to be dealt with by you and God together. In doing this you will gradually change for the better – understanding (and then losing) your old ways and gaining new and better ones.

Therefore, stop feeling guilty about being depressed. Appreciate that you will need to go through a learning process which will teach and mature you. In understanding why you are like you are, you will learn to change yourself, shaking off old habits and attitudes from the past.

Above all, begin to learn that there is no guilt attached to being depressed. It comes at you from the past, and may have no relation whatsoever to the current state of your Christian life.

EXERCISE

Were you surprised that I suggested that you *didn't* read the Bible, or pray last night? Did it feel easier, not having the burden of "but I ought to *try*" – then hating every minute of it because you 'couldn't get through' or couldn't concentrate properly on the Bible passage?

I hope you felt relieved that you were no longer duty-bound to do it, and that the sky wouldn't fall in if you didn't say your prayers.

It sounds daft to put it like that, doesn't it? But you would be surprised how many Christians adopt this approach, especially when tired, fearful or threatened. We are very easily led into superstition, and the idea that God will not look favourably upon us unless we have a quiet time each day should be seen for what it is – a silly superstition. As if God could be bribed with a prayer or two! He knows your needs already, and what is in your heart – you don't have to tell Him. Later on, prayer will have its place, but you will feel differently about it by then, and it won't be so exhausting. If you want to pray, fine. God would like to hear from you! But if you *can't* then don't worry – He understands.

So what do you do with your quiet time? A depressed person can't concentrate well, and if your attention span is only three minutes at a time make sure that your quiet time is scheduled for *less* than this. Otherwise you'll get discouraged and feel guilty for letting your mind wander.

What should you study? Here we have a problem – depressed Christians are much more likely to draw out of their daily reading criticisms rather than blessings and promises. ("Look what happened to Saul because he was disobedient......") Guilt feelings are easily and unnecessarily aroused by such passages.

Therefore:

1. **It may be easier to study the more historical sections of the Bible** – where there is not quite so much spiritual confrontation. You will be surprised how much you can learn about God through the apparently less theological bits of the Bible, especially with the help of a good commentary.

2. **Pick something that interests you** – at least, as much as anything interests you at the moment: perhaps the feasts of the Israelites (not just the Passover – try the Sabbath, the feast of Tabernacles, etc.). Early church history is another useful area, and Acts is a lively, interesting and not-too-threatening book. But it's whatever you want. If you suddenly have a passion to learn all about Daniel, Belshazzar and Babylon, then do so!

3. **Read what the commentaries say.** It's not a bad thing for you to read the Bible through someone else's eyes – their (non-depressed) summation of a passage may be more accurate than your own subjective, depressed and guilt-ridden assessment.

4. **Don't set yourself tasks that are too difficult.** At first it may be best not to set yourself any tasks at all. Read the Bible if you feel like it – and if you can't summon

up the energy, don't bother, and don't feel guilty about it either. If Daniel and Belshazzar don't turn you on as they did yesterday, try a parable, or Esther, or read about the Shekinah Glory of God. If you are depressed, with your concentration shot to bits, then God is not going to take you to task for not keeping to your Bible-study plan. It is far better that you should read something of the Bible enjoyably than plough wearily through a passage to the bitter end. If you *do* try the 'nose to the grindstone' technique, you won't get far. You won't remember much for all your time spent trying, but you *will* feel guilty that you're not enjoying it or concentrating on it.

The main thing is not to let yourself feel threatened by your quiet time, either through what you are reading, or because you feel guilty for not being able to spend much time on it. *Don't worry!* Remember, you really *are* in the centre of God's will at the moment, so all those threats about hell, damnation and exile don't apply to you!

So do what you want – and what you can manage to concentrate on. If, on the way, you manage to acquire a bit more knowledge about the Bible, about the Jews, about Jesus or about God, then good for you! And if you don't, it doesn't matter. God isn't counting.....

5. **Don't set yourself a target of more than a few minutes for your study.** By all means study for longer if you genuinely want to, but don't feel you *have* to. Alternatively, split it up throughout the day – a few minutes here, a few moments there. This will allow you to do quite a lot within the limits of your span of concentration.

The same applies to prayers. Short, sharp and sweet. Ten seconds each. "O God, I'm lonely and sad, but I know You know. Help! Amen." – this is about the right length. A few like that interspersed through the day will be a lot more effective than, "Dear loving and merciful heavenly Father, Thou knowest how I, Thy most unworthy servant.........." By the time you've got halfway through the first paragraph your mind will be off on other things. Then you'll feel guilty for not concentrating, so you start again... and the same thing happens... so you feel worse... so you'll try again...

Short and sharp. As Jesus said , "Don't be like the heathen. Don't pray with vain repetitions, thinking that the more you say, the more God will take notice."

Happy studying. Enjoy it.

3

SYMPTOMS

Anxiety is a state in which the mind is over-roused, and reacts excessively to a minor stimuli. **Depression** is the reverse – the mind works sluggishly. You might be forgiven for thinking that these two conditions are opposite to each other – but they're not, because it's common to get agitation in depression!

It doesn't help to try to define the terms too closely. Doctors often talk about anxiety-depression as being one entity. It may help to think of them as a spectrum, with pure anxiety and pure depression at opposite ends, but mixing together in the middle. This is how I think of them in this book.

★   ★   ★

There are many different symptoms of anxiety and depression. Your main problem may well just be lethargy – everything seems far too much trouble. You have no interest in doing things – or, if you would like to be doing something, you can't summon up the energy to prepare yourself for it: just undressing for bed becomes an ordeal, to be put off as long as possible, even though you feel tired out, and long to be asleep. Yet when you get to bed sleep may elude you, even though you're dog-tired. It may be difficult to get off to sleep, or else you wake in the early hours of the morning and can't get back to sleep again.

Other symptoms include lack of concentration, irritability, lack of sexual drive, and exhaustion. There is a sensation of profound and utter despair; yet often the sufferer knows that he has nothing to be depressed about. There may be a sense of hopelessness, or of the uselessness of everything, a fear of death, phobias, obsessional behaviour, or a permanent sense of anxiety. You may feel as if you want to cry, but can't. There may be thoughts of suicide, or (more commonly) a *fear of committing* suicide, where you are afraid that one day you'll get so desperate that you'll kill yourself, almost against your will.

The symptoms can sometimes be worse at a particular time of day: depending upon the type of depression, it can be worse in the morning or at night.

There can be hormonal links, too. In women depression can vary with the monthly cycle, being worse around the time of the period. It can also occur at or after the menopause.

Depression is more likely to occur at times in your life when there is great emotional stress – particularly in adolescence; and sometimes in the so-called 'mid-life crisis'.

The depressed person may start to get bodily malfunctions – headaches, alterations in weight, tiredness unrelieved by sleep, heart palpitations, sweating, diarrhoea, constipation, backache, a feeling of a lump in the throat or a choking feeling.

You may feel that your friends are avoiding you, or whispering about you behind your back. In the very severest of cases the sufferer may start to hear voices when there is nobody in the room.

For the man who has a creative job, such as an artist or writer, there may be a lack of creative drive. Such problems are worse in a man who is working with his brain rather than his hands. A minor depression that will hardly affect a manual labourer may be quite sufficient to stop a creative writer completely. However, in a really severe depression the manual worker can suffer just as much as the creative person – sometimes more so since he cannot always articulate his feelings nor express them creatively.

Paradoxically, a depressed person can also be agitated, and this gives a difficult diagnostic problem to the doctor. Is the patient suffering from anxiety alone, or is it really depression manifesting itself as anxiety? In some people there is a very fine line between the two. The problem is that if the doctor treats the anxiety without dealing with the underlying depression he may well make the patient worse.

The depressed *Christian* often feels that God isn't listening to his prayers, but seems to answer everybody else's, gloriously, just to rub it in. He may well begin to doubt his salvation, citing this as evidence. There is often an overwhelming feeling of sinfulness – manifesting itself either as a concentration and rumination on past and present sins (especially the 'recurrent' ones), or alternatively as a sense of total personal failure or worthlessness unrelated to any specific sin. There is often a heightened awareness of the possibility of having committed a sin through what you've said or done, and it is common for the depressed Christian to be apologising left, right and centre for having given offence over something which the 'recipient' hadn't even noticed, let alone found offensive. As an extension of this sense of sinfulness it is common for Christians to fear they have committed the unforgivable sin – blasphemy against the Holy Spirit. (If this is you, take heart. It is a truism that anyone who fears they might have blasphemed against the Holy Spirit hasn't done so. We'll deal with this in the chapter on Guilt.)

It is important to distinguish between depression and sadness.

Those who have experienced both say that sadness is a *rich* experience, whereas depression is just empty and numbing. You can be sad, or depressed, or both together. But sadness is not the same as depression, and here lies a trap for the inept helper:

Gaffe number one: "But you've nothing to be sad about."

He may well be right – you *don't*. But then, you're not sad – you're depressed. Our Job's comforter hasn't recognised the difference between the two (if indeed he knows there is a difference) and has just made things worse for you. You now feel guilty for being depressed because you've just been told that you have no sensible or logical reason for it. Be warned – 'helpers' like this can do a lot of damage to depressed people. Ignore them!

Of course, there may be reasons why you are depressed – you may have lost a loved one; or be out of a job; or have failed an important exam – but there is not *necessarily* a cause-and-effect relationship between recent life events and depression. Unfortunately, non-medical people often think there ought to be.

EXERCISE

Do you feel unforgiven? That no matter how hard you try, God isn't really very pleased with you?

Once God forgives, He forgives and *forgets*. (Someone once said that He throws the sin into the deepest part of the ocean, and then puts up a sign that says 'No Fishing'!) You don't have to persuade God to forgive you – you only have to ask, simply, once, and once only. The forgiveness is there – it's just that you don't feel it. The real problem is that it's *you* that is not forgiving *yourself*!

So, simply ask God to forgive you for the things you have done wrong – both the things you know about and the things you don't. Then tell Him about the things that you know are wrong, but that you find you can't give up. He understands. He doesn't ask for the impossible. He knows that you are tired, and that your mental resilience is low, and He won't kick you in the teeth when you sin yet again. (It's you that's kicking yourself in the teeth, not Him!)

Now write down your prayer, simply. Something on the lines of:

> "Dear Lord, please forgive me for *all* the things I've done that I shouldn't – especially .... and ... and .... Forgive me for the things that I don't know about, and those I've forgotten about. And please forgive me for the fact that so often I still want to do these very same things again.
>
> Please give me the grace to accept forgiveness, and release me from the feeling that somehow I've got to earn forgiveness by trying harder. I ask for all this in Jesus' name."

Fold it up and put it away carefully: pick a place where no one else will find it, and where you won't routinely come across it yourself: either, say, the top drawer of your wardrobe, or at the back of your personal files. You should know that it's *there* – but no one else should see it, and I don't intend that you nor anybody else should ever look at it again.

When you are tempted (and I *mean* 'tempted') to go over and over your misdeeds, as most depressed people do, remember the piece of paper. You meant it when you wrote it. That paper is a testimony to the fact that you meant it. Therefore *every sin that happened before that piece of paper was written is now dead, buried and paid for.* There is no question that it's gone, and you have the piece of paper to prove it – not that you need to look at it. All you have to do is discipline yourself to remember that you have been forgiven, and that to review your past sins is not appropriate any more – in fact, under the circumstances, ruminating on your past (forgiven) misdeeds is in itself sinful, because you are doubting that God has forgiven you! Consciously think of other things. And start to accept forgiveness.

When Jesus said, "Love your neighbour as yourself", He also implied, "Love yourself". Would you treat your Christian neighbour as you treat yourself? No, you wouldn't. So learn to love yourself, to look after yourself, to forgive yourself. It's what being a Christian is all about and, as they say, charity begins at home!

4

CAUSES

Christians are often wary of psychiatry and psychology because they fear that these subjects might 'explain away' religious beliefs and render their faith null and void. Speaking both as a Christian and as a doctor, I see Christianity, psychiatry and psychology as entirely compatible.

God made us with brains – and gave us a longing for Him as well. Those brains have to work in a certain way, including the longing! Finding out how that brain works is merely following in the footsteps of God – we need not fear that it will somehow show us that God is not necessary, nor that religious feelings can be explained away.

It helps to think of our minds at three distinct levels – physical, mental and spiritual. They are separate concepts but the boundaries between them are blurred, just as a painting can be described in terms of the chemical make-up of its pigments, or of its effect on the viewer (which in turn depends upon the layout of those same pigments). Where does the painting start and where do the pigments stop?

So let's begin with a few definitions.

BODY, MIND, SOUL AND SPIRIT

The body and brain are the physical parts of ourselves. The mind is that part of us which thinks. Part of the mind is conscious – we are aware of the fact that we think! But an important part of the mind is *sub*conscious – we don't realise what goes on in it, but it's still there, calculating away. (It's this bit that's at work when we can't remember someone's name, then half an hour later it comes to us, apparently out of the blue. All that time the subconscious mind has been beavering away, trying to find the answer.)

The mind has two important aspects, logic and emotion. Logic is a calculating type of thinking, whilst emotions are an inner sensation, much as heat or sound are external sensations. (However, in common parlance 'emotional' is also used to refer to the overall feelings we have and I've sometimes used it this way. It's obvious from the context which one I mean.)

It is not easy to make a clear distinction between brain, body and mind, because each aspect of our person and personality interacts with the others. For example, hormonal changes in the *body* of a woman with premenstrual syndrome affect the way cells in her *brain* function, which in turn affects the logic and emotional workings of her *mind*. Similarly, purely mental changes (such as anxiety over an impending exam, or of speaking in public) cause nerve cells to release adrenaline. This in turn causes the blood pressure to rise, makes us sweat, and gives us the feeling that we want to go to the toilet. Mental stress is also thought to affect the working of the immune system.

If it's difficult to define 'mind' precisely, it's even harder to define 'soul' and 'spirit', especially as the English word 'soul' is used to translate both a Hebrew word and a Greek word, each of which has different connotations. (The Hebrew word which we translate as 'soul' actually means 'whole person', as in the archaic English usage, "Twenty-three souls were lost when the ship foundered.".)

In this book I use the word 'spiritual' to refer to those aspects of the individual that are God-directed and God-orientated.

★   ★   ★

So let's look at the causes of depression from the viewpoint of these three aspects of the mind – physical, mental and spiritual.

1. **Physical causes of depression** include premenstrual depression; postnatal depression; some types of manic depression which have been shown to have a genetic basis; hormone deficiencies such as thyroid disturbances; generalised illnesses such as kidney or liver disease; lack of natural light during winter in certain susceptible people; alcoholism; drug dependency; food allergies and peculiar reactions to medicines, chemicals, and food additives. Treatment is by relieving the biochemical or hormonal abnormality, where that is possible.

2. **Mental causes** – Here there is no obvious biochemical abnormality, but a mental problem (conscious or unconscious) is weighing the person down. There are three main ways this can happen.

   a. Some psychologists (**Freudians, Jungians,** etc.) think that our behaviour is particularly influenced by *unconscious impulses,* especially those relating to early experiences in childhood. For example, if a nine-month-old child is separated from her mother while she has an operation, then although she cannot recall the event, she may later become insecure and frightened because deep down she fears that she will lose her security, just as she 'lost' her mother so long ago.

   b. The **behaviouristic** approach says that psychiatric problems are caused by present-day problems when the patient, instead of coping properly with these difficulties, *has learned the wrong* *responses*. For example, a woman begins to be frightened of going out (perhaps because the last time she went out she got lost); the next time she tries to go out, the memory of the panic comes back to her so she becomes even more fearful, and when she goes out she begins to fear the same thing will happen again. She has *learned to panic* when going out, and the more she is frightened, the worse it becomes. The panic builds up and up until just the thought of going out makes her so afraid that she cannot venture outside her door, though by this time she may well have forgotten quite what it was that caused the fear in the first place.

Another behaviouristic approach is to think of depression as 'learned helplessness'. In this, a person just can't seem to learn how to control the stresses placed upon him; after a while this extends to become a belief that he won't be able to control *anything* that happens in his life. He retreats into himself and becomes mouse-like, passive and unresponsive, unwilling to do anything to take control. If anyone challenges him, he'll always have a good excuse as to why any suggested course of action won't work: "Yes, but that would mean....."   Treatment consists in showing the patient *how* he can control his life, so that he can change back from being passive to being active again.

c. Finally, *sheer overload* ('stress') can overwhelm the mind's ability to cope.

Note that 'mental' problems like this can have very physical results on the brain: 'mental' problems can be greatly helped by antidepressants, probably because the increased strains of extra mental activity cause the brain to use up its own chemicals too quickly. As I said earlier, the boundaries between physical and mental are sometimes very fuzzy!

3. **Spiritual causes** of depression can affect Christians and non-Christians, *but are much more common in non-Christians*.

For the non-Christian there can be an overwhelming sense of despair at the apparent futility of life, a despair which is incapable of relief with drugs or psychotherapy. All drugs do in these cases is numb the mind to the problem; but it doesn't go away, and psychotherapy may well only serve to bring the problem into sharper focus, and make it even worse. Spiritual depressive crises may develop with the death of a loved one, a contemplation of one's own impending death, severe illness or injury ("Why me?") and at times when there is a feeling of fate being against you – the sense of nature (or God) being implacable and remorseless. Often the sufferer tries to numb himself with alcohol, prescribed drugs, illegal drugs or cigarettes – and it is noticeable how quickly the use of these can disappear once religious conversion has occurred and the original underlying spiritual problem or spiritual insecurity has been healed.

For Christians, depression hardly ever has a spiritual cause. If you remember this, you are unlikely to fall into the second trap, namely:

> *Gaffe number two: "If you're a depressed Christian there's something wrong with your spiritual life."*

Wrong. Wrong. Wrong. (But ever such an easy assumption to make, both for the sufferer and his Christian adviser.) *In Christians, spiritual effects follow from the depression, and seldom the other way round.* I repeat – in Christians, nearly always the depression comes first, followed by a sense of remoteness from God, rather than depression being the result of 'falling away'.

This idea forms the central theme of this book. Many Christians just do not understand that depression is hardly ever caused by problems with your spiritual life. People like this make out that there *is* a spiritual cause – so it's *your fault* that you're depressed. It's an easy mistake to make, but it is still a mistake, and one with far-reaching implications. It also pushes the depressed Christian even more deeply into his depression and loads him (quite unfairly) with an extra burden, making his situation even more intolerable. Depression is painful enough, but now the sufferer feels that God is angry with him for being like this: so he prays for forgiveness, for obedience, for guidance, for wisdom...... and gets no better. (In his eyes, there's only one reason why – he's not addressing his own sin, so he's not getting better. God must be *very* angry indeed with him.) So he tries to pray even more...... and gets nowhere – *because his spiritual life is not where the problem lies,* and he's trying to correct something that probably doesn't need correcting.

For the Christian, *truly spiritual* causes of depression usually involve behaviour which the Christian knows to be wrong, but which he still deliberately and arrogantly persists in – such as an affair, fiddling the books, or really hating a fellow-Christian. Note the words 'persists' and 'arrogantly'. I am *not* talking about repeated sins that the Christian wishes he could control but can't – such as addiction to alcohol, a quick temper, impure thoughts – but *a deliberate and continued rebellion against God.* There is a very important distinction between the two, and depressed Christians often get them muddled up.

Every Christian sins. *Every* Christian has weaknesses that he wishes he didn't have – his own Christian Achilles heel. (Remember St Paul?

– "The good I want to do I find I can't, and the bad things I don't want to do I find myself doing. O wretched man that I am! – but praise be to Jesus who forgives us for our every weakness.") No one would say that St Paul wasn't a Christian! Yet he obviously encountered exactly the same problem.

The answer to Achilles-heel-type sins is that Jesus doesn't condemn, but understands us, and forgives us *readily*. Achilles-heel sins are not the type of sins that lead to *spiritual* depression. But often the depressed Christian loses his sense of proportion, blaming himself mercilessly for his failings, thinking that these are the root cause of his problems. They're not.

Bear in mind that in times of stress 'comforting' behaviour is often used as an antidote to the emotional pain we feel. This is why depressives hit the bottle, go gambling, overeat, go on spending sprees and so on. I must emphasise again and again that Jesus understands this sort of comforting behaviour, even when it involves something that is sinful, and does not condemn you for it, nor reject you. Comforting behaviour is *not* the cause of your depression. The best test is – do you regret it afterwards (even if you know you will probably do the same again in the same circumstances)? If you do it's an Achilles-heel-type of problem. However emotionally upset and dejected you become as a result, it is unlikely to be a cause of your depression.

On the other hand, the sort of Christian behaviour which does lead to spiritual depression is the deliberate, unregretful cocking a snook at God, which is quite different. The Christian who won't follow the guidance he *knows* he's been given; the one who deliberately enters into sinful situations that he needn't do, especially those *un*related to his own Achilles heel. Sinful activity which causes spiritual depression is quite different from repetitive Achilles-heel-type sins. *Please* understand the difference, if you're depressed. It will almost certainly remove a whole load of unnecessary guilt from your shoulders.

There is an additional problem here. Many apparently 'spiritual' causes of depression should really be classified as **religiously orientated mental problems,** as described in "Mental Causes" above. For example, a Christian may have difficulty relating to God, not knowing whether to apply 'God as Judge' or 'God is Love' to a specific problem. Or he may have a crisis over whether God is there at all.

Finally, and *very rarely,* demon possession can occur (see Appendix 2). However, the overwhelming majority of Christians with depression are depressed for completely different reasons and it is unusual for Christians to become possessed, so don't get worried. If any of the conditions in Appendix 2 apply to you, (particularly involvement with the occult), see your minister or an elder. If they don't apply, then *forget it*.

However, this doesn't mean that the Devil is inactive – far from it! He has a great interest in keeping Christians miserable. Don't forget that the Bible tells us that it's the *Devil* who stands before God and accuses us. It's the Devil who tries to make us feel we are unforgiven, unforgivable, and beyond the pale, especially with regard to our Achilles-heel-type sins . He's the one, not God, who is accusing us, trying continually to make us feel wretched and condemned, trying to get us to feel we're so bad that Jesus cannot love us any more.

Remember this – for the Christian, anything that splits you off from God, that tries to make out that you are unforgivable, that accuses and condemns, comes from Satan. With Christians God *convicts* – He never condemns.

True spiritual causes of depression are not common. Most Christians with an apparently religious content to their depression in fact have one of the mental/emotional causes (sometimes based around a religious problem such as whether God is there or not) rather than a true spiritual cause. *I cannot emphasise enough that solely spiritual causes of depression are infrequent in Christians:* these depend upon a *continuing* sin that you are not addressing, (such as the refusal to terminate an adulterous relationship) and are *not* a matter of a repeated sin which you can't control *but wish you could,* such as problems in controlling your sexual thoughts. It is true that a drifting-away from God can result in a lacklustre feeling within our lives but this is not in the same category as depression. Unfortunately, all too commonly other Christians imply that if you're feeling depressed then there is something wrong with your relationship with God. They are almost certainly wrong.

As an example of this, I well remember one occasion when I was depressed. I knew God was there – I knew He cared about me and loved me; but I didn't feel that it mattered whether I lived or got hit by a bus. Living seemed pointless.

So was this a spiritual falling-away? Shouldn't I have cared about living to do Christ's work? Wasn't this a spiritual depression? No, it wasn't. Two weeks later we found out that it was caused by an unusual reaction to some medicines I had been prescribed for a chest infection, and the depression lifted as soon as the tablets were stopped. So much for a spiritual cause of *that* particular incident....

I repeat – those who try to make out that your depression is the result of your poor relationship with God have almost certainly got things the wrong way round: it's the depression that makes you *feel* as if you're cut off from God, not a cutting-off from God which gives you the depression.

The important lesson to learn from this is that *God is on your side.* You have not offended Him. The fact that you don't feel particularly well or happy is a result of quite different problems, and nothing to do with your relationship with Him.

But it is a problem, isn't it, when you meet other Christian friends and they say with eyes aglow, "Wasn't that a super service; isn't God good; don't you feel just great knowing that your heavenly Father is there looking after you?" – and you feel like saying "No" to all three! Ebullient Christians sometimes unwittingly make depressed Christians feel even more terrible, left out, spiritually frail.

Don't blame yourself if you feel like this. Your feelings are unrelated to the real truth about your relationship with God. Even when you feel totally lost, He is still there. He has not forgotten you, He is not blaming you, and you are still very loved – even if you don't feel it!

Remember Elijah. He stood up single-handedly against a pagan king and a pagan nation; and in the contest with the prophets of Baal, he'd called down fire from heaven to burn the sacrifice, and God had answered him.

So what does he do? He crawls into the desert, sits down and says, "Oh God, I want to die. What's the point in going on?" Blasphemy? Spiritual failure? A falling-away of his spiritual life? He'd just had his position wonderfully and miraculously confirmed by God. What could possibly be better? How could he possibly say this to God?

The reason he felt like this was simply because he was exhausted – and for very good reasons: he'd just had an intense spiritual and mental battle.

So what does God do – criticise him for his lack of faith? Tick him off? No - He tells him to go to sleep, then feeds him. Does he feel OK after this? God doesn't think so! He repeats the treatment – rest and food. Only then is Elijah ready to do anything more. *And all the time there is not a word of criticism from God* – just encouragement. "Elijah, my beloved servant, you're shattered. Let me look after you..."

It would be so easy to interpret Elijah's despair as a lack of faith; but God didn't think of it like this. Similarly it is easy, but wrong, to dismiss the depressed Christian in the same way. As with Elijah, for Christians spiritual problems are seldom the cause of depression; but very frequently depression caused by other events causes spiritual dryness.

In other words, *it is not a sin for a Christian to be depressed.* You have to look elsewhere for its causes. And just knowing this simple fact may be enough for the burden of "if-you're-depressed-what's-the-matter-with-your-spiritual-life" to begin to lift from your shoulders, thus starting you back on the road to recovery (and Christian self-respect).

When you're tempted to despair, remember Elijah.

EXERCISE

Have you someone in whom you can confide? It doesn't necessarily have to be your minister (but it's a good idea for him to know about your situation anyway). Your confidant could be your minister, an elder, someone within the church with a specific ministry for (or responsibility towards) those with spiritual and emotional problems; or a close Christian friend. It may well be that if you approach someone 'official' within the church, he (or she) will put you in touch with another church member who has particular gifts in helping people in situations such as yours.

What you need ultimately is someone to whom you can unload, to whom you can go for support and guidance, whom you can ring up when the going gets tough. He or she needs to be a *mature* Christian who can keep confidences, and preferably of the same sex as yourself.

Go to him, and tell him about your situation. The adage about 'a trouble shared is a trouble halved' is very true, especially in this sort of situation. You may want to talk about things; confess things; or just cry on his shoulder (literally). It will be helpful to have him pray with you and for you; and it's good for you to know that there will be a smiling, sensitive face welcoming you when you go round or ring up. You need to know that at least one person loves you, accepts you for what you are, understands you, doesn't condemn you, and will help you through your present troubles.

But your friend is not just there to listen to your perpetual moans and groans, however helpful this may be at first. He also has the important job of helping you retake control of your life. As we have discovered, some depressed people have learned to be helpless. *Your friend is also there to help you win back control of your life for yourself!* If he is wise and mature, he will give you good advice, so listen to him.

Relearning how to make (and carry through) decisions is part and parcel of the recovery process. You won't get better overnight, but keep plugging away, and over the months you will find that your life returns more and more into your control.

Start with little things – if necessary, like deciding what to have for supper (some people can't even do that at first). Then, with your friend's help and advice (because he can see things more clearly and objectively than you can) learn to extend this decision-making process to other areas of your life. Go slowly.

Don't be afraid of making mistakes. Many people are so afraid of making mistakes that they'd rather do nothing at all than risk actively doing something that may go wrong. They end up being extremely passive. Refusing to make decisions is a typical 'helpless' way of behaving.

Be prepared to take risks! (sensible ones) You will certainly make mistakes, but you will progress much more quickly than if you try to do everything perfectly first time round.

5

TREATMENT – PHYSICAL CAUSES

Strictly speaking, anxiety and depression are not diseases in their own right, but symptoms produced by any one of several different diseases. It is not really correct to think of them as single ailments. This is important because it affects the way we choose the appropriate treatment. There is little point in treating depression due to thyroid problems by delving into your childhood relationship with your parents! Equally, there is no point in trying again and again to seek a physical cause when the real problem is mental. Trying to find the origin of a depression is no easy task, even for a skilled doctor. (Just establishing that the patient *is* depressed can be hard enough, never mind finding the cause.)

The last thing you need at this stage is another layman telling you what the matter is. Do the exercise at the end of this chapter, then *go to your doctor, tell him the symptoms, and ask his advice.* Depending upon what you say, he may or may not want to do some investigations. Ask him what he thinks is the matter. If there is a physical cause for the depression then you needn't waste time and energy trying to 'make yourself better': once the physical illness has been sorted out you will be back to normal.

Let's go through the physical causes of depression in detail, and talk about what can be done.

1. **Post-viral depression.** Depression and exhaustion coming after a viral infection can be profound and last for a long time – usually many weeks, sometimes months, occasionally years. Usually, however, post-viral depression lasts about six weeks. Rest and patience are required. The symptoms will pass eventually, and there is nothing much that you can do to speed things up. Look after yourself physically – your resistance and energy will be a lot lower than normal. Go easy on yourself – make fewer demands upon your resources. Eat a well-balanced diet, even if your appetite is not great, to ensure that you don't get a vitamin deficiency to add to your problems. If you eat a balanced diet already then there is usually no point in taking extra vitamin pills, unless your doctor suggests them.

   ME (myalgic encephalomyelitis, disdainfully known as 'yuppie flu') is a specific type of post-viral infection in which any activity (physical or mental) results in profound exhaustion which can last for several days. Muscle cramps are common, and the condition can last several years, if not for life. There is much debate in medical circles as to whether ME actually exists or not, but opinion seems to be swinging towards it: it now appears that it is related to a persisting viral infection. Sufferers initially tend to be labelled as neurotic hypochondriacs (which doesn't help them at all!) and it is a great relief to them when they are properly diagnosed, as the sense of guilt evaporates!

Post-viral depression is common and self-limiting within six to twelve weeks: true ME is rare and prolonged.

2. **Glandular fever** is like a *severe* viral infection – the depression can be profound and in some cases may last for many months. A blood test in the initial stages will tell you that you have contracted glandular fever. The treatment is the same as for post-viral depression, and even more patience may be required as the problems can be much more severe and more prolonged than with ordinary viral illnesses.

3. **Thyroid problems.** Your thyroid gland sits on either side of your windpipe, in the neck, and is responsible for controlling the speed at which your biochemical reactions work. Too much thyroid hormone, and you'll become overactive and anxious. Too little, and you'll be sluggish and depressed. Treatment for an underactive thyroid consists in giving tablets containing the hormone thyroxine. An overactive thyroid can be calmed down in a number of different ways – with medicines; by surgical removal; or by burning out the extra capacity of the gland with a carefully controlled dose of radioactive iodine.

4. **Premenstrual tension (PMT)** affects most women at some stage in their lives. It can lead to anxiety and/or depression, and is usually worse in the latter half of the monthly cycle. The condition is well recognised, but not yet fully understood. Diagnosis is not always easy, nor do all doctors accept PMT as a valid diagnosis. The crucial observation is that the swings of depression or anxiety are related to the monthly cycle, usually being relieved with, or shortly after, the period. Keeping a chart of the intensity of each symptom, noting the day-number of the monthly cycle, may demonstrate dramatically the relationship between the two.

It is important to recognise those who are affected by PMT, as treatment for PMT is quite different from the treatment of depression on its own. Just recognising that you have PMT will improve matters, because this helps to lift the burden of guilt about being ill. Often the PMT sufferer gets more practical support from her husband and family once the diagnosis has been recognised. There are a variety of treatments, all of which work in suitable cases. Diuretics (to make the patient pass more water), hormones, vitamins, and certain other drugs may be appropriate, individually or in combination.

5. **Hormonal upsets** – particularly in certain susceptible women around the time of the menopause – can cause much more than hot flushes! Depression, anxiety, a sense of not being able to think straight – all these can result. The cause can either be a lack of the right hormone, or an imbalance in the proportions of hormones. Hormone replacement therapy (HRT) with oestrogens and progestogens can produce a rapid and dramatic transformation. However, depression in menopausal women can just as easily be related to emotional problems – there will be no more babies; the children are leaving the nest; older age is coming nearer. So HRT may or may not be the answer for depression occurring at or after the menopause.

6. **Postnatal depression.** Everyone knows about the 'baby blues' which hit the new mother about three to five days after her child has been born and usually make her suddenly feel very tearful. It's quite normal, it's related to the abrupt drop in hormone levels following delivery, and usually doesn't last for too long. This transient tearful state is *not* a true depression. However, in some mothers it can last quite a time. This more extended version of the 'baby blues' is the true postnatal depression. The problems are compounded by the exhaustion and interrupted nights that occur with a new-born baby.

   The treatment is firstly, to recognise that this is in fact postnatal depression, and secondly, to allow time for rest and recuperation – a supportive family is a blessing here. Thirdly, anti–depressive therapy and/or hormone therapy may be appropriate, especially where symptoms are prolonged.

   Postnatal depression can be severe, so if you are suffering from it for any length of time tell your doctor, midwife or health visitor.

7. **Food allergies** are increasingly recognised as a potential source of trouble, but not all doctors are convinced of their importance. They are responsible for only a small proportion of cases of depression. Further information about the diagnosis of food allergy is given in Appendix 3.

8. **Preservatives and colourants.**   The comments on food

sensitivities also apply to preservatives and colourants in food, and the method of detection is the same.

9. **Idiosyncratic reactions to drugs and medicines** are quite common: they can be difficult to recognise, especially if they creep up on you slowly. There is no set pattern to this sort of reaction: a drug that is harmless in most people may have the most unpleasant effects on someone else. (A few years ago I had to have a short course of steroids when I developed a particularly bad chest infection. Steroids usually make people feel good, if not actually 'high', but in me a black depression descended and it took a long time before I realised that it was the steroids that were doing it. I've never met anyone else who has had the same problem with steroids!) Essentially *any* drug is capable of producing an odd reaction.

10. **Cancer** is depressing enough, but it can also give a purely physical depression: **radiotherapy** and the **drugs** used to fight cancer can also lay you low in the same way. Tell your doctor.

11. **Alcohol** is a depressant. (You might think it was a relaxant, but what it actually does is depress those areas in the brain which are responsible for 'holding you in check'.)

Apart from the obvious dangers of getting drunk, alcohol probably only causes problems in those who are really hooked on it. Occasional or moderate drinkers don't need to get concerned. Warning signs are when you can't do without it; when you need a drink early in the day or before you go to work; where your intake is progressively increasing; where you constantly make excuses for your drinking; where you hide alcohol in secret places; or where your tolerance to it is dropping (in other words, it only needs a few drinks to get you inebriated).

Alcohol causes damage in several ways: firstly, by pickling the liver, which is no longer able to detoxify waste products in the body; secondly, by affecting the brain directly; thirdly, by the stress it produces at home and at work through reduction in the reliability and mental stability of the patient; and fourthly, by the financial strain it puts on the family where excessive amounts of money are spent on alcohol, especially where the earning power of the patient may be dropping due to his undependable personality. Finally, alcoholics often don't eat properly and may run short of essential vitamins.

The depression produced by alcohol is typically when the patient is *not* under its influence (which is why he continues to drink – a drink makes him feel better).

The treatment for alcoholism is to abstain permanently from alcohol for the rest of your life, which is easier said than done. High doses of vitamins can be useful in the early stages, to replace what is missing, and your doctor may prescribe certain special tranquillisers to help you through the initial drying-out period. The support of your doctor and organisations such as Alcoholics Anonymous is *vital* as the emotional pressures on the alcoholic are intense, and drying out can be very unpleasant, both physically and emotionally.

Once the patient is off alcohol there is usually a gradual reversal of the damage to liver and brain – but it takes time, often many months. The depression is usually relieved once the drying-out period is over – but if the patient was drinking in order to forget the pressures upon him, he may need help to deal with the source of the pressure itself.

12. **Drugs,** whether prescribed or illegal, can have much the same effects as alcohol. *Do note that anti-anxiety drugs (tranquillisers, sleeping tablets) can have the side-effect of making you depressed.* Drugs that can do this include the barbiturates and the benzodiazepines (such as chlordiazepoxide, diazepam, nitrazepam, Librium, Mogadon, and Valium as well as many others). Some of these drugs can be *very* helpful in short courses, but in certain patients can produce considerable depression. This is particularly the case where the doctor hasn't realised that he is dealing with a depression, and is treating the patient for anxiety. (Surprisingly, the two often look very similar, especially where there is anxiety caused by depression.)

Tranquillisers *do* have a place in the treatment of both anxiety and depression: just be aware that they can have depressive side-effects, that's all. If in doubt, ask your doctor.

The contraceptive pill can also cause depression in some people. Altering the proportions of the two main constituents (i.e. changing to a different version) may be all that's necessary to rectify the situation.

13. **Illegal drugs** (heroin, cocaine, barbiturates etc.) work in much the same way as alcohol, only more quickly – usually they give a kick to the user, followed by unpleasant withdrawal symptoms, and the time of being depressed is, like alcohol, in the withdrawal phase. Where drugs are injected there may also be the problem of infection – boils, hepatitis and AIDS – to add to the feelings of malaise.

14. **Undiagnosed chronic illness** can present as depression – hepatitis is one such, but there are many others which make the

patient feel awful. If there are other symptoms besides the depression (skin rashes, for example) then consult your doctor. Usually a couple of blood tests will establish whether there is an underlying physical problem.

15. **Lack of sufficient natural light** is increasingly recognised as a cause of depression in some susceptible people. It goes by the wonderfully appropriate acronym SAD – which stands for Seasonal Affective Disorder – and is thought to be related to the activity of the pineal gland, which regulates the body's timing mechanisms.

SAD manifests itself as depression which hits in the wintertime when there is little natural sunlight; typically the condition improves in the spring and there is often a burst of activity around April, just before the depression resolves. The treatment is to expose the patient regularly to special bright lights – or to send him to the tropics for the winter! Normal antidepressants are ineffective.

EXERCISE

You can help your doctor to diagnose you quickly and accurately if you answer the following questions. *Write the answers down,* so that you can refer to them in the surgery without forgetting anything.

- When did your depression start? Did anything obvious trigger it, like a bad exam result, or a death in the family?

- Have you had anything like this before?

- Are other members of your family depressed? Is there a tendency to depression in your blood relatives?

- Have you recently had a bad illness, or a virus infection?

- Do you work with chemicals?

- Are you losing/gaining weight?

- If you are a woman:

  - is there any relation between your depression and your periods? (It may be helpful to keep a diary for a couple of months, scoring your symptoms each day, and noting where your periods come.)

  - are you on the contraceptive pill?

  - are you menopausal?

- Are there other physical problems – such as altered bowel habit, cough, excessive sweating?

- Are your symptoms worse in the winter?

- Are you an allergic person? Do your blood relatives tend to have allergies, asthma, hay fever, hives, irritable bowel syndrome, migraine?

- How much alcohol do you drink? Is your intake increasing? If you stop drinking does it bother you or make you unwell?

- How much coffee, tea and cola drinks do you take in a day?

- Are you taking any medicines?

- Are you using any illegal drugs?

Be brief! Depressive people are often hypochondriacal as well – but a concise summary will help your doctor immensely.

6

PSYCHIATRIC TREATMENT
WITH MEDICINES

There are two main aspects to psychiatric treatment. Firstly, there are the purely chemical treatments, in which drugs and medicines are given in an attempt to control chemically the abnormal workings of the brain. The second type of approach is for the therapist to concentrate on the 'mental' aspects of the sufferer and to attempt to identify hidden sources of worry and conflict within his mind. In practice many psychiatrists employ a mixture of these methods, but there are some who prefer to use drugs exclusively, and others, especially psychotherapists and psychoanalysts, who concentrate on resolving hidden or overt mental conflicts.

In this chapter I want to concentrate on the use of drugs and medicines in helping to relieve depression and anxiety. Don't be put off by the name 'drug' – I don't mean the illegal ones!

First, let me tell you in outline how nerves work. Signals are carried round the brain, spinal cord, and peripheral nerves by electrical impulses in nerve cells, which are extremely long and thin. Especially in the brain and spinal cord each nerve cell is in contact with lots of others and looks rather like the branches of a tree. Where one nerve touches another there is a junction called a synapse, and here the message in the nerve is converted from an electrical impulse to a chemical one: the signal is carried across the gap in the form of tiny packets of chemicals. When these chemicals hit the receiving nerve cell they cause a change in its reactivity: some types of chemicals stimulate the second nerve, whilst others reduce its excitability.

If the amount of chemical in these packages is changed, the messages will be not be transmitted normally. If the nerve-ending is depleted of its normal transmitter chemical then it cannot pass messages on efficiently. Similarly, if the receiving nerve is not responsive enough then the normal release of stimulating chemical will not be sufficient to excite the nerve to action.

In practice the situation is a lot more complex, but we don't need to bother with the details here: suffice it to say that there are several different types of nerve-endings: some inhibitory, some excitatory, some working with one type of chemical, some with another. In addition, there are substances that block the effects of transmitter chemicals and others that destroy the transmitters immediately after they have done their job, so that active transmitter chemical doesn't hang around for too long and restimulate the nerve after the impulse has been passed on.

Complicated, isn't it? But the basic picture is simple. I'm sure you can see how changes in the amount of these chemicals in the brain can have large effects on the activity of the nerves. If there is a reduction in effectiveness of these chemical transmitters all over the brain, a generalised depression will ensue.

We can treat depression by using drugs designed to correct abnormalities in these brain chemicals. There are too many drugs to mention by name, but amitryptilene, dothiepin, mianserin, the monoamine-oxidase inhibitors, and the benzodiazepines such as diazepam and chlordiazepoxide are frequently used. (You may know their trade names better – these include, in no particular order, Tryptizol, Prothiaden, Parstellin, Valium and Librium, Bolvidon and a host of others.)

These drugs fall into two main groups – the **antidepressants** (amitryptilene, dothiepin etc.) and the **anti-anxiety drugs** (particularly the benzodiazepines. They have quite different effects, and are used for quite different reasons; both groups can sedate, though some antidepressants have an immediate stimulant effect, as well as a long-term stimulant effect by correcting the imbalance of brain chemicals.

Anti-anxiety drugs can be addictive if taken in high doses over a period of time, so tranquillisers (particularly the benzodiazepines) should be used with care and preferably over short rather than long periods. On the other hand the true **antidepressants** often need to be taken in quite high doses for many months, but do not seem to have the same addictive properties and therefore present much less of a long-term problem.

Antidepressants increase the effectiveness of the transmitter chemicals, either by increasing the amount of chemical in each packet of transmitter substance; or by reducing the speed at which they are broken down after their passage across the synapse, so allowing the same amount of chemical to act for longer, and thereby exert a greater effect. **Anti-anxiety drugs** work by damping down the overactivity of brain cells.

Surprisingly, antidepressants can work well in the type of depression where there is a clearly defined *psychological* cause (such as a bereavement), perhaps because the intense grief and mental activity that occurs at these times exhausts the supply of available transmitter chemicals. Because of all this, 'mental' and 'biochemical' causes of depression are not mutually exclusive: presumably in both varieties of the illness there is a final common pathway in the reduction of overall effectiveness of synapse chemicals.

Manic depression can be due to a specific type of brain chemical abnormality. In many cases it seems to spring from an underlying inherited biochemical defect which can be traced through many generations of affected families. In manic depression the sufferer swings from the heights of elation, energy and activity through to moods of numbing black depression – made worse because the sufferer recognises with horror that he is going 'down' *again*. The condition is often lifelong, and the cycles of mania and depression can be quite regular: fortunately medication is now available to stabilise the mood so that the swings in temperament are much less violent. Lithium is the basis of treatment here, though other drugs such as haloperidol may be appropriate. It should be said, however, that some forms of manic depression do have a 'mental' cause.

So far the drugs we have talked about all affect the synapse chemicals directly. There is another type of depression which improves with drugs that work on the body generally, rather than affecting the brain directly – in other words they change the biochemical make-up of the body as a whole, which has a knock-on effect on the workings of the brain. This is particularly the case for women with premenstrual tension and depression: in some cases the use of diuretics to reduce excess body fluid will relieve depressive symptoms, possibly by reversing the previous overdilution of body chemicals.

Additionally, the treatments for physical causes, mentioned in the previous chapter, all work through a general effect on body chemicals (and this includes hormone treatment).

Finally, there is **electro-convulsive therapy (ECT).** This was developed quite by chance when doctors noted that patients who had convulsions (epilepsy) seemed to be less prone to depression. We now know that there is in fact no relationship between the two, but the assumption was made that convulsions might ward off depression – and as an electrical shock can bring on convulsions, maybe (done under anaesthetic) this would help patients with intractable depression. It did! – but not for the reasons that were given at the time.

Nowadays electrical shock treatment is carried out in the following way. The patient is anaesthetised and a muscle relaxant is given to stop muscular spasm. Electrodes are placed across the non-dominant side of the brain (i.e. the side away from the speech centre) and an electric shock is given. This causes no pain as the patient is anaesthetised throughout. The patient then has a fit (not very dramatic to the onlooker because the muscle relaxant reduces the limb twitching).

He is then left to recover from the anaesthetic. On waking from the anaesthetic it is common for the patient to feel confused, but by the next day this confusion has usually disappeared.

ECT is normally given in courses of treatment spread over a number of days.

We don't know why ECT makes patients better – it's a bit like kicking the telly when it won't work: sometimes it jiggles a dry joint into contact again. But it does work, and often very well, especially in older people who are often extremely resistant to other forms of treatment. ECT has of late had a bad press, and some (usually lay people) think it should be outlawed. I don't agree with them. ECT still has a part to play – and for some people is the difference between living in the community and being a permanent in-patient in a mental hospital. The need for ECT is much reduced now that we have powerful antidepressant drugs, but in certain cases it is effective and appropriate: it can work *very* well.

EXERCISE

Although depression makes you feel mentally lethargic, you will find you have energy for physical things. It will help to take physical exercise, and the more strenuous, the better. Play squash, swim, chop logs, go for a bike ride, weight-train - it doesn't matter what it is, except that it should tire you out completely by the time you've finished.

Try to do this regularly - daily if you can. You will feel *much* better afterwards.

There are two reasons why this is helpful. Firstly, depression is often described as 'inturned anger'. It can be very helpful to dissipate this anger and tension in physical work. Secondly, especially when accompanied by anxiety, there is often a lot of adrenaline swilling around the body, leading to a heightened 'fight or flight' response: if your body is in a constant state of arousal, but has nothing to do, the adrenaline just sits there, getting you worked up. If you give your body some hard exercise you will use up this 'readiness for activity', so that when you have finished you feel more relaxed than you did before.

Finally, you will probably sleep better for taking physical exercise during the day.

Unfortunately, just planning to do something physical can take more mental energy than you've got! So ask a friend to take you to the swimming pool, or to come and encourage you to take a brisk walk together over the common. In this way you may be able to summon up the energy to get started. Once you have embarked on the physical activity itself you will usually have no trouble in continuing – it's summoning up the energy to get going that is usually the problem, hence the need to involve your friends.

7

PSYCHOTHERAPY AND PSYCHOANALYSIS

Just as each psychological discipline has some good insights into one or more aspects of the workings of the brain, so each has different methods of treatment, which seem to be appropriate for different types of patient.

There are people who have had searing experiences in their early years which have overshadowed their way of thinking about life in general: once the source of their problems has been found and brought out of their subconscious into the conscious by **psychoanalysis,** their fears and problems have ceased.

Equally, there are people who can be helped by **psychotherapy** – which helps them to understand at a conscious level why they are behaving in a particular way, and what they can do about it. Psychotherapy and psychoanalysis at first seem very similar – the difference is that psychoanalysis tries to get the patient to disperse hurts at the deepest emotional levels, whereas psychotherapy attempts to get the individual to deal with his own problems logically, by recognising the problems and conflicts for what they are and changing his behaviour accordingly.

Behaviourists seek to deal with problems by relearning maladapted responses. This helps the patient to sort out what to do in set situations – such as how to cope with someone who is angry with you, or what to do when confronted by a spider when previously you have gone into a panic.

These, then, are the main types of psychological therapy: there are lots of offshoots from each.

PSYCHOANALYSIS

Psychoanalysis attempts to delve into the subconscious to discover the unconscious motives that colour our thinking, especially those formed in early life. The psychoanalytic method is the origin of the joke-book idea of 'the psychiatrist's couch', and therapy consists essentially of a one-to-one relationship between psychoanalyst and patient. The patient lies on a couch, and the analyst remains out of sight, behind him (so that his presence is less obvious). The patient is encouraged to talk about whatever comes into his head: the analysis of dreams is a central theme. (Freud considered that dreams were the 'royal road to the unconscious'.) The analyst attempts to guide the patient into seeing the connections between various aspects of his thinking. During therapy the patient often relates to the analyst as though the analyst were a particular person in the patient's life – e.g. father/mother/brother etc. This phenomenon is common, and is called 'transference'. The skill of the analyst consists in handling these transference reactions, which are often very powerful, and in guiding the patient into *coming to his own conclusions*. The healing effect of psychoanalysis comes when deep-seated problems, which have previously been pushed into the unconscious (because they are too frightening to think about), are allowed to bubble up to the surface and dissipate – if you like, the mental equivalent of lancing a boil to allow the pus to escape. At the end of the therapy, the patient will (hopefully) behave in the 'right' way and make the right decisions because he is no longer impelled by subconscious forces into the wrong course of action, now these 'incorrect' subconscious drives have been dissipated.

Analysis is long, tedious and expensive, taking between one and five hours a *week* for perhaps five years. It is of use particularly where there are very deep-seated problems.

There are a number of different types of psychoanalysis, which vary in the emphasis given to particular aspects of mental life. **Freudians** major on sexuality. **Jungians** are concerned with the need for individuals to attain a sense of completion, and it was they who developed the ideas of introversion and extroversion. **Adlerian** psychoanalysis is concerned with the way in which the infant knows himself to be powerless and how he tries to overcome this in either a good or a maladaptive fashion. The term 'inferiority complex' comes from Adlerian analysis.

There is good and bad in all these approaches. Analysts do *not* have to be medically qualified: psychoanalysis is taught *by the analyst undergoing the analysis himself*. This is good, in that the analyst has first-hand experience of the effects of psychoanalysis, and of the intensity of the emotional struggles that go on, so he has 'been there before you' and understands what you are going through. The danger is that analysts become a self-perpetuating, non-self-correcting faction, convinced that their own interpretation of mental activity is the only true one – 'quango' psychiatry, if you like!

Although psychoanalysis (especially Freudian) is almost revered by the media, there is no great body of scientific evidence to support it. It is not founded on much independently derived scientific evidence other than the anecdotal. A cynic would argue that Freud had a fixation about sex and that Jung was trying to explain away his own frightening dreams. So be wary of treating the pronouncements of psychoanalysts as though they were absolute truth – they are nowhere near this. In practice their work may prove helpful – but it is another matter whether the suppositions on which it is based are always accurate. Psychoanalysts may be doing helpful things, but possibly for the wrong reasons.

PSYCHOTHERAPY

Psychotherapy is rather like a quick version of psychoanalysis. Rather than concentrating on dreams and the subconscious, it is much more concerned with the logical connections of mental problems. Whereas a psychoanalyst will ask non-directive questions such as, "Tell me what you're thinking about?" or, "What does the colour red mean to you?", a psychotherapist is more likely to ask "How do you feel *now* about your mother?" or, "Why does this make you feel so angry?" Although a good psychoanalyst is actually very active (but seems to be passive), a good psychotherapist is much more obviously active, and will need to talk a lot more.

Psychotherapy is a good deal quicker than psychoanalysis. A course of treatment may be fewer than ten sessions, and at the end the patient should possess a much more logical understanding of his problem; he should be able to see *what he should do* in the future, and why he should do it.

I am fond of psychotherapy – perhaps it's my logical approach to things – and I see a lot of advantages in understanding how your own mind works. It also appeals to the teacher in me – the saying "Give a man a fish and you feed him for a day – teach him to fish and you'll feed him for a lifetime" works just as well for his mental needs. If you realise that the reason you react in a certain way to particular types of people is because of *this...* and *that...* and *that...*, then in future when you observe yourself starting to behave like this you can say to yourself, "Careful, now, you're doing it again", and change the way you act.

TRANSACTIONAL ANALYSIS

There are a number of offshoots of psychotherapy, but my particular favourite is called transactional analysis. This analyses the mental and emotional transactions that go on when people interact. In essence it states that each person operates from one of three different modes

– in a parental, adult, or child-like fashion – *but a normal person switches from one mode to another, as appropriate*. Therefore a person operating in the adult mode gives logical, emotionally uncharged statements or questions such as, "How much is this?" When acting from the parent mode the emphasis shifts either to protection or proper condemnation: "Don't forget to put your safety-belt on, Thomas"; "Don't do that, Henry." In the child mode there is an emphasis on emotion, needs and fun (which are all *normal* in appropriate circumstances): "Shall we?" "Oh yes, let's ..."; or else whining and subjugated: "Why pick on me ...?"

Often the distinction between adult, parent and child mode is not *what* you say, but *how* you say it, e.g.:

"Don't do it like that" said without emphasis is Adult.

"*Don't* do it like that" (with condemnatory, how–many–times–have–I–to–repeat–myself emphasis) is Parent.

"Don't do it like that" (whining) is Child.

An *abnormal* response is when you speak or act from the wrong mode – such as giving a peevish (child) reply when asked a logical (adult) question; or going into parental mode to try to push other adults into behaving in child mode, and thereby dominate them.

Other aspects of transactional analysis include the idea of 'the games people play' (meaning 'games' in the malicious sense).

I can't do justice to transactional analysis in just a few lines – it is the nearest thing to do-it-yourself psychotherapy that I have come across, and I recommend it heartily to those who are diligent enough to read it up and put it into practice. But beware – you have to be honest with yourself! An excellent guide to transactional analysis is the book *Born to Win* by Muriel James and Dorothy Jongeward, published by Addison-Wesley.

BEHAVIOURAL THERAPY

Behaviourism takes a problem and by a process of desensitisation relearns wrong patterns of behaviour. A woman who has a dread of spiders would first be encouraged to talk about them positively ("Think of all the flies we'd have if it weren't for spiders."); read about them; then handle pictures of them and draw them. All the while she would be in a supportive atmosphere, and if things got too upsetting she would be able to withdraw a bit until her level of panic subsided enough for her to go on. Eventually she would be encouraged to look at and get closer to real spiders and finally to handle them without panicking. Sensitively handled, the feelings of fear disappear as the old, fearful memories are supplanted by new, good ones. (It is sometimes helpful to use anti-anxiety drugs at the same time, to reduce the level of panic and speed up the process of relearning confidence.)

Behavioural therapy is rather like getting into a very hot bath – jump in and you jump out again quickly, howling! But lower yourself in slowly, acclimatising yourself to the heat, and you will eventually be able to tolerate the high temperature.

Behavioural therapy works well for selected patients, especially those with phobias.

Family Therapy

A lot of problems can stem from abnormal relationships and responses within the family, but because we are all part of our own family we find it hard to step outside the family circle and view what happens objectively.

The normal way in which a child matures is for him gradually to split off emotionally from his parents, acquiring his own independent identity in the process.

But not all children do this. Sometimes they are discouraged by their parents from splitting off; sometimes they don't get the chance, as when a parent dies when the child is still young.

If adequate individualisation does not occur then members of a family can get wound up with one another to such an extent that they lose some of their own individuality and identity. Moreover, because they cannot step outside the family, they can't see what is happening from an objective viewpoint. Abnormal relationships and ways of handling problems occur as a result.

Family therapy is all about the way in which members of the family become separate individuals. Where members of the family are not sufficiently independent, it is common to hear statements such as, "When Emily died something died within me" – a statement which shows graphically how 'the patient' and 'Emily' were emotionally overlapping individuals.

A particular technique of family therapy is to encourage the patient to get to know the rest of the family 'from the outside' – i.e. seeing them as other people rather than as members of the family. In this way, in the eyes of the patient, each member of the family is seen as an individual, rather than a relative. This allows the patient to react to them in a much more appropriate fashion.

Family therapy is of use particularly where there are obvious difficulties in the maturing of the individual and in his establishing an independent existence and identity. Its aim is to allow each member of the family to enjoy being *both* a part of the family *and* an independent being in his own right.

EXERCISE

Do you still feel unforgiven, in spite of the exercise you did at the end of Chapter 3? Although you may be forgiven, it's quite another thing to *feel* forgiven – but that is what you are!

Still don't believe it? Try this as a prayer/meditation. You remember your list of sins which you've sealed in an envelope? Shut your eyes and imagine yourself standing in the presence of Jesus. You're holding the sealed envelope tightly in your hands. Now slowly open your hands and offer it to Jesus; imagine Him taking it away from you, turning away and nailing it to a cross; the nail has gone through the centre of the flap so that it can never be opened again. Now Jesus turns back to you and, with a smile (and a grin!) gives you a parcel in return. You unwrap it – and inside there's a gold cross, which you take and hang round your neck – inside your clothes, so that only you and He know that it's there.

Now imagine returning to your home. In your mind's eye, walk around your house, along the street, into the church, off to your job, talking to people, doing all the things you normally do – but aware all the time that you have the gold cross round your neck, even though no one else can see it. It's your secret possession. Thank Jesus for it.

Now you can open your eyes.

When you next go for real into these situations you've been imagining, remember the secret gold cross; imagine it hanging round your neck again, secretly, as a gift and a token of love from Jesus to you.

PART 2

WHY AM I LIKE THIS? AND WHAT DO I DO ABOUT IT?

8

MENTAL ENERGY

We all know people who seem to have bags of mental energy, and others who get exhausted just waking up! No one really understands what this mental energy is, but nevertheless it is a useful concept in helping us understand how our minds work.

Think of a person's mental energy as being like the electricity stored in a battery. A battery works well if it is the right size for the job and is connected up properly – but if the battery cannot deliver enough power, the work it can do is limited.

Some people have bigger 'mental batteries' than others. They have more energy to do things, and are less easily floored by adverse events because they have a greater reserve of energy to call on.

Conversely, some people don't have enough mental energy. If you think how an electric circuit works you will see that failure like this can happen in three ways:

1. Overload – the job may be too big for the size of the battery.

2. The battery may be run down.

3. A short circuit may dissipate most, if not all, of the available energy, leaving little for external work. When a short circuit occurs, the battery delivers large quantities of energy through the short circuit, to the exclusion of the rest of the system. Although there is a lot of energy around, none of it is being expended usefully: the light won't come on, or the motor doesn't work very well, if at all – but the battery and the site of the short circuit get very hot indeed.

These are good parallels with the mind of a person who has met some form of crisis.

1. OVERLOAD

Just as the battery may not be big enough for the job, so a crisis may overwhelm an individual's mental reserves, simply because of its size. *Every* person has his or her cracking point, but the exact point varies from person to person – some can withstand more than others.

When overwhelmed, people do one of two things. The first is to spend a lot of energy on small tasks while not dealing effectively with bigger and more important ones. For example, during one of the

Arab-Israeli wars an Egyptian field commander who had completely lost control of the battle was found expending his entire energy in the positioning of a single field gun. He had been pushed beyond his limit – he could no longer cope with the overwhelming problems of the battle strategy and had sidetracked himself into the only thing he could cope with. (He could also justify his actions in an odd sort of way – "At least I'm doing something.")

The other reaction is to lose control in a *positive* way – by becoming irresponsible, with worsening language and behaviour, even to the extent of behaving unpredictably and in a bizarre fashion.

The treatment is simple – remove the pressure if you can, share it if you can't. I recently went through a very traumatic, stressful period involving just about all aspects of my personal, professional and church life, and became *very* tired. I could keep going at the tasks I had to do, but had no reserve for anything else. I needed a holiday – but I just hadn't got the energy to choose and organise one. The remedy? We were intending to go on holiday with another Christian family, so I explained my lack of mental energy to them. They took care of the early preparation, the groundwork and the booking. We got the holiday – I lost the stress. In turn, I had taken certain problems away from them.

Christians, both lay and ordained, often take on too much, and are made to feel guilty if they shed work. Two services on Sunday, the Sunday School teaching, the young people's meeting, meals on wheels, pastoral care, sick visiting, evangelistic work, conventions, meetings, fellowship meals... How much of what you do is worth it? Are your *real* talents being used, or are you just a pair of hands, or (worse) – just pew fodder?

Sometimes you may need to learn to say "No". Church leaders (who ought to know better) are very prone to measure the success of their church by the attendance at meetings. In some fellowships there is immense pressure for members to come to mid-week meetings, complete with criticism from the pulpit or in the church meeting for those who don't attend. (It's all very well for the pastor to criticise, but he doesn't *have* to work *all* day and then attend a meeting in the evening – *and* he gets a day off after the rigours of Sunday church activities, unlike the rest of us.)

Don't be made to feel guilty by people who want you to take part in meetings, or ask for your help in running them or doing various 'Christian' activities. Ask yourself instead – does God *really* want me to take part in this? Are my talents *really* suited to that? Am I doing too much? Have I allowed myself enough time for rest? Is my family seeing enough of me?

On the other hand you must answer honestly! It is important that you get enough Christian input in terms of fellowship, friendship and teaching. It would be unwise for you to cut yourself off completely from the church's activities. But do make sure you know *why* you're doing *what* you're doing.

Peter Meadows in his excellent book *Pressure Points* (published by Kingsway) gives graphic examples of how pressured he became through the insensitivity of the elders of the church he was attending at the time. He points out very wisely that church members with young families are most at risk; often the adults started off running the youth club when they were first married, but then the family came along – *yet the church still expected them to run the youth club,* and made them feel guilty for giving it up.

The problem is likely to be worse where the church is run by deacons or elders who have extended families within the church. With an extended family there are lots of built-in baby-sitters, so it's easy to continue with church work, knowing that Aunt Hazel will look after the baby/do the shopping/fetch the children from school. People in this fortunate situation don't always appreciate that other families *without* family connections within the church don't find it so easy to take on the same amount of church activity. And because members of extended church families often have a great influence on the running of the church – frequently being deacons or elders – they may start criticising publicly the 'inactivity' of other families within the church, not realising that these other families have much less extended-family support than ever they had.

As far as possible you should be using your time and efforts on those things to which you are specifically called, leaving others to do those things which are not in your sector of work. Learn to say "No" without feeling guilty. If the women's meeting falls apart because you don't attend, then it can't have been much of a meeting anyway. If you die of a coronary at forty through running the youth club *and* doing an eighty-hour week, then how, at the age of fifty, will you be able to use your *real* talent of counselling?

Learn not to get involved in those things which do not concern you. (In badly run churches probably half of them don't matter anyway.)

However, God does not call us to an easy life, and there may be times when you end up tired and exhausted having done precisely what you are supposed to be doing. As always it's a matter of balance – there is no point in exhausting ourselves on things which God is not calling us to do. There *is* a lot of point in using up our energies on the things that are important to Him.

2. The Battery is Running Low

This parallels the biochemical causes of depression where not enough transmitter chemicals are formed: therefore nervous impulses travel less well round the nerve connections, and a bigger stimulus is required for a given response to occur. A rest from excess stress (and in some cases replenishment of the synapse chemicals with appropriate medicines) allows 'topping up the mental battery' to take place: after this the nerve messages will run freely again.

3. The Short Circuit

Here there is a crisis which takes a lot of mental energy to solve – or, more likely, to *try* to solve, because as it stands it seems insoluble. Under these conditions so much mental energy is diverted into dealing with the problem that there is no longer enough available to deal with other things.

The treatment is simple – in theory, at least: find the cause of the short circuit and solve the problem. This is easy to say but often difficult to do! If the problem is 'on the surface', such as which house to buy, then sheer logic should be able to deal with most of it; in which case assemble all your information, pray, make a decision, sleep on it, pray, review it and then stick to it. *Making* the decision is much harder than *keeping* to it, so it's downhill all the way afterwards!

However, most problems are a bit deeper than this.

"Why don't people like me?"

"Is God really there?"

"If He's there why doesn't He listen to me?"

"Why did He let my baby die?"

These are questions that have no easy answers – there is always room for uncertainty or misunderstanding.

Sometimes psychotherapy can highlight a problem and enable the patient to deal with it directly – such as the person who is miserable, but doesn't realise that the root cause of his misery is his inability to decide whether to leave his ageing mother in order to build his own life and fulfil his own dreams. Once the source of the crisis is recognised for what it is, and once the decision is made (in whichever way), the crisis dies down. On the other hand, highlighting a problem may make you realise just how insoluble it is – which isn't very comforting.

If the problem is insoluble as it stands – such as coping with the death of a relative – then a modified approach must be used. By its very nature, this sort of problem cannot go away.   Instead of trying to believe that the event hasn't happened, the patient must learn how to accept the new situation and cope with it.

Once a major problem has been solved or deflected, or dies down with time, then the mental short circuit disappears and there is energy available to deal with other things.

★   ★   ★

A combination of short circuit and running down sometimes occurs in the person who is chronically overtired through overwork or long periods of stress. Under these circumstances the tired mind cannot deal with stressful situations as efficiently as it once used to – so decisions take longer to reach, the time needed for a given piece of work spreads out, leading to less time for relaxation and hence greater tiredness, which leads to even further inefficiencies in work, and guilt feelings for not achieving as much as before, so he tries to work harder or longer... and round and round it goes. Paradoxically, in this situation conscientious people often try even *harder:* their sense of guilt makes them feel that they shouldn't have a rest because they haven't earned one *because* they are so far behind. It is not easy to realise that a rest is just what you need in order to get back to full efficiency.

History shows us that when men try to work more than six days per week, after a time they find that they can't keep it up. In the last war munitions workers were put on a seven-day instead of a six-day week – and output stayed the same. They just couldn't work in this fashion, so they 'paced themselves'. After the French Revolution it was decided to adopt a ten-day week: they soon went back to seven!

It is not for nothing that God gave us a rest on the seventh day, though we don't always appreciate the wisdom of this. If you combine the Old and New Testament doctrines about the Sabbath, it comes out something like this: "Six days shalt thou labour... and on the seventh thou shalt have a beanfeast!"   Sunday should be for recreation (re-creation); a recharging of the mental batteries; a time for relaxing and doing something different. Jesus said that the Sabbath was made for man, not man for the Sabbath. How often do we find as Christians that Sunday is the hardest day of the week? (Up earlier, try to get the children neat and tidy for morning worship; Sunday School lessons to prepare for the afternoon; an evening service and the after-service fellowship squash; then collapse into bed exhausted to begin *another week of work...*)

Tell me – where in the Bible does it say that you should attend worship *twice* on Sundays?

One of my friends has a much better idea. "Sunday morning is specifically for God ... the rest is for us – we play with the children, go for walks, play on the computer, see friends ...*relax!*" It's very Scriptural! Our high-pressured existence is very exhausting, and the temptation to 'do a little bit more' is very great. Would you run a machine in this way, without giving it time to cool down and be oiled? I think not.

Nothing gives us more pressure than the wristwatch. In the days before clocks we measured time by the day, or alternatively by forenoon and afternoon; now we all wear clocks on our wrists and measure time in minutes. "There is no time to stand and stare", because the dictator on our wrist says that in two minutes and forty-five seconds we will be exactly five minutes and twenty-seven seconds late for our meeting. Because we split time up into such small fragments, we feel that we waste time if we don't use up each and every fragment. If we went back to measuring time by the day we would see things with a broader perspective. When I'm on holiday, I try not to wear a watch; then I don't have to bother about the minutiae of time. It's very relaxing, and I recommend that you try it.

Medically, the alternatives to rest are quite horrifying: continued stress shortens your life. It causes coronary thrombosis, raised blood pressure, strokes and ulcers. Increased stress reduces concentration – so accidents increase. The psychological effects of stress lead in turn to problems with sedatives such as cigarettes and alcohol, or temporary illicit relief in the form of affairs or wild behaviour; marital disharmony, broken homes and emotionally deprived children follow. Not a pretty tale.

So learn to use Sunday *for yourself* as well as for God. He intended it that way.

EXERCISE

I want you to make several lists. First, write down the long-term things that you think God may be calling you to do, and the areas in which you feel He has given you special gifts. Think long-term rather than short-term, so you'll be putting down items like 'work among deprived youngsters', 'marriage counselling', 'being a mother to my young family', 'studying to be a fully qualified computer programmer'. Include a wide range of items – job, family, church.

Now list your hobbies and interests.

Finally, make a list of what you *actually* do at the moment, and roughly how much time you spend on each item per week.

Now compare the lists. It ought to tell you a lot about how well you are allocating your time by comparison with what your overall aims and objectives are.

Now ask yourself a few questions:

1. Am I getting enough recreation time?

2. Am I getting enough time to myself, just being quiet? (I don't mean your 'quiet time' for Bible study and prayer; I mean time just to be you, without pressures, jobs to do, stresses or strains.)

3. How far are my ultimate aspirations, my Christian calling, mirrored in my actual activities?

4. Am I missing out time for things that are important?

5. Is the amount of time I'm spending on church activities related to what I feel to be my gifts and calling?

6. Should I be changing anything? Should I be saying "No" to some things? And should I be developing my involvement in other areas?

9

STRESS

The more I practise as a doctor the more I become convinced that it is unwise to put psychiatric labels on patients, because it limits our ability to understand them. There is no clear distinction between anxiety and depression; and even apparently specific ailments such as phobias can often be successfully treated with antidepressants. Therefore I prefer to treat any psychologically upset patient as an individual case, without a label, remembering that each and every aspect of medicine may have an impact on his or her mental state.

Stress is a case in point – it can lead to depression, to anxiety, or to both. So what is stress? And why do we suffer from it?

WHAT IS STRESS?

We all have in us a "fight-or-flight" reaction. Like the animals, if we are threatened our body gears us up either for standing our ground and fighting, or running away very quickly. This fight-or-flight reaction is caused by the release of the chemicals adrenaline and noradrenaline and it is these that make your heart pound, your blood pressure go up, your mouth go dry, and your muscles tense up for action. This is great – it means that you're on top form, alert, and ready for anything. The fact that you also want to go to the toilet is useful too – it relieves you of the extra weight of urine or faeces, so that you can sprint more quickly! The mind is affected, too, creating a state of maximum alertness.

This adrenaline-mediated reaction normally occurs when we meet any potentially threatening situation, whether physical or mental. If the threat is met with physical action – such as fighting, or running away, then this chemical preparation of the body gets used up and afterwards we go back to our normal relaxed state.

On the other hand, if there is no resolution through physical action, if the threatening agent doesn't go away or if it is replaced by a further threat, then we end up in a permanent state of over-alertness, with muscles that are too tense – "All dressed up, with nowhere to go".

Whilst the fight-or-flight reaction is a definite advantage in an emergency situation, continued over-alertness is very definitely not good for us. It leads to anxiety, irritability, lack of sleep, headaches, muscle pains and, in the more prolonged cases, ulcers and high blood pressure.

In short, too much stress is bad for you.

If you're stressed – uptight, irritable, on edge – then what you're doing is holding on to the stress you've experienced: you haven't found an adequate way of releasing it. (This is particularly true for those with sedentary but mentally stressful jobs. Because there is no *physical* method of resolving the tension that you feel, the tension stays with you.)

Therefore the keyword for stress relief is – *exercise*. Use up that adrenaline by indulging in physical activity – the harder the better. Swim, run, jog, chop wood, do circuit training in the gym, sail a dinghy – it doesn't matter what it is: but physical exercise that leaves you feeling really tired afterwards will get most, if not all, of the effects of stress out of your system.

What about removing the causes of stress? Here we are into much more difficult territory. For a start, each of us can cope with different levels of stress. Some people even enjoy it – there is a definite addiction to adrenaline in some people who like pushing themselves to the limit: the sort of person who enjoys hang-gliding, motor racing, gambling or other activities involving psychological or physical risks.

Other people like a quieter life! But everybody has their own level of stress that they can cope with and enjoy. A life completely without stress would be very boring indeed. Equally, a life too full of it wears you out!

I cannot emphasise enough that stress is a *relative* phenomenon, and everything I say in this chapter has to be read with this in mind.

Different jobs have different levels of stress. The more responsibility you carry and the more time-pressured you are, the more your job is likely to be a stressful one. (Housewives suffer stress because they have so many activities to attend to in the course of a day.)

Life events create their own stresses as well – on a scale of 0 to 100, the most stressful is the death of a spouse (score 100), with divorce and marital separation at about the 70 mark – but Christmas scores 12 (!), and an outstanding personal achievement 28[1].

Death of spouse	100
Divorce	73
Marital separation	65
Jail term	63

[1] From Holmes and Rahe in the *Journal of Psychosomatic Research*.

Death in family	63
Personal injury or illness	53
Marriage	50
Losing job	47
Marital reconciliation	45
Retirement	45
Illness of member of family	44
Pregnancy	40
Sex problems	39
New baby	39
Business readjustment	39
Change in financial circumstances	38
Death of a close friend	37
Change in work	36
Increased marital argument	35
Large mortgage/loan	31
New responsibilities at work	29
Children leaving home	29
In-laws trouble	29
Outstanding personal achievement	28
Spouse begins or stops work	26
School or college ends or begins	26
Living conditions change	25
Personal habits change	24
Trouble with boss	23
Change in working conditions	20
Change in residence	20
Change in school or college	20
Change in social activities	18
Change in sleeping habits	16
Change in eating habits	15
Holiday	13
Christmas	12
Minor law violation	11

Add up the points from all the items that apply to you. If you score more than 200 then you're under a lot of stress and should try to reduce the amount of it you experience.

Too much stress exhausts. Overworking leads to overtiredness, which leads to inefficiency, which leads to discouragement, which leads to self-pity, which leads to giving up, which leads to guilt, which in many people leads to trying harder, so you exhaust yourself more, so that you get even more overtired, which means....

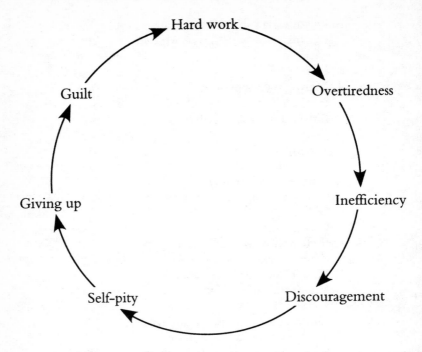

STRESS FROM THE CHURCH

For the Christian, one of the biggest sources of stress can be the church itself. Sometimes the church handles stressed/anxious/depressed people excellently – but on other occasions it does just the opposite, even to the point of making church members psychologically unwell. Peter Meadows in his excellent book *Pressure Points* (published by Kingsway) graphically describes how, in the middle of a hectic lifestyle with lots of family problems and much national Christian responsibility, he was brought to task by the elders in his church for not attending twice on Sundays! What the poor chap needed at the time, as he says, was a walk in the park and a long sleep. (Remember Elijah!)

Although most churches are not as legalistic as this, they can still stress their members unnecessarily by seeking their involvement in all sorts of good works. In this context, do remember that a request for your involvement which comes from the church, or from an individual Christian, does not necessarily come from God. Sometimes we have to step back and say, "Does God *really* want me to get involved with this?" The answer may well be "No", especially if you've already got a lot on your plate.

God gave us our bodies. He wants us to use them properly, and just as we shouldn't abuse them with drug-taking, so we shouldn't abuse them by overstressing them.

STRESS, ANCIENT AND MODERN

It's always said that we live in a very stressful world – the pace of modern living and all that. I don't know that I entirely agree. It must have been very stressful in the sixteenth century when you quite literally didn't know whether you would still be alive at the same time next week. Any number of illnesses could strike which are easy to deal with now, but were fatal then. A quick attack of pneumonia, so easily aborted with penicillin now, was a killer; so too was TB. Today, apart from the shadow of the bomb, which is a relatively theoretical fear, we have nothing like the shadow of death hanging over us that was the case even a hundred years ago.

On the other hand, we are stressed in other ways. We have more gadgets to help us – but then we have to work harder in order to pay for them. And jobs are often more responsible – there's more to go wrong and more people to kill when you're a bus driver, a ferry captain, or an air traffic controller than ever there was in the days of horses and carts.

There is also the stress of the new. Everything is new, different, a fresh experience, when holidays are taken to a different part of a different continent rather than always to the same boarding house at the same resort. (There is in fact a syndrome of tourist stress in places such as Florence, where visitors from abroad see so much in so many museums in such a short time that they become totally overwhelmed and physically collapse.) On a more mundane level, what about the stress that confronts the average housewife doing the shopping? – not just for 'soap', but for the best / cheapest / biological / non-biological / money-off / will-it-suit-my-washing-machine / will-it-get-rid-of-that-nasty-stain / does-it-come-with-coupons soap! And that's just the washing powder!

What can we do against this ever-changing sense of novelty? One answer is **ritual**. I don't mean ritual of the religious type, but ritual of the family type. This is where having a stable life-pattern helps. If bedtime for the children is always the same – in our house it's always one story followed by prayers followed by two songs – it induces a sense of stability in the children that allows them most easily to relax and go to sleep.

There are many rituals that fall into this category and provide a sense of security in an otherwise constantly changing world: going to church on Sunday; washing the car on Saturday afternoon; going to the swings on Wednesday afternoon when the children visit the grandparents.... It's the very regularity of these events which helps so much, reassuring because of their familiarity.

(Having said this, there is one specific area where *lack* of change can bring stress: the stressed man whose job never varies is more likely to experience burnout (see below). In this case, *increasing* the variety within his job, or the ways of carrying out the job, reduces his level of stress.)

THE STRESS OF TIME

We also get stressed because we are time-poor, and this is definitely made worse by being members of the church. We find we really do *not* have time to stand and stare. We can get very busy rushing around doing hundreds of things. It's important to stop and say to ourselves, "How many of these are things I really ought to be doing?" I've dealt with this in a previous chapter but it's worth saying again. It's also worth saying that God's time is not necessarily our time and that there is a right time for doing things. We often try and rush God instead of waiting for His perfect sense of timing.

Anne Townsend describes the time leading up to her breakdown as being like this. She particularly remembers a student-type poster about Christian service – "The need is the call." The need is very definitely *not* necessarily *your* call! Get it right! God gave you talents to do certain things, and He has a plan for you – one which won't overload you, but which will use the talents He's given you (either naturally or supernaturally) to do the things *He's* called you to.

In dealing with stress it helps to review your life style. What are the *really* important things in your life? Make those a priority. Other things can be left to the end of the queue.

Finally, stress is often our own fault. People often externalise stress ("It's my boss who makes me do it.") but in reality it's *we* who are allowing our boss to stress us. There are very few jobs where responses are required instantly: firemen, the police, ambulancemen, and the medical and nursing professions must top the list. For most of the rest the pressure is entirely self-generated. How I wish, as a doctor, that I had the ability to say, as can workers in so many other walks of life, "I can't do it now: it will have to wait until tomorrow", and go away with a completely clear conscience, knowing that nobody is suffering as a result. *Most jobs are like that*. There are very few occupations where you really cannot put your work down, and pick it up the next day.

This is a most important principle in dealing with stress. There are only twenty-four hours in a day and you cannot stretch it to twenty-four and a bit. If you are working hard then there is no way that you can work harder in the same amount of time. If you are working at full stretch, then *any* more work becomes stressful. Therefore, learn to deal with it appropriately. Is your boss asking you to do another report for him? If you haven't the time, *say so*. If he insists, tell him that you haven't got the time, at least not today, and if he still insists, ask which of your other tasks he would prefer you to put aside for the moment. Then, if that second task is not done properly, you have the perfect alibi – "But you told me to do it this way."

Stress comes when you say "Yes" to something that you really should be saying "No" to.

Get into the habit of assessing your ability to withstand pressures – whether these pressures be time, finance, emotional/intellectual energy, physical energy, or whatever. If you cannot do it properly then by saying "Yes" you are laying up future stress for yourself. Be honest (that's what Christians are supposed to be, isn't it?) Let your "Yes" mean yes and your "No" mean no and be honest and honourable to your employer, your client, your family, and God in honouring the body that God gave you and the time He gave for you to do things in.

Techniques for Coping with Day-to-Day Stress

A. Attitudes

1. **Be reasonable with yourself.** Remember the prayer of alcoholics anonymous – "God grant me the serenity to accept the things I cannot change, the courage to change the things I can, and the wisdom to know the difference."

2. **Avoid perfectionism,** which (surprisingly) is often the enemy of good standards. Perfectionism in one area (in all its nit-picking detail) is often accompanied by a reduction in standards in another area, because there's no time or resources left. For example, there's no point in spending hours editing the church newsletter in meticulous detail, getting the layout just right, if in doing so you haven't time to prepare that talk properly. Perfectionists often expect too much of both themselves and others – which can get very wearing on the others!

3. **Don't panic** at what you have to do. If you panic you add yet another problem to those you already have to deal with.

4. **Know your own stress symptoms** – so you don't find they take you (or others) by surprise. If you tend to become a perfectionist when tired (and thus take even longer to complete a task), you should learn to recognise this and make yourself stop before you get even more tired, even slower, even more of a perfectionist and even more stressed!

5. **Talk problems through,** don't bottle them up.

6. **Learn from those who know how.** I can't mend cars, but once I had been shown how to dismantle the carburettor to get rid of dirt, I became a dab hand at it. Learning good techniques will always help you to do your job in a less stressed manner, because you will almost certainly achieve better results more quickly than by any other method. (Third babies are generally easier to look after than first or second ones, for the same reason.)

7. **Have some sort of physical exercise each day.**

8. **Don't have too much coffee, tea or cola drinks,** especially before bed, because caffeine stimulates your brain and stops you relaxing.

9. **Have a hobby** – it doesn't matter what. Collect things – they don't have to be expensive: polished rocks, for example. Build things; make models. Express yourself in music/painting/drama/art etc. Read. Be an individual!

10. **Make your surroundings peaceful** – take time to make your home (and your place of work, if possible) gratifying to the eye and ear. Edith Schaeffer's book *Hidden Art* (published by Norfolk Press) gives an excellent account of how to put precious creative touches into your life – cheaply!

11. **Spoil yourself** from time to time.

12. **Know where you're going.** Be at peace with God. This doesn't mean being out of this world, nor being in easy situations – but knowing that you are right where God wants (because you've asked for His guidance) means that you can adopt a much more peaceful approach to the stressful situations you encounter on the way.

13. **Don't take your worries to bed with you.** Learn to shut off. You won't ever help anything by worrying about it, and lack of sleep makes you function less well the next day. Anyway, what are you doing taking problems to bed when you should be giving them to God? Don't work mentally and then immediately go to bed. Have at least an hour to unwind – watch a TV programme, or read a book. Don't work in bed, either.

14. **Learn to forgive yourself** – it helps to be forgiven by God, too! And if God has forgiven you, who are you *not* to forgive yourself?

15. **Prevent stress in your partner** by showing physical affection, by touching (see Chapter 19 about baby elephants!), by voicing positive thoughts and encouragement; with reassurance, congratulations, forgiveness and appreciation; by giving gifts (little ones are just as important as big ones); and through understanding and sympathy.

16. **Prevent stress in your children** in exactly the same way as for your partner. A secure home gives a child the security to develop his own personality properly.

B. Time Management

1. **Beware of constantly working against the clock,** trying to beat deadlines – it causes *a lot* of stress. Was working to a deadline really necessary? Was it reasonable to set it so close, or should you have given a longer period? It's much better to say, "I'll get it to you in ten days", knowing you probably could do it in five, than to suggest, "I'll deliver it in four", hoping against hope that somehow you might be able to fit it in.

2. **Concentrate on this moment.** What must I do *now*? It's very Biblical! "Today's problems are for today – let tomorrow worry about itself", said Jesus. On the other hand, we do have to plan sensibly for the future in order to minimise fuss later – just don't go overboard about it!

3. **Sort out your priorities.** Learn to distinguish the important from the urgent (but unnecessary); and the truly urgent from the rest.

4. **Try to avoid multi-tasking** – which is a computer term meaning 'doing several things at the same time'. It isn't always possible to avoid fragmentation of your time, but the human mind works best when it can concentrate on only one job at a time. The main source of stress in housewives is having to look after many things at once. (If the baby's crying or teething, you can't cook Crêpes Suzette, so make do with bananas instead!)

5. **You need time for silence and thinking** – quite separately from the time you set aside for Bible study and prayer.

6. **Have a day of rest each week.** ("Six days shalt thou labour and do all thy work and on the seventh thou shalt have a beanfeast!") It's not just for religious purposes that the Bible teaches us to have one day off in every seven. Man needs the rest, and doesn't

function properly or effectively without it. But it should be positive recreation, not just the absence of work. For the Jew, the Sabbath is a day which is full, not one which is empty.

7. **Too little to do** (which of course includes unemployment and retirement) is a stress in its own right. Learn a new skill; take a course or qualification; do voluntary work. This may sound obvious and easy – but unemployment saps your mental energy, so it's harder to get yourself in the mood to start.

C. Work

1. **Work stress.** Causes include bad working conditions (noise; bustle; interruptions; too much/too little light; too hot or too cold an environment; non-ergonomic work-station design); too demanding a job; too undemanding a job; a job which demands different talents to the ones you really possess (for example, the excellent ward nurse who's been promoted to become a nurse administrator, but hasn't got much of a 'feel' for organisation or management). If you identify any of these things as a problem, change them if you can.

   Then there are the interpersonal office problems – over-demanding bosses, lazy colleagues, and sexual harassment (see the chapter on Assertiveness Training for advice on how to cope with this sort of situation). Too much work also provides the classic starting point for burnout (see below).

2. **Too much to do?** Say "No" more often; delegate; take on fewer committments; employ someone else to do what you're not good at, thus freeing you to do what you *are* talented at.

3. **Try not to mix your home and work life.** Taking your marital problems to work makes you less efficient as a worker because your mind is not fully on the job. Taking your work home means you can't concentrate fully on the needs of your family, nor can you relax properly. *However,* this is a counsel of perfection and no one with problems in either area can cut off completely. If your child's sick, you can't help but think about him or her at work. And for those in the professions it is almost impossible not to let work encroach on family matters, because that is in the very nature of the job. Try to minimise it where you can, though.

4. **Take holidays.**

5. **Try to get off to a good start in the mornings.** There's nothing like being three minutes late for work to make you start the day feeling incompetent, rushed and behind!

D. Money

1. **Failure to make ends meet.** This is obviously related to failure to prepare properly for earning, and failure to budget properly. Take stock – be realistic. If you're in debt, it may take a couple of years to get out. Don't 'worry' it – get financial advice, which may include debtor's advice agencies. Whatever you do, stick with your plan of action. Don't take the easy way out (alcohol, gambling etc.) – this sacrifices long-term goals for short-term ends.

2. **Minimise your use of credit.** There's nothing like the lure of easy borrowing to make you overcommit yourself. Borrowing is expensive in the long run, because you have to pay back the money together with a lot of interest.

3. Conversely, **try to save something for a rainy day.** Unexpected bills are so common as to be expected – if you see what I mean! And knowing that there's a bit in the bank to pay them means you can afford to relax.

STRESS FROM FEAR

People who are stressed are often fearful – fearful of failing as a person, of failing in society, of failing to make ends meet, of being ill, of dying, and, for the religious person, a fear of failing in the eyes of God. Too often mental stress leads to various escape routes – typically into cigarettes, drugs, alcohol, food, sex, or gambling as a way of relieving the pressures. Stress at work can lead to irritability at home. Irritability at home leads to marital and family rows, which reduce the amount of relaxation you get, which makes you more tired for going to work, which means you do your job less quickly, which makes you more irritable.... Eventually excess alertness wears out the ability of the brain to continue to pass messages. Too much mental stress reduces the brain's ability to cope, rather like a short circuit in mental energy (see Chapter 8), and down you go into a depression.

Here's how to deal with some of these:-

a. **Fear of failing at a specific task.** Counter this with adequate preparation (particularly for predictable stresses like exams). Discipline in preparation helps enormously for future pressured situations: after the loss of the *Sheffield* in the Falklands war, the Navy practised extensive fire drills and this subsequently saved at least one ship that was set on fire.

b. **Overall lack of confidence.** The *average* school-leaver goes out feeling "sub" (and many of the more jaunty ones are hiding internal insecurities). Why do so many feel like this? Perhaps because we're too introspective, too self-orientated. Contrast this with the techniques of the hustler (see Chapter 18), which can be summed up as, "Others can do this successfully – why shouldn't I be able to?"

Another way to increase your confidence is to concentrate on the other person, not on how well/badly you are doing. It's very Biblical!

Confidence also comes through preparing things properly, so you're not immediately at a disadvantage. Taking pride in your appearance is not unchristian (unless done to excess), and knowing that you are well turned out, with clean shoes and neat hair, gives you an instant "I am starting off on the right foot" feeling, and allows you (paradoxically) to forget yourself more than you would if you were worrying about what others were thinking of your grubby shoes.

The same principle applies to housework. Your house doesn't have to look like something out of *Dynasty*, but it certainly shouldn't look like an imitation of the local Tidy Tip. (Don't just put things down, put them away!)

Another way to create confidence is to have an accurate appreciation of time and work. Constantly failing to meet deadlines because you don't realise the amount of work involved gives you a definite loss of confidence. Starting the day in a rush, two minutes late, immediately sets you off on the wrong foot.

c. **Fear of failing in society.**   It's easy to get subconsciously brainwashed by the TV: one of my friends used to think that life really could be like the Martini adverts, and doubtless felt somewhat disillusioned when he found it wasn't. And although we don't *really* think that life is like *Dallas* or *Dynasty*, we are often affected by hidden messages carried in the most innocuous places (that's why they're so devastating – *because* they're innocuous).

There used to be an advert for a well-known breakfast food, which centred on "Would baby Jimmy like it?"   It showed a family at breakfast, with little Jimmy (aged fifteen months) being offered the cereal.   He takes it – immediately smiles, and wants more.   Cut to picture of the packet: end of commercial.

Simple enough, you might think – but wait! Mum is there, with her make-up on, wearing a smart dress. Dad is there too – in a neat suit, ready for the office. The other two children are at the table as well, neat, dressed and ready for school. *Everything*'s tidy! (Not like our household, I can assure you!)

The overt message may be, "Buy our cereal." But the *hidden* message is, "This is how a normal ordered family behaves" – and mothers watching may not realise that they're getting this message; they unconsciously absorb its neatness and niceness. The next day they look at their own family at breakfast in total despair.

This sort of thing *unconsciously* gives a set of impossibly high standards to aim at *without the viewer realising it,* and without him or her realising the hours of background preparation that it took to create these 'ordinary' scenes. (It probably took two weeks to film what was seen on screen in thirty seconds.) Don't think that I'm knocking the advertisers – I'm not. They may not intend to send these hidden messages – but the messages still come across, all the same.

While we're on the subject of television, one of the sources of stress/depression in the viewer comes as a result of the 'balanced' viewpoint of current affairs programmes, which, in trying to be fair to all parties, find fault with all approaches to a problem, leaving the viewer with the feeling that there *are* no answers: it is but a short step from this to total despair, feeling that the world is full of faults for which there is no remedy. Don't forget that one or more of the remedies discussed may be completely right – and the *objectors* may be the ones in the wrong. (Imagine the reaction in the studio if someone dared to point out that the cause of pollution is to be found in man's inherent sinfulness....)

d. **Fear of being ill.** This is often related to fear of dying or of being in pain. In general, don't read too many medical books! You haven't the depth of knowledge nor expertise to interpret them properly. All medical students go through a phase in which they think they have picked up some awful disease, which they usually haven't. A little knowledge is very dangerous when applied to medical matters! Do the obvious things with regard to your health – eat sensibly and wisely, with little junk food; take regular exercise; go for routine check-ups when appropriate for blood pressure, cervical smears, teeth, etc. Then actively force yourself to concentrate on other things whenever you start worrying about your own health.

e. **Fear of dying.** Christians often have a real fear of dying, despite their faith. This is related to the natural instinct of self-preservation that all of us have. Christianity is, after all a *faith* (however well based on evidence) and even the strongest believers have periods of uncertainty and doubt. It takes a very firm belief to *want* to die, especially when you're young.

f. **The fear of failing before God** is to many a very real and frightening prospect.

Don't imagine that God didn't know you'd feel like this when He first called you! You can't delude God into thinking that you're better than you are (or worse than you fear). He has no illusions about you! He called you, as an individual, knowing every one of your weaknesses better than you know them yourself. He didn't look down from heaven and say, "What an awful job lot came forward at the end of that crusade..." He *called* you, personally and individually: you didn't sneak in while His back was turned! He knew all about you from the very beginning ... and still called you! Isn't that reassuring?

In the long run, if a man knows that he is at peace with God then he loses the fear of dying – and in fact most of his other fears. But knowledge and faith like this is not always easy to come by: it may take a long period of search and struggle. Additionally, the *sensation* of peace with God is often far removed from the feelings most depressed Christians experience. Paradoxically, you may be at peace with God without in any way *feeling* that you are! Particularly in depression, it's a truism that your feelings don't necessarily mirror the truth of the situation. In these circumstances it's often better to try to forget how you *feel* and concentrate on what God has *promised*. Grab at the promise of salvation/ new life/ heaven *logically*, rather than trying to experience it *emotionally*. Feelings can be deceptive.

BURNOUT

Burnout is where the mental faculties are so drained by continued stress that the sufferer can no longer cope properly in his job. If he functions at all, it's very badly. Those in management and the professions are most susceptible.

There are three related but independent parts to burnout. Firstly, there is emotional exhaustion which can include tiredness, irritability, accident-proneness, and depression. Secondly, there is depersonalisation – which is where you treat people as if they were objects, forgetting that they have feelings and sensitivities. Lastly, there is poor productivity, together with feelings of low achievement.

Burnout is most common in high-pressure situations, and especially in those who have jobs with immense emotional and social responsibilities – doctors, social workers, ministers, teachers. It is most likely to occur when there is little job variety. People who burn out are often emotionally isolated. The more they become burned out, the more isolated they get – if nothing else, because of the manner in which they treat others.

Burnout is surprisingly selective – a man who is burned out as, say, a teacher, may find a new lease of life if he turns his hand to writing, or social work.

The cure for burnout may simply be to change jobs; or it may require rest, a period of absence from work (probably measured in months rather than weeks), and a change in working practices, avoiding excess stress, emphasising the team approach and the sharing of emotional responsibility, and varying the ways in which the job is tackled.

★   ★   ★

Here are some ideas which you may find helpful in dealing with your own personal sources of stress.

Ten Rational Ideas[1]

1. I want to be loved or liked and approved of by some of the people in my life. I will feel disappointed or lonely when that doesn't happen, but I can cope with those feelings, and I can take constructive steps to make and keep better relationships.

2. I want to do things well, most of the time. Like everybody, I will occasionally fail or make a mistake. Then I will feel bad, but I can cope with that, and I can take constructive steps to do better next time.

3. It is sad that most of us do some bad things from time to time, and some people do a lot of bad things. But making myself very upset won't change that.

4. It is disappointing when things aren't how I would like them to be, but I can cope with that. Usually I can take constructive steps to make things more as I would like them to be, but, if I can't, it doesn't help me to exaggerate my disappointment.

5. My problems may be influenced by factors outside my control, but my thoughts and actions also influence my problems, and *they* are under *my* control.

6. Worrying about something that might go wrong won't stop it from happening, it just makes me unhappy now! I can take constructive steps to prepare for possible problems, and that's as much as anyone can do. So I won't dwell on the future now.

7. Facing difficult situations will make me feel bad at the time, but I can cope with that. Putting off problems doesn't make them any easier, it just gives me longer to worry about them.

8. It's good to get support from others when I want it, but the only

[1]As devised by Albert Ellis. Ph.D. and Robert A. Harper, Ph.D. and expanded in their book, *A New Guide to Rational Living*, Copyright © 1989, 1975, 1961 (see pp. 198-201), and used by permission of the publisher, Prentice-Hall, a division of Simon & Schuster, Englewood Cliffs, N.J.; also quoted in *How to Close Your Church in a Decade*, by David Cohen and Stephen Gaukroger, to be published by the Scripture Union in September, 1991.

person I really need to rely on is myself.

9. My problems may have started in some past events, but what keeps them going now are my thoughts and actions, and they are under my control.

10. It is sad to see other people in trouble, but I don't help them by making myself miserable. I can cope with feeling sad, and sometimes I can take constructive steps to help them.

Care for the Caretaker[1]
(especially for those in the caring professions)

1. Be gentle with yourself!

2. Remind yourself that you are an *enabler* not a magician. We cannot change anyone else – we can only change *how* we relate to them.

3. Find a hermit spot. Use it daily.

4. Give support, encouragement and praise to peers, subordinates and to management. Learn to accept it in return.

5. Remember that in the light of all the pain we see, we are bound to feel helpless at times. Admit it without shame. Caring and being there are sometimes more important than doing.

6. Change your routine often and your tasks when you can.

7. Learn to recognise the difference between complaining that relieves and complaining that reinforces negative stress.

8. On the way home, focus on a good thing that occurred during the day.

9. Be a resource to yourself! Get creative – try new approaches. Be an artist as well as a technician.

10. Use supervision or the buddy system regularly as a source of support, assurance and redirection.

11. Avoid 'shop talk' during breaks and when socialising with colleagues.

12. Schedule 'withdraw' periods during the week – limit interruptions.

13. Say, "I choose" rather than, "I should", "I ought to", or "I have to". Say, "I won't", rather than, "I can't".

14. If you never say "No" – what is your "Yes" worth?

15. Apologies and indifference are far more harmful than admitting an inability to do more.

16. Laugh and play!

---

[1]Source unknown.

A CHRISTIAN APPROACH TO STRESS

Nowhere does the Bible ever suggest that Christians will have an easy life. On the contrary, look what happened to St Paul – imprisoned, beaten, chained, reviled, sleepless, shipwrecked – life wasn't easy for him. Nor was it easy for Jesus. But He coped with it – and the Bible gives us an insight into how He managed to do it.

We often think of Jesus as 'the man for others' but the Gospel accounts show us how often He took time out for Himself – time for relaxation, time for refreshment, time to let His hair down, time to go off and be quiet, time to be alone with God. He often got up early to go to the hills and pray. Doubtless He could have spent all day every day in healing people – yet He said to many of those He healed, "Go away, and don't tell anyone." And there are occasions when, although it is clearly stated that the need was there, Jesus obviously felt that enough was enough, that He had to stop, go away and *get a rest*. Equally, when it was necessary, he was prepared to be stressed – the obvious occasion is the garden of Gethsemane.

Jesus also delegated – such as when He sent out the seventy in His name.

With this in mind let's look at how you, as a Christian, can reduce the level of stress on yourself without denying your calling, or developing guilt feelings!

Firstly *take time for yourself*. The first miracle took place at a wedding reception. Jesus let His hair down just like anybody else! Think of rest and relaxation as being active, and not just the absence of work. It is right and good that we should spend some time and money on enjoying ourselves. It is false modesty to think that all your money should go on someone else or to worthy causes. God intends you to look after yourself and to do it properly and well.

At the wedding in Cana, Jesus could quite easily have said, "You've run out of wine? Make do with water and it will remind you of those who haven't enough" – but He didn't. He could have gone round healing all day and all night and all the next day and all the next night... but He didn't. He knew that He had to get away to recuperate and rest, otherwise He would be good for nothing the day after.

Jesus delegated. Don't be afraid to do so yourself. At work, my idea of delegation is that I would normally *never* do anything that could properly be done by one of my more junior staff. In other words I do *only* those things that I alone can do, and I let one of my staff get on with those things that either of us could do. This is not to say that I won't muck in when it's necessary – because I do! Nor do I treat my staff like dirt. The more I delegate, the more my staff get interesting work to do – which they enjoy because it stretches them. The more you delegate the more you can achieve, the happier you will be in your work and the happier, too, will be your staff (assuming you are delegating appropriately, of course).

Individual Christians sometimes behave as if they are called to save the world on their own – home missions, mission abroad, help for the socially outcast, the old, the lonely, the preaching, the teaching... *Even Jesus didn't save the world on His own*.... (What?.....) Yes, of course He saved mankind on His own on the Cross, but *then* He used all His helpers, His disciples, His followers, His apostles to heal the sick, preach the gospel, do social work, and carry on the Christian message. He didn't try to do it Himself (at least, not in His earthly body). Each Christian has his own niche, his own part to play in God's plan. No one does everything. So don't let other Christians or the church try to overload you with work that is not your calling. In His earthly ministry Jesus didn't take on more than He could deal with – nor should you.

Psalm 23 for Busy People[1]

The Lord is my pacesetter, I shall not rush.

He makes me stop and rest for quiet intervals.

He provides me with images of stillness, which restore my serenity.

He leads me in the way of efficiency; through calmness of mind.

And His guidance is peace.

Even though I have a great many things to accomplish each day I will not fret, for His presence is here.

His timelessness, His all-importance will keep me in balance.

He prepares refreshment and renewal in the midst of activity.

By anointing my mind with His oils of tranquillity, my cup of joyous energy overflows.

Surely harmony and effectiveness shall be the fruits of my hours,

For I shall walk in the pace of my Lord, and dwell in His house forever.

[1]Source unknown.

EXERCISE

Find a hill where you can walk, sit, and be on your own: go there without a book or anything else to 'occupy' you, and spend three hours just looking around – maybe watching the sun go down. I guarantee that afterwards you'll feel as if you've had a day or two away from your work!

Do you get the point?

CIRCUMSTANCES

Depressions are often 'reactive' – in other words they are a response to some outside influence on the individual's life, such as a bereavement, financial problems, exam failure, a bad marriage, difficulty with the children, illness, sleepless nights – to put it at its widest, any stress that the individual finds too much to cope with. In treating a reactive depression it is obviously important to try to relieve external causes of stress. Later in this section we shall be considering how to do this for specific causes. First, however, let us look at some generalised suggestions as to how you can cope with stress, whatever the circumstances.

SUPPORT FROM FRIENDS

Friends are important in depression, particularly if amongst them is someone who can help you to start to sort out your immediate problems. It is surprising how something which to an outsider seems comparatively small, may look like a mountain to the depressed person who has to get over it. It's always the little things that cause the greatest emotional side-effects – such as a fuse blowing, or the need to wash the children's football kit by the weekend. It's the straw that breaks the camel's back. Paradoxically you may find you can cope with the main problem (such as the death of your spouse) but all the little problems seem insurmountable: so it's a help to have someone come in and do the washing, or take the children off your hands for an afternoon, and it can give you breathing space to enable you to organise a little bit more of your life, or alternatively just to have a rest.

A supply of understanding friends is essential! You need friends to listen to you, to love you unconditionally, to help you out when one of those silly little things is dragging you down. They have to be *understanding* friends because they need to know just how much those little things do affect you – how your emotions explode in all the wrong directions, and over the wrong things – and not criticise you for it.

Just before I started to write this book, our eighteen-month-old daughter started having fits – very odd ones where she would get immensely irritable. At one time there was the possibility that she had a brain tumour. Coping with her was a nightmare, made worse because at first we couldn't find any drugs that would stop the attacks. When she started a full-blown attack, which she did every five or six days, we knew she would be intensely irritable for the next twenty-four hours, and that we would probably get woken up twenty or more times that night. One evening, after three months of this, she was starting to get a bit irritable again and couldn't go off to sleep ... and wouldn't settle ... and wouldn't settle. Finally, in desperation, I phoned a friend. She stopped her ironing, came round, looked at our exhausted and worried faces, told us to sit down, make a drink and watch the TV... and then patiently sat with our daughter until she went (finally) off to sleep.

That's the sort of help I'm talking about. We could cope (just) with the thought that our daughter might have a tumour – but when she wouldn't go off to sleep we were tipped over the edge again. It's always the little things that do it. That's when you need friends to take the burden off your shoulders for a bit – and *let them*. It's no crime that you're collapsing under the strain. Don't feel you ought to be able to cope – you're depressed, your resources are low, you can't be expected to cope. Don't add pride to the problem – let others help you: and don't apologise for yourself all the time, which is so easy to do.

I always feel very sad when people apologise for needing my help – it's as if they are saying, "I'm not worthy to be helped". The answer is always the same: "Apologising for yourself is the only silly thing you've done this evening – anyway, you're worth it". Just because you are depressed doesn't suddenly make you an outcast, a non-human, unentitled to love, care and attention. You're a frail human (aren't we all!) and you need more care and attention when stressed and depressed than at other times. Let others help you – don't feel abashed that you need them. When you are better you will be able to return their kindness by doing the same for someone else with problems.

PS. Our daughter is fine now, and doesn't have fits any more. Thank you for your concern.

Support from 'Experts'

It is amazing how much it can help having assistance from someone who 'knows the ropes'. Just sitting down with someone who is financially clued-up can make all the difference to your family finances: he can help you work out where all the money is going and just how much you have free to spend on yourself each month: in turn this shows you what you ought to be doing in the future. Perhaps it will demonstrate in black and white that things are not as bad as you feared: you can also become aware of what financial danger signs you ought to be looking out for. If you have got yourself organised financially, then when the 'unexpected' bills come in (that perhaps aren't quite so unexpected but just overlooked, like the quarterly telephone bill), they don't come as such a shock any more, now that you have learned how to plan for them.

It may well be useful to get the help of somebody who can give you specialised advice. If you are embroiled in a complex financial problem or have legal difficulties, you will obviously need to speak to an accountant or a solicitor, but skilled advice is often appropriate for many other sources of trouble. If you have housing problems, or long term personal financial difficulties, then maybe talking to Social Services or the Citizens' Advice Bureau will help you organise your life a bit better, make you aware of benefits to which you are entitled, or just give you a shoulder to cry on.

Getting sensible informed advice (not necessarily expert advice) on what to do about the rising damp, or the crumbling wall, or the car engine, may make all the difference in the degree to which that particular problem occupies your mind, to the exclusion of everything else. Once you understand your problems, they become tamer than they were before and you can at least begin to see the light at the end of the tunnel. It is often the unformed problem, the unresolved, uninvestigated conflict that worries us. This is really another way of saying, "Better the devil you know than the one you don't". The devil you don't know is always sixteen times bigger than reality – in other words you get more concerned about the fear of what you *might* find than the reality of what you *do* find. So, make sure you get the advice you need from the people who really know how to deal with the particular subject – you'll find it a great relief.

REMOVING THE CLUTTER

In depression it is often very useful to clear the decks a little – certainly if you are pressurised over time or money. Ask yourself – is this essential? Is it necessary? Do I want to do it? Would I like to do it? (Note that I'm *not* saying that you should only do things that are essential – it is just as important to do something that is totally inessential, if *wanting* to do it is very important to you.) However, it's important that you try to see the whole of your life with a sort of large-scale, wide-angle lens so that if you are too pressurised in time or money you can discard the things that are least relevant to your present life style.

I include the church in this. Christians often allow themselves to get roped in for the most stupid things – things for which they are not particularly gifted, but are used just as a pair of hands or as pew fodder. It may be more Christian for them *not* to do that particular activity because they need to get some more rest, see the family, put their feet up, watch the telly or just go to sleep. So, make a plan of your life. Make sure that your time is spent correctly – doing the things that you feel you ought to be doing and that you *want* to do, and not necessarily those things into which other people are trying to pressurise you.

However, when you're depressed it's easy to feel that you *should* be doing everything. This is not the way that God sees it. He knows you haven't got infinite time, nor infinite energy, nor infinite money and He won't ask you to do more than you are physically capable of doing. Therefore learn to say, "No! I haven't the time". It may be the beginning of the end of your depression! Learn to look people straight in the eye and say, "Sorry, I can't do it."

On the other hand, *don't* say, "I haven't the time" if you really mean, "I don't want to do it", because that's just a lie (and anyway they will come back next week and ask if you've got any more time yet). Much better to say, "I'm sorry, that's not one of the areas that I feel called to get involved in" (which is the truth), and then the questioner will go away *not* feeling rejected: what is more, he won't worry you later for further assistance.

This little word "No" is very helpful. It stops you getting overloaded. While I was in Medical School I came to the conclusion that God was telling me very strongly that He did *not* want me to go into the missionary field, and from that day onwards I have taken Him at His word and refused to get involved to any degree with missionary work other than purely for interest's sake. I am delighted to see it done (by others), I am delighted to hear it encouraged (by others), I am delighted to see that money is collected for it (by others), but I am not prepared to get involved with it to any degree – because that is not the area to which God has called me. Presumably He has other activities on which He would like me to spend my time, work that perhaps other people can't do. Because I've been able to say "No" to missionary-related activities, I've cleared the decks for involvement in other things. It has been a very liberating experience: I have been able to look other Christians squarely in the eye, with a completely clear conscience, and say that I am not able to get involved in their missionary project, whatever its merits, however important in the Christian sphere it is – it's not my scene, and I'm not going to allow myself to get detracted from the things that really are my calling.

So learn to say "No" without guilt. Understand that you are doing it for *positive* reasons (to allow greater involvement in the activities that you really should be involved with), rather than thinking of it in a negative sense. These positive reasons are important, so be honest with yourself, and give yourself time and breathing space to get on with those things that only you can do – such as playing with your children, or studying for those important qualifications, or taking part in a particular church activity that's very dear to your heart and for which you have specific gifts; or even just to give yourself a break.

EXERCISE

More lists! This time, write down all the things that are troubling you – problems you face, things that have to be done.

You can't deal with them all at the same time, can you? So list them in order of urgency. (Deciding whether you are called to be a missionary will just have to take second place to paying off that overdue gas bill.)

Can you reasonably delegate any of them? And if you can't delegate any of them straight away, could you, if you spent a little time teaching someone else how to do it?

Make a *reasonable* timetable for doing all the remaining items. Now go down the list, and carry out each and every item, one at a time. Don't bother about any other item on the list – just do the one you're working on at the moment, finish it off, and cross it off.

If you're ahead of schedule, you have two options: you could start the next one on the list – or you could go and enjoy yourself. If you start the next one on the list you will give yourself more leeway if you get held up later – but you'll probably be better having a rest! You'll be able to enjoy yourself much more, knowing that today's tasks have been completed. Tomorrow's can wait.

Do you remember what Jesus said? "Don't worry about tomorrow. Tomorrow has enough problems for itself, without them spilling over into today." Splitting up your tasks into reasonable day-sized chunks helps you to carry this out and live for today.

11

SLEEPLESSNESS

One of the most troublesome symptoms of anxiety and depression is sleeplessness. There are four main types.

The first, almost diagnostic of depression, is early waking. In this, you go to bed tired, get off to sleep moderately quickly – and then **wake in the early hours** of the morning, still feeling tired but unable to get back to sleep again. The time of waking can vary – in some people it is four or five, but in others it may be as early as one or two a.m.

The second type of sleep problem is in those who find it **difficult to get off to sleep,** but once they are asleep they stay asleep. It is very common for people with this sort of sleep pattern to lie in bed for an hour or two desperately trying to get their feverish thoughts calm and go off to sleep. This tends to be the pattern in those who are anxious – but don't forget that anxiety can also be present as part of depression.

A third form of sleeping problem is where you appear to sleep normally, or even longer than usual – you can go off to sleep and you can keep asleep – but **when you wake up you still feel tired.**

Finally, there is the problem of **nightmares,** which can be particularly vivid and recurrent.

It is possible to get sleep disturbances without having a psychiatric illness – for example, in an elderly person who has got into the habit of cat-napping during the day, and hence cannot sleep well at night.

Major sleep problems are usually not diseases in their own right as much as a knock-on effect from other problems such as anxiety or depression. If this is the case, the cure is to treat the underlying anxiety/depression: once that goes, the sleep problem will also go.

DEALING WITH SLEEP PROBLEMS

There are four ways to attack the problem of sleeplessness.

1. Adjust your life style to give yourself the best chance of sleeping properly.
2. If sleeplessness is associated with underlying anxiety or depression, then treating the underlying complaint will ultimately relieve the problem. (This is especially true in early waking.)

3. The medicines used to help the anxiety/depression may also relieve sleeplessness directly, as most of them are slightly sedative (see below).

4. A sleep-inducing agent taken before bed may be appropriate *in the short term*.

Although it is usually better to start by trying non-drug methods first, it's easier to explain the treatment of sleeplessness if we first look at the use of medicines.

The non-drug methods may not work, especially if there is severe underlying anxiety or depression, and it may be necessary to deal with the sleep difficulty with medicines of one sort or another. Ideally, the doctor will try to give medicines that help the underlying psychiatric problem. If you are depressed, then adequate antidepressant medication may make your sleep problem go away automatically, as the depression lifts.

A neat trick with antidepressants is for the doctor to use their sedative properties (where present) and get the patient to take the whole day's supply all together, just before bed. This means that you don't need to take extra sleep-inducing agents. (Of course, you shouldn't alter the way you take your tablets unless your doctor suggests it.) Personally I favour this approach, and use it a lot.

As with the underlying depression, so with underlying anxiety – an appropriate dose of anti-anxiety medication will relax your mind and enable you to go off to sleep quickly instead of lying awake ruminating.

If you sleep a lot but are still tired when you wake, it may be that your *depth* of sleep is at fault and that you are in need of something to help you sleep slightly more deeply. In this case, paradoxically, although you may be sleeping for ten or twelve hours a day, your doctor may give you something to make you sleep! This will increase the *depth* of your sleep, allowing you to sleep for a shorter time, but yet have a more effective, deeper sleep giving greater relaxation and greater refreshment on waking.

Sleeping tablets can make you feel a bit hung over in the morning and if this happens it may be wise not to drive for the first few hours. And don't take sleeping tablets with alcohol as you will tend to double the sedative effects of both.

★   ★   ★

Going short of sleep is a terrible problem – and it gets worse and worse as you go on. A single night without sleep is bad enough – you feel jaded the next day, and often the day after that as well. But it is soul-destroying to continue day after day, week after week, knowing that each time you go to bed you almost have to fight to get to sleep. Then you begin the following day feeling hung over, tired, listless and generally rotten. As a result your decisions are not as good as they could be, you don't feel as capable of doing physical work, and it reduces your inclination to do something interesting, relaxing and recreational because you feel so tired you can't be bothered to start. The more these things affect your life, the more you will look back at the end of the day and think that you have done only a small proportion of what you really ought to have done. So you go to bed that night feeling guilty for underachieving – and as a result of worrying about your underachievement, you stay awake even more... and so it goes on.

Difficulty in going off to sleep can be caused by getting into a cycle of sleep deprivation – the more tired you get the harder it is to relax. In these cases a *short* course of sleeping tablets may be all that is needed to get you back on the right track. Using sleeping tablets for four or five consecutive nights may give you enough sleep and relax you sufficiently, so that the next night you will be able to go off quickly without them. This method minimises the amount of sleeping tablets required.

There is a great overlay of panic in the person who is trying to get to sleep and can't. Will I get to sleep tonight? If so, how long will it take? Am I going to lie awake until three in the morning, tossing and turning like last night? In these circumstances going to bed becomes an ordeal. It may help to have a supply of sleeping tablets to hand so that if you are not asleep within half an hour you can give yourself something to help. Just knowing that they are there may relax you sufficiently to allow you to go off to sleep without taking any! One word of warning however – if you do use sleeping tablets like this, and particularly if you happen to be using barbiturate sleeping tablets (uncommon nowadays but there are still people who use them) then *don't put them on the bedside table.* Some sleeping tablets impair your memory, and there are cases where people appear to have overdosed themselves unintentionally by taking a sleeping tablet from the bottle by the bed, then going to sleep, waking up again, forgetting that they have already taken a tablet and reaching for another ... and so on. If the bottle of tablets is in the bathroom cabinet then a mistake like this is much harder to make. (In addition they're out of the way of the children.)

★   ★   ★

Now on to the non-drug methods of helping you to get to sleep. There are several important principles. If you can, indulge in physical activity during the day so that you are physically tired when you go to bed. Many people with anxiety and depression don't have physically exhausting jobs (maybe that's why they notice the anxiety or depression more).

Try not to do mental work for the hour or two before you go to bed. If you try to go to sleep immediately after doing intensive mental work then your mind will be tired yet alert, and problems from your work will be whizzing round your mind, preventing you from going to sleep. Instead, read a relaxing type of book, watch the telly, play games, or just chat.

Coffee and tea late at night don't help either. Most people think that tea is relatively harmless, but in fact it contains about half as much caffeine as does coffee: so in terms of stimulant effect two cups of tea are the same as one cup of coffee. Cola drinks also contain caffeine. You may well be better not having any tea, coffee or cola later than about midday. Instead, have a milky drink at night. As well as omitting the caffeine, the milky drink provides you with a full stomach, and this in turn helps you to settle. Going to bed on a full stomach is sometimes very sleep-inducing, but having too big a meal at night can also be a problem. In other words, don't go to bed hungry, but don't overdo it either!

Our bodies have an internal time-keeping system – a body-clock. When this is altered it can take a while to reset: this is the basis of jet-lag. The less you mess around with your sleep times, the more likely your body-clock is to settle into a constant pattern. Therefore, try to get up at the same time each day, regardless of whether it's the weekend or not. Resist the temptation to lie in: it re-sets the clock and disturbs your sleep pattern. So set your alarm clock for the same time each day – and get up when it goes off!

You can also help your body-clock to keep a stable, regular rhythm by going out in the sun – the bright light keeps the body-clock in time. It isn't necessary to do this every day, but if you've got a sleeping pattern which is very haphazard, this may help in restoring order from chaos! If you're having difficulty going off to sleep, expose yourself to sunlight early in the day. On the other hand, if your problem is that you wake in the early hours, try getting a good dose of sunlight in the late afternoon or evening.

Alcohol (and also some of the very short-acting sleeping tablets) can help you get off to sleep, but paradoxically may let you wake up more easily in the early hours. This is why it's not a good idea to have a lot of alcohol before bedtime.

Some people think that cheese at night doesn't help either. I've never been sure whether this is an old wives' tale, but as there are lots of active biochemical substances in cheese it may well be wise to avoid it.

If when you get to bed you find that sleep does elude you, it is probably better not to toss and turn and get angrier and angrier, but to put the light on, grab a good book and read a bit until you feel drowsy. To increase the chances of getting to sleep, it's often better to read *in bed* rather than *prior to going to bed* because if you feel drowsy and tired when you're in your lounge, you can't roll over and go to sleep – you've got to get yourself up, lock the house, put out the cat, get changed into your night things, clean your teeth ... and by then you're fully awake! So save the reading for bed – then if you're tired you can go to sleep on the spot.

Sleep problems can be particularly difficult if you're married – and especially if your spouse doesn't have the same problems, nor the sleep pattern that you have. It may be appropriate for you to buy one of those night lights that clip on to the top of a book so that you can read without disturbing him/her. Alternatively, when you are having particularly bad bouts of sleeplessness, use the bed in the spare room. However, I am most reluctant to encourage this on anything but a temporary basis, because of the rifts it causes in the togetherness of marriage. Which reminds me – lovemaking is a very good preparatory activity before sleeping! It's physically tiring, it relaxes you very effectively, and afterwards allows both of you to drift off into sleep in a much more natural and peaceful manner. It's much better than sleeping pills!

DREAMS AND DREAM THERAPY

Nightmares often plague anxious and depressed people. No one really knows what dreams represent, though there are several schools of thought. One group feels that dreams are nothing more than a subconscious disentangling of the day's memories; a sort of automatic sorting and filing routine, which you happen to be aware of in a disjointed way. Others, particularly the psychoanalysts, believe that dreams are 'the royal road to the unconscious' where hidden problems and conflicts are allowed to surface, often in symbolic form. Perhaps the truth lies in a mixture of the two.

If you think about it, apart from dreams that are a direct revelation from God (and not many of them are), your dreams are entirely created by your own mind. Therefore *every* part of your dream comes from within yourself. Your dreams will be connected with your hopes and fears – *but they may be 'dressed up' because you find the subject matter too hot to handle*. By analysing your own dreams you can often work out what is going on within yourself – what unapproachable fears you have, and so on. The secret is to work out what each piece of each dream represents.

So how do you analyse your own dreams? Firstly, write them down as soon as you wake up – otherwise they'll disappear. Now, remembering that every part of your dream comes from within you, and therefore represents something in your psyche, try imagining yourself in turn to be each person represented in your dream. What are you feeling and thinking as that person?

For example, let's imagine a dream in which you're being invited by a man to come inside a strange house. When you get inside there's no one there, but all the rooms have been vandalised. In the corner of one of the rooms is a baby; you pick him up and carry him out of the house.

Firstly, who are *you* in the dream? What age are you? Is this now, some time ago, or in the future? Do the events have any relationship to the past (especially to the previous day's events)?

Now, imagine yourself to be the man. Think and behave as though you are the man. Who is he? What is he doing in the house? Say what comes into your head first ("I'm the man, and it's my house. I see this person coming towards me, and I'm asking her to come to me because I'm lonely. But she's scared of me, which makes me feel sad, so I keep following her to try to get to know her....")

What about the baby? "I'm a helpless baby, vulnerable. I need rescuing." Remember, *you're* creating the baby. So do you need rescuing? And if so, from what?

Now for something very odd. *Imagine you're the objects in the dream, and do the same thing.* "I'm the house. I was once beautiful, but I've been bashed about, interfered with, destroyed. I'm empty: there's no life in me." Is this you?

These might be your feelings about the people and the objects in the dream. Another person having a similar dream might interpret it quite differently. Her personality is different, so her subconscious has created the dream for quite different reasons. "I'm the house – I'm not very nice at the moment, but if you look under the surface you'll see how beautiful I could be – so I can soon be restored to my former glory."

Do you see how the dream mirrors different aspects of the personality of whoever is dreaming? One feels the house to be a shadow of its former self; the other sees it as a foretaste of what could be.

If you're trying to interpret your own dreams like this, do it *quickly* – spontaneous responses to what is happening in the dream may give a more accurate idea of what it means than attempts to think things out logically. *Feel* the dream, rather than analyse it. But don't try too hard – and don't lay too much emphasis on the interpretation of any one dream, because you might have got it wrong. However, if you suddenly have a feeling of "So *that's* it...." then maybe you've hit gold!

Once you start to understand what your dreams represent, you are then in a position to deal with the underlying conflicts and problems they bring up. (In the example, if you realise that you feel like the house – once beautiful, but now abused and destroyed, then you can start to work out logically how to deal with the situation. In this case you might want to offer your present state to Jesus, and ask Him to take you *as you are*.)

Once you have identified and resolved the conflicts represented by your dreams, you will find that the nature of your dreams changes, and in particular those disturbing recurring dreams may disappear.

Acting out your dreams like this is called a Gestalt experiment, and there's another example in Chapter 14, this time from real life. If you think that Gestalt experiments like this might help you further, do read a lovely Christian book called *Healing Dreams* by Russ Parker, published by SPCK; it's well worth getting.

Recurring nightmares can make sleep a torture rather than a rest. If you are particularly troubled by them, tell your doctor. He may want to give you a sedative to increase the depth of sleep and make it more restful for you.

EXERCISE

Analyse your dreams! Try it – it's not as daft as it sounds. In particular, write down any recurring themes. Then consciously try to deal with the problems, attitudes and emotions these dreams have revealed.

If you're troubled with sleeplessness, count how many cups of coffee/tea/cola you're drinking during the day. You may get a shock.

And having carried out all the things mentioned in the chapter, if you're still having trouble sleeping, *go and see your doctor*. A short course of sleeping tablets may put you on the right road very quickly, without risking any problems of addiction.

12

LONELINESS

It is very difficult to describe the intensity of the isolation and loneliness experienced by a depressed person. It consists of an overwhelming feeling of emptiness, but of such intensity and of such a pervasive character that *everything* that you touch or do is contaminated by it.

This all-pervasive finger of death interferes with every single part of your life, from the moment you wake up to the time you try to go to sleep. Because this sense of futility saps the emotions, it frequently prevents you from finding the energy to do anything. Then at night, when you look back over the day, you feel that you have achieved absolutely nothing – which may well be true. Then you worry that you've wasted the whole day, which makes you feel even more depressed, so you are less able to cope with things the following day....

The most common and intense feeling of loneliness comes directly from the depression itself. Along with the sense of depression there is an inner sense of desolation and despair. Nothing seems important any more: everything seems a waste, futile, without purpose. Everything you do feels wrong. Because everything seems so hopeless, you may find it impossible to join in activities with the same intensity as anybody else, and things that others find of value feel to you just boring or pointless. All the enjoyment goes out of life, all the banter, all the wisecracks. However, this feeling doesn't stop *others* enjoying life: and when you see them bouncing around having a rare old time you feel even more out of it. Not only do you not enjoy life as much as your friends, but you can see an increasingly wide gulf opening up between you and them. They enjoy things – you don't. It becomes difficult to laugh and because depression is a flattening of the emotions generally, it's almost impossible to cry as well. When you can't respond emotionally to what is going on around you, it makes you feel more isolated, and what's more, because others see you not joining in they may feel that you are intentionally isolating yourself – so they ignore you even more. This, of course, only increases your loneliness.

There is a further sort of loneliness in depression – the loneliness which imagines that nobody else has ever experienced what you are going through. Increasingly you may feel that your friends don't understand what is going on within you. This can often be made worse by the attitudes that well-meaning but inept friends can have towards depression. Their attempts to help (the "pull yourself together" routine) only serve to make you feel that nobody really understands you at all. It's true! People who say things like that don't understand! But many others *do* understand what goes on in depression, and it is important for you to realise that others have been through what you are facing and have come out on the other side.

All these sources of loneliness conspire to create a considerable barrier between you and the outside world. Inside this shell the sufferer retreats to mope. And the more you retreat, the more isolated you feel; the more isolated you feel, the more you behave in an isolated fashion; the more isolated you become, the less other people contact you, and so it goes on.

What are the remedies for this situation? Firstly, an awareness that *you are not alone*. Knowing that other people have gone through the same problems will give you heart – at least you know you aren't *actually* alone. This is rather like Elijah, who, having single-handedly faced the priests of Baal, complains to God that he is all alone: whereupon God tells Elijah (with, I suspect, a slight twinkle in His eye) that, actually, there are two thousand others that haven't bowed the knee to Baal...

Knowing that you are not alone means that you can take some comfort in the fact that others have been there before you, and therefore at least *some* people understand what you're going through.

Once you know that loneliness is an important feature of depression and that it tends to set up this vicious circle, you know how to fight it. When you feel insecure you may tend to cut yourself off from other people: therefore make a conscious effort to do exactly the opposite. Make time to meet other people – and I don't mean time to meet them so that you can talk endlessly about your own problems. I mean making time for other people to talk about *their* problems, and *their* interests. Two things will happen if you do this – firstly, you will look back over the day and feel that life is not quite as desolate as it once used to seem, because you have actually been able to talk to one or two people and have valuable conversations with them. Secondly, you realise that they are actually interested in having a conversation with *you* (so long as it's not about your depression!) and so they feel more friendly and warm towards you. This is likely to make you feel a lot better, a lot more wanted, more accepted and more human.

It is very important to make this effort. Just having a little bit of time for other people stops you becoming introverted and selfish, which is unfortunately what can happen if you get a severe depression. In addition, getting out of yourself, meeting other people, and talking about other things will provide a lot of background support for you whilst you are working through your own problems. It will also provide new interests. It will also give you fresh heart to face your own internal battles if you feel supported and encouraged by friendship.

But in many ways the one thing which you need more than anything else is a lot of love. It will carry you a long way to know that you have friends who care for you, come what may, who are not put off by your moods, and who come back smiling even after you've been rude or offhand with them. In this context a close friend is a great help – and it doesn't matter who it is: husband, wife, boyfriend, girlfriend, or simply a deep platonic friendship – even a pen pal will do. It's the feeling of being needed, cared for, *understood,* loved *for yourself* that is the crucial thing.

Physical contact is very important too, much more so than we might at first think. We're going to deal with the importance of touching later on (see Chapter 19) so I won't repeat myself except to say how important physical contact is in giving someone a sense of being cared for. Which do you think helps more when somebody is sobbing their heart out? To say, "I'm terribly sorry" – or to put your arm round his shoulder? What do you think helps a depressed woman most – her husband saying, "Cheer up" from the other end of the room – or a cuddle? We English are very biased against touching, so there are certain social barriers to climb over before you can feel at ease in doing it. Nevertheless, simple things can work wonders – like putting a hand on a depressed person's arm when you're talking with him.

Just holding hands can help. In this respect I'm sure that couples are much *less* vulnerable to the worst effects of depression than their unattached colleagues. Unfortunately, when you're depressed these relationships come under strain and, in the case of courting couples, don't always last. I certainly wouldn't suggest you go looking for a boy/girlfriend as an antidote to depression – you may well team up with someone for all the wrong reasons, and choose someone with all the wrong attributes to help you through your current situation (remembering that if you pick someone who is similar to yourself, he or she may be just about to go through a depression too!)

EXERCISE

1. Start to make positive efforts to make contact with others *without* discussing your depression. Join a society or two – not necessarily connected with the church. Go bird-watching, make music, play bowls, do pottery, etc. Learn to join in with others doing 'third-party' things, such as decorating the church or doing some gardening for the old people in your neighbourhood – in other words, do things for others. Depressed people can get very introspective, and 'third-party' activity creates a good antidote to this, as well as providing stimulation, and interesting you in new areas.

2. Keep a diary in which you put only the *positive* things that have happened to you: the outings you enjoyed; the sights you've seen; the people you've met; the promises you've come across during your Bible study; the guidance; the answers to prayer. Nothing negative. Just the successes. In doing so you'll realise how fortunate you actually are (more so than you thought!), and what's more, you'll start looking for successes to write down, rather than concentrating on the failures. You'll find it helpful to re-read your diary from time to time to remind yourself of the good things that have happened to you.

13

BEREAVEMENT

Of all life events the death of a spouse is the most stressful, and the death of a close relative is almost as bad. (See the table in Chapter 9.) However, bereavement only causes problems if the bereavement itself is badly handled. It is very important that the emotions it generates are handled properly and brought to the surface at the right time, as otherwise they will burrow deep into the psyche and may come out as a depression later on. (See Chapter 14 on Emotions.)

For the Christian, bereavement is sometimes easier, but sometimes much more difficult, than for the agnostic or atheist. If you have lost a loved one who was a practising Christian, then there is great confidence that they have gone to be with Jesus and a knowledge that you do not have to worry about him or her on that score. However, *it does not stop you from missing them,* and it is just as important for a Christian as for an atheist to grieve over their physical death. *This grieving is for your benefit,* not for the benefit of the dead person. The fact that they are dead and with Jesus is, as far as you're concerned, only a partial comfort – they have left your life, permanently, and they aren't coming back, this side of heaven. That's a big blow, and mourning is all connected with reorientating your life to accept that fact. I just do not believe that a Christian who has loved somebody very deeply can turn round in the *immediate* stage of bereavement with their eyes aglow and say, "They are with Jesus", with the sole exception of someone who has been through a long and painful illness and has now been released from it. If anybody takes this attitude towards death then either they're hiding their worst fears from everybody else, or they didn't love the other person very much in the first place.

Christians have to mourn their loved ones just like anybody else. However, there is a big difference in the mourning of a Christian and a non-Christian. The Christian mourns the personal loss knowing that their loved one is going to be with Christ forever. Their death is a temporary stage at the beginning of everlasting life. On the other hand, the non-Christian has no certainty of anything after death, and although many agnostics hope that there is a life beyond, nevertheless they are living on hope rather than living by faith. Bereavement to a Christian is intense, personal and sad – but not hopeless.

If, as a Christian, you have not been able to come to terms with the death of a loved one, then it is not a demonstration of your lack of faith, but an expression of your difficulty in coming to terms with the loss of somebody who physically, mentally and spiritually meant a lot to you. Therefore you must concentrate on that aspect of the grieving process – the effect on *you*. Did you ever cry over their death or did you try to keep a stiff upper lip? Maybe you need to do some crying now. Even if you think you're going to hit rock bottom by immersing yourself in the sadness that you feel, nevertheless it is important to go down before you come up again. Therefore do allow the hurt and sadness – and the anger – to be dissipated through the mourning process.

Even when you are a Christian mourning another Christian there are still potent causes for anger, often directed against God. Why did God take my baby? Why did God allow my husband to die in that road smash? It is important not to get guilt-ridden about telling God of your anger. Far better to go into it honestly and say to God that you don't understand why He allowed it to happen, than to deny that you have these feelings, because in denying your feelings you are not being honest and you will be sowing potent seeds for later problems through your own internal dishonesty. (God knows how you feel anyway, so you might as well be honest, face up to it and tell Him openly.)

Ultimately of course your anger is misplaced, because it is not God that has created the problem but sin. It's worthwhile remembering what Jesus Himself felt when confronted with the death of a friend – Lazarus (see John 11). Jesus *knew* that He was going to raise Lazarus from the dead. Yet what did He do? He wept. What did He weep for? Surely not for Lazarus, because He was just about to raise him. No, he wept because of what *sin* had done in the world. It was sin that had killed Lazarus, it was sin that was causing his relatives to mourn and Jesus was weeping for the disaster that sin had brought upon the whole world, on the good and the bad, the Christian and the non-Christian alike. He wept. He was upset. He was sad.

When confronted with bereavement there is no reason why we should not emulate His actions. We should not fear that we are in some way doing the wrong thing. As always, God understands. He would rather that you were honest about it than hide it. And if you are honest about your feelings and questions, you will find that He will eventually give you some very good answers. My experience is that God never dishonoured nor disowned anyone who asked honest questions, and in times of bereavement it is often very difficult questions that are asked very honestly – so don't be afraid to do it.

What about the times when a Christian loses a non-Christian friend? This is very much more difficult in many ways. For the agnostic at least there is the hope that there may be *'something'* on the other side of death. For the Christian, there is only the feeling that

the person who dies Christ-less is doomed – which is *real* hopelessness.
I think it is wise on these occasions to give the problem over to God.
After all, it is God who is going to do the judging of that person and
the Bible tells us that God will judge according to the lights that the
individual people had. Only God can tell the state of a person's soul;
only He can judge. He gave us very strict injunctions against judging
our fellow man, and I sometimes think that we employ these
injunctions in exactly the wrong way, implying that we should not
judge our fellow Christians, but that in some way we are entitled to
turn round and judge non-Christians in the most vehement terms
imaginable. It is not up to us to judge, it is God who will do it – justly
and lovingly.

If you have a non-Christian friend who has just died, then tell God
the whole situation and let him deal with it. Don't get yourself
muddled by trying to make the decision for Him on inadequate
evidence.

In any case the distress may not be necessary – there are a number
of occasions in the Bible when we are told that people close to us are
in fact God's by virtue of the fact that they are related to us – we are
told specifically that our wives and husbands and children belong to
God because we are Christians (see 1 Corinthians 7 : 12–14), (though
it has to be said that opinions vary as to the implications of this
passage).

In the period immediately after personal bereavement it is very
common to say and do apparently stupid things – like laying two
places at the table instead of just the one. Quite frequently the
bereaved person experiences hallucinations in which they see or hear
the dead person; this happens especially on waking or going to sleep.
These phenomena are so common as to be normal, so if you are
experiencing them don't worry – you are not going mad! It also has
nothing to do with Satanic influences. The person is not there, and
the voices that you hear are in fact memories from your subconscious,
but they can be very vivid and in some cases very worrying.
Gradually these hallucinations and experiences will disappear as the
grieving process continues. (Incidentally, the resurrection appearances
of Jesus cannot be due to this phenomenon because Jesus appeared
to several people together and they wouldn't all have had identical
hallucinations! You will recall that on one occasion Jesus was given
a piece of fish, which he ate. This is not the sort of thing that happens
in the hallucinations that accompany bereavement.)

Good grieving is important. If you don't let out the emotions you
feel at the time you experience them, they are likely to emerge later
in a different form, perhaps as a depression: the emotion will be harder
to deal with in this form. It is important to forestall these later knock-

on effects: a set period of mourning can actually be a great help – such as the formal time of mourning that used to be common in the Victorian era. The great thing about a formal period of mourning is that it actively comes to an end after an appropriate interval (unless you're Queen Victoria) and then life is expected to resume. This encourages you both to feel the depth of your grief, then come up out of it. People who are depressed often find difficulty in experiencing the heights and depths of emotional sensation and, because they are too frightened of the intensity of their misery, they are not prepared to experience it fully. (It's rather like fitting a compressor in an audio-electrical circuit – it won't allow the troughs to be that low, but it won't let the peaks get too high either.)

If the sufferer is not prepared to plumb the depths of his grief, when he eventually 'comes up' he will be unable to experience happiness to any great degree, either. Proper grieving releases you from this situation and allows the natural swing of emotions to occur: thus the mourner gets it all out of his system in a permanent fashion and is left without the tendency to secondary effects later on.

EXERCISE

If you are experiencing problems related to bereavement there are several books which may be of help.

Good Mourning by Judy Gordon Morrow and Nancy Gordon DeHamer (published by Word) sensitively explores the difficulties encountered with miscarriage and stillbirth.

A Grief Observed by C.S.Lewis (published by Faber) consists of reflections on the inner turmoil he experienced following the death of his wife. If you've recently lost a loved one, and find yourself wondering if you are going to go out of your mind with grief, doubting God, goodness, and just about everything else, you may find this book a real comfort. He explores the questions death throws up with deep and disconcerting honesty, but at the same time, in sharing his feelings he shows that others share in what you are currently experiencing: that you aren't going mad, and that God is still there.

14

EMOTIONS

Emotions are strange and complex things. On the one hand, we know we shouldn't trust them because they are 'emotional' not 'logical', (though this is not strictly true, as we shall see later). On the other hand, they are by their very nature intense, personal and demanding. We 'feel' apprehensive, we 'feel' confident – yet these emotions may not be a true reflection of what we should logically be feeling, bearing in mind the circumstances.

We also think of emotions as being allied to some form of sixth sense, some form of 'gut reaction' which tells us the 'real truth' of the situation, and because we think that this sixth sense is in some way infallible, allied to Nature, (or the Universe, God, Guardian Angels, the Life Force or what have you) we think that these emotions are therefore to be trusted. This sounds pretty pagan, doesn't it? However, in our society emotions have become invested with an almost magical quality and unfortunately *this attitude has been aided and abetted by a misunderstanding of certain church teaching*. More of this later.

WHAT ARE EMOTIONS?

Emotions are generated by some of the apparently more primitive areas of the brain and are best thought of as being *internal* sensations, in much the same way that touch, pain, and temperature are sensations derived from *external* sources. The emotions are mainly related to conditions within the brain – reflecting the type and degree of mental activity. Perhaps the most primitive emotion is fear – this will be generated when there is real danger present, such as a large and angry dog coming towards us; or alternatively when we are reminded of previous danger, such as the fear of falling – which brings back painful memories of the occasions when it was *we* who went bump in the night!

Emotions often work very logically indeed, although we are not always aware of their logicality. For example, whenever I'm driving along a particular stretch of road near where I live, I start to feel apprehensive. I know why – it's because I had to assist with a particularly unpleasant car crash there, in which a badly injured driver was trapped inside his car for a considerable time. Every time I pass that particular spot the intensity of the emotion that I felt on that occasion is brought to mind (whether I want it to be or not) and it makes me feel uneasy and apprehensive. I am aware also that, given the choice, I'd rather not use that particular road, in case the same thing happens to me.

In this particular instance I am fortunate because I know precisely why I am apprehensive. On the other hand, if the mental connections were a lot less obvious then I might misinterpret my state of apprehension and feel that some sixth sense was warning me of something unpleasant that was about to happen.

Feelings are often generated by quite logical (if unconscious) connections like this. It is therefore not right to think of emotions as being illogical – they are not. However, their logic is often buried very deeply and may take an awful lot of winkling out; particularly if the memories upon which that logic is based occurred very early in life. For example, a six–month–old child in his pram gets half smothered by the family cat when the cat decides that the child's face is a lovely warm spot on which to go to sleep. Should we be surprised if later on that person develops an anxiety state about things that are black and furry? Or if he develops claustrophobia – a fear of being in a confined space? It's very logical – but it may not be easy to spot what has happened, particularly as *the child may have no conscious recollection of the original incident* and there may have been no external witnesses to the event.

Dissecting out the logic behind the emotion is the region of psychotherapy and psychoanalysis. When the individual understands *why* he starts to feel apprehensive, then he is halfway to controlling his inappropriate emotional fears; although true and accurate as far as the past is concerned, they are no longer relevant for the future. (Adults don't have to worry about cats suffocating them while they sleep, for example.)

FEELINGS – REAL OR IMAGINED?

Our problems about our emotions are compounded by one very important fact. If you think about it, our emotions are one of the few *objective* things that we experience about the universe. When we look at somebody else *we* may *think* that they are apprehensive (whereas in fact they may not actually feel this way). We have therefore misinterpreted the truth about their bit of the universe. On the other hand when we feel apprehensive we *know* we are apprehensive! It is *true* that we are apprehensive. (We may not *need* to be apprehensive, but that's not the point at issue.) We *know* we are apprehensive. This very immediacy and intensity makes us sense that these feelings are all the more relevant and true; and because we *know* we have these feelings, it is but a short (but illogical) step to assume that we are right to have these feelings, and that they mean something significant.

So our emotions are very logical, very real, but not always relevant. Yet we rely greatly on them: how often have you done something because you just 'felt' that it was the right thing to do? You had a 'gut reaction'? Or alternatively, how often have you been frightened to do something for the same reason? "I really had this feeling that I was saying the wrong thing." This gut feeling may well be accurate – we may have worked out the answer subconsciously while our conscious mind hasn't fathomed out what to do. Alternatively, we may be aware of the 'non-verbal communication' coming from others, where the posture, manner of speech and physical behaviour send messages to us that we perceive subconsciously.

But equally, our emotional reactions may be welling up from our personal memories of events good and bad. We may be feeling apprehensive because something about the situation reminds us of an event in the past that ended with problems. Memories like this can be very useful when we are confronted with bull terriers! They are *not* helpful when there is a more oblique relationship – such as the one I always experience whenever I smell the printing ink from toy printing sets. It reminds me irrevocably of my first encounter with death, because at the age of eight I was playing with such a set when I heard my next-door neighbour had died. A whiff of printing ink will (almost subconsciously) colour my emotions without my even realising that I can smell it.

Unfortunately, *there is no way of telling whether our gut feeling is occurring for good or bad reasons*. Therefore, although it is wise for us to be aware of our emotions, we must remember that they are not always true to the situation, and we have to be prepared to use our logic in order to work out what our next course of action should be.

GUIDANCE, EMOTION – OR BOTH?

The gut sensation of anxiety or apprehension (for the wrong reasons) can often be exacerbated in depression, and sufferers often have that dreadful uneasy feeling that all is not well, but for no obvious reason. Unfortunately, unease often colours what we choose to do or say. If for emotional reasons I feel uneasy about going out today, then I will probably be less confident in what I say and do when I do go out. At a more obsessional level I may feel that my actions after going out are sinful because I feel I ought not to be in that particular place, and therefore everything I do is totally wrong because I shouldn't be there at all.

Go on, admit it, you've felt like that, haven't you? Unfortunately the depressed person usually feels that *everything* he does is wrong. This can be compounded by misunderstanding some of the teachings of the church. How many times have you heard a speaker say, "I felt the Lord was leading me to do ...". In this context, what does he mean by the word 'felt'? Unfortunately the English language mixes up two quite distinct ideas in one single word – 'feel' meaning 'I sense', and 'feel' meaning 'I came to the conclusion that'. We often have no easy way of separating the two meanings, nor of being sure of which one was intended – and if we guess wrongly we may totally misinterpret what is being said.

Let us assume that our speaker was perfectly correct and that God was in fact leading him. (Whether he was led or not is not the issue at stake. It is *how* he was led, and how he knew he was led, that we have to investigate.) "I felt the Lord was leading me ..." can mean one of two things. The first means *as a result of the logical working out of a problem* – "I felt (came to the conclusion that) the Lord was leading me..." Alternatively, the word 'feel' describes our internal emotional state, unrelated to logic – "I feel (emotionally, not logically) that God is leading me ..."

Therefore his statement can be misinterpreted. The speaker may think he has said, "As a result of logically working it out, I came to the conclusion that...", whereas you, the listener, may think that the speaker felt a rosy glow inside him. This may lead to a lot of unhappiness when you, as the hearer, try to emulate the speaker's attitude to Christian living. We are told the importance of 'waiting on God'. The danger is that a Christian (especially an anxious or depressed one) may think he is being told that it is better not to do anything until he reaches the point where he 'feels' (emotionally) that it is the right thing to do. Now 'feeling' in this sense is quite different to 'feeling' in the coldly logical sense. Therefore our anxious or depressed Christian listening to this sort of address will go away and think to himself, "I mustn't act until I feel (emotionally) that God is telling me the right time has come." What he *should* be saying, instead, is, "I mustn't act until I feel (come to the conclusion, logically) that God is telling me the right time has come. This is where the Devil gets in and makes hay. Because our feelings and emotions are so subject to subtle events and memories from the past, our current emotional state is not an accurate guide to our next course of action. If we wait until we feel good about something then we may *never* act – particularly if we are scared of doing things that are unusual or abnormal, or if we suffer from 'floating anxiety' due to anxiety or depression. If we tend to fight shy of doing anything new, we will never 'feel' that it is right to start and because we never 'feel' ready to start, then we will never make new efforts or essay the unknown.

(I should add a rider to this – there are occasions when God really speaks to people, perhaps with a word of knowledge, or prophecy; when this happens the speaker is aware of feeling quite different about what he is saying or experiencing. But this more direct experience is not usually what is meant by "I feel that God was leading me".)

FAITH, LOGIC AND EMOTIONS

It is vital for Christians to understand that our emotions are not necessarily a good guide to what is going on, nor to what we should be doing in the next few minutes or hours. Unquestionably this is where logic should apply first and foremost. For example, in the case of the person who is scared to do anything new his emotions may be saying, "Don't do this, it's the unknown, it's frightening – don't do it", whereas his logic may be saying, "This is an obvious and excellent opportunity to do something – grasp this opportunity immediately because you may not get another one like it for some time."

Faith is often like this. The Bible talks about those who are tossed around by the wind in terms of faith; such people often depend entirely upon their emotional appreciation of God for the depth of their faith. When their emotions are in an upheaval their faith will be too, so at the time when they most need God they will *feel* as though He's not there!

There is a modern parable about this, of three tightrope walkers called Faith, Emotion and Logic. When Emotion went first along the wire with Faith and Logic afterward, Emotion got very worried, wavered, and fell off, dragging the other two down with him. On the other hand, when Logic went first with Faith second and Emotion bringing up the rear, everything was on a much more even keel. Emotion was steadied by the effects of the other two.

It may be a rather simplistic analogy but it does illustrate the point rather well. It is so easy to think that our emotional feelings are in some way very 'true' reflections of our faith (or lack of it!), and it can be quite difficult to wean ourselves away from depending upon our emotions at times when we really should be relying upon our logic.

However, I don't want to discard emotion. True emotion is *vital* – the danger is that we will rely on it for the wrong things at the wrong time. We sometimes pay too much attention to our emotions at times when we should really rely upon our logic, yet on other occasions when we should be *expressing* our emotions we try to keep cool, logical and distant, particularly when preserving that English stiff upper lip.

CARING FOR YOUR EMOTIONS

Depression is in many ways a disease of the emotions, and getting the emotions back into trim should be the prime target for any depressed person. It is important that we learn to laugh when we want to, to cry when we need to, to be joyful and to be sorrowful when appropriate. As Ecclesiastes says, there is a time for everything under heaven – a time to weep, a time to laugh, a time to sow, a time to reap. There is a time to be joyful and there is a time to shed tears. There is a time to be happy and dance; there is a time to wail and weep.

Unfortunately, in depression the emotions are flattened and this is a characteristic signature of the disease. Not only can you not be happy, you can't be very sad either. It may well be that the mind is trying to avoid dealing with something that it finds intolerably sad – such as the threat of death or disease, or the loss of a loved one; the mind protects you from feeling unbearably despondent. Unfortunately, this is at the cost of not being able to show much emotion in *any* direction – which means that although you are not able to be too sad, you are not able to be too happy either.

Most people when faced with a depressed person will try to make them feel happier. Perhaps we're going about it the wrong way – maybe what we ought to do is to enable and encourage them to feel sad, yet supported enough so that their sadness does not destroy them. Once they have experienced the depths of that sadness that they were trying to protect themselves against they will no longer fear it, and their mind will no longer try to shut it out of their conscious thinking. Once the barriers to these feelings are released, the sufferer can at last begin to appreciate the depth and intensity of *all* emotions, both pleasant and unpleasant.

We English are a silly lot as far as emotions are concerned. For some reason our society has come to the conclusion that a display of emotion is in some way barbaric. We speak admiringly of those who *don't* break down under conditions of stress, who *don't* cry when told of the death of a loved one, and we applaud stoics. This is not natural, nor is it very helpful. Is it *really* honouring the dead person if a close relative doesn't shed tears on hearing of their death? Is a public display of emotion that bad? What happens is that the emotion is there, but gets repressed, and instead of coming out at the appropriate time, manifests itself later on, perhaps as a depression, or as unrelenting grief, at a time when others feel that the degree of grief or depression is totally inappropriate, and when there is far less sympathy and support for the depressed person as a result.

Instead of keeping a stiff upper lip, how much better to let your fears, anxieties, sadness and despair all flood out so that you *can* cry when you hear of the death of someone close to you. In that way all the emotion, anger and sadness will be liberated, to go away permanently. By comparison, if you keep those emotions to yourself then in six months' time you will still have them! You may find that you feel unbearably sad, without being able to understand why.

In terms of looking after their emotional health after a bereavement the Italians and Israelis win hands down over us English. When there is a death in the family they shout and scream and cry and wail, and there is a great public show of sadness and grief which releases all these deeply felt emotions, and dissipates them.

As an extreme example of what can happen if we button up our emotions, consider the case of the man whose grief came out at least twenty years late. His grandmother died. Initially he had had to take charge of the situation, but was then shut out of all aspects of the death, and his grief only came out twenty years later, on the day his dog died – it triggered off all those pent-up emotions which had been held back for so long.

Using Your Emotions Properly

Our emotions need feeding and our emotions also need listening to. We need to respond to how we feel – not how we feel in terms of memories from what has gone on in the past, but from the emotion that we feel as a result of what is happening *now*. If something today is making you upset, then *react to it*. Display your anger (if it is justified and if it is righteous anger – see Chapter 15). Don't push it down and out of the way.   If something *today* is making you feel sad, then let it out – cry. If something *today* is making you feel almost unbearably happy, then be prepared to laugh and dance and jump around and have a party to celebrate it.   This is what I mean by feeding the emotions – reacting with appropriate emotions to *today's* events.

What I do *not* want you to do is dwell on the emotions that you have as a result of things that happened in the past. If there is no good reason for you to 'feel' sad today, it is not appropriate for you to go around expressing that sadness. (It may be appropriate for you to try to work out why it is that you feel sad, and under certain circumstances let out the sadness that you feel, but that is another story.) I don't want you to go and feed the emotions that are from yesterday or the day before, or maybe twenty years ago – because these emotions should by now be dead and buried.   Appropriate emotion should be connected with things that are happening *now* rather than things that happened in the past.   Feed today's emotions, express today's emotions, enjoy today's emotions, whether they are happy or sad.

They will make living that much deeper and that much richer. To go back to something I said earlier, those who have experienced both sadness and depression say quite categorically that sadness is an enriching experience (if painful), whereas depression is just numbing. So to benefit from your emotions use them, and enjoy them. God made them, and they're good for you.

Using your emotions properly in this way will give you great satisfaction. You will be living for here and now – a good Biblical principle! In addition you won't be storing up emotions that you cannot handle, which will surface to plague you later.

So start to use your emotions for today. In this way you will not be adding to the backlog of emotions you have so far been unable to deal with. Rejoice when you want to; cry when you need to; allow yourself to feel apprehensive too, but only react to it when it's appropriate – such as when you are attempting a difficult or dangerous task. Otherwise, ignore illogical feelings of apprehension.

HEALING THE EMOTIONS

Even if you have got into the good habit of using your emotions for today, you may still need healing from the backlog of stored memories and emotions that were too hot to handle at the time you originally experienced them.

A little bit of delving into the past may be necessary. There are two approaches, which can easily be combined. The first is, with appropriate counselling, to explore those memories which seem to be causing most trouble, and to uncover forgotten and 'hidden' memories of things that are too painful even to remember with regret. The second is to do the same thing, but with a Christian counsellor gifted in the 'healing of memories' – in which, through prayer and counselling, God reveals either to the patient or to the counsellor aspects of the situation that need attention. These hidden memories can then be brought to God in prayer, forgiveness can be requested (if appropriate) and then the memories handed across to Him to deal with.

There is no reason why these two methods cannot be used in conjunction. God sometimes uses supernatural means to deliver healing, and sometimes ordinary human means. (In passing it's worth noting that if all healing were supposed to be supernatural, then God wouldn't be calling Christians to be doctors! It is important to see the spiritual and the human methods of healing as being complementary, not opposites.)

Going back into the past is a region where psychoanalysis and psychotherapy come into their own. By unearthing sources of emotional crisis – times when emotions have been stored up because they have been too difficult to deal with – the therapist unearths the source of the patient's problem and in helping the patient to experience or re-experience those emotions, allows them to dissipate, as they should have done so long ago. Good and careful psychotherapy can be of immense benefit here.

You can do your own counselling on yourself, you know! If you start to feel a particular (usually unpleasant) emotion for no obvious reason, ask yourself why you should feel that emotion at that particular time. Is it because of your circumstances, or because somebody has reminded you by thought, word, or deed of something that was unpleasant or saddening or difficult to cope with in the past? You can establish a routine of questions to ask yourself. What is it that makes you feel like this? What does it make you want to do? What does it make you think of? What events in your life spring most quickly to mind? These may give you a clue as to the source of your emotion.

If you're feeling panicky, *why* are you feeling panicky? Is it because you're on your own? What does being on your own mean to you – being left by your parents, being lost in a crowd when you thought you'd never get them back, being shut up in a cupboard by mistake (or on purpose), being friendless, being bullied, feeling left alone by God as well as by man? Explore your feelings, explore your memories, explore the connections that you find developing. It may help to go into a quiet room where you won't be overheard, and act out some of the memories again, just to see what happens, and what further memories it unlocks.

If you find that there are a number of recurring themes then try to work out where these recurring themes come from – you may need to have the help of a doctor, psychotherapist or counsellor, particularly if the connections are not that obvious.

Alternatively, try a Gesalt experiment. Gestalt therapy is a form of psychiatry in which you act out your feelings. We've already touched on this in Chapter 11. One of my friends had a recurring dream which involved a tree. After a few nights' dreaming of trees in various guises he decided to try to work out what it was all about, but couldn't logically think of anything he was involved in connected with trees. So he did a Gestalt experiment. He stood in the middle of the room with his hands up in the air and said, "I am a tree", and with that, he said, the floor seemed to give way underneath him: the flood of realisation dawned upon him that a tree was strong and upstanding and that in his current situation he was expected to act in this fashion – tree-like, firm and secure. However, his worry was that he might not have the inner strength to be supportive enough –

hence the dreams.

Things are not always as dramatic as this! But if you are able quietly to find possible reasons for your current upsetting feelings, then you will be further along the road towards helping yourself.

Back to emotions and feelings in general. One of the principles of transactional analysis (see Chapter 7) is the concept of 'sweatshirt messages'. These are the beliefs about yourself that you carry around, as if written on the front of your T-shirt. You project these statements about yourself onto yourself or onto other people. One person may have a sweatshirt message with "I'm great" written on it; another has the message "I hate myself "; yet another, "I hate everyone else". These sweatshirt messages present our basic feelings about ourselves and about life, and it is quite revealing to work out what sort of life style and sweatshirt messages each of us possesses. (Some people have several – in layers, just like layers of sweaters. The top layer might say, "I'm great." The next layer might be, "No, I'm not." And the third....)

Finally, a word about healing of the emotions and the Christian. It should go without saying that God is God of the whole universe and quite capable of healing things that are in the far distant past, of forgiving them, and of forgetting them. If He forgets them, who are you to remember them? If, on your travels back through your emotions and through your own personal history, you come across things that you wish to God (literally) had never happened, then tell Him! If they have bothered you for such a long time they must be very emotional, very worrying, very guilt-making subjects. Approach them, grab hold of them firmly with both hands, bring them to God – then open your hands and *let them go*. He is quite big enough, He is quite capable enough, He is quite competent enough to forgive you for them. There is *nothing* that He cannot forgive. The only requirement for being forgiven is that you are sorry for what you did. Do not worry about whether you're sorry! The fact that you have been scared stiff to approach the problem for so many years means that you *are* desperately sorry for what happened, to the extent that you can't cope with it at all. There should be no question under these circumstances of not approaching God in the right manner! So go to Him, tell Him about them, *and then let go*. Having asked for forgiveness, ask also for the grace to be able to accept the forgiveness that God willingly and freely gives you.

And then forget about it. *He* has. Resist any attempt to think of the event as being an unforgiven sin: remembering it as such is in fact sinful. The event happened; it has now been forgiven. Perhaps you did something that was silly or downright evil, but it has been forgiven and although the event and its physical consequences cannot go away, the importance and the implication of it has, permanently. Once the sin has been forgiven, memories of the event will lose a lot of their sting and remembering it will not be half so painful. In fact, you may not need to bring it to mind any longer; it will probably have much less significance for you now that the sin itself has been forgiven.

'Healing of the memories' like this is an important part of Christian therapy. Sometimes our minds block off things that are too painful to remember. It's not that we don't want to remember them – we *can't* remember them – our subconscious mind is preventing it. Yet the effects of these memories fall like a shadow across our lives. It may seem strange that a searing event can be forgotten – but believe me, it happens frequently.

Psychotherapy and psychoanalysis may unlock these memories, by allowing the patient to get nearer to them in a very supportive atmosphere, so that when the door finally opens, it's not as terrifying as the patient once feared.

Prayer can also unlock these closed areas of the mind, and it is surprising how often this can get to the bottom of things very quickly.

The memories can be anything – sexual assault by a parent; the day you nearly killed your friend in a fight; what your parents said when you told them your exam results...... They will all be frightening, shameful, or hurtful – which is why you've had to lock them away as though they never happened: they've been just too painful to recall.

Most importantly, these memories, once unlocked, have to be dealt with, swiftly and sensitively. They can't just be left there. Tell God about them. Ask His forgiveness for the things you've done which were wrong: ask Him to heal you from the hurts they represent.

Sometimes the memories that surface are not of things that you have done, but of things that have been done *to you*. You may still be harbouring resentment against those who have offended against you. This resentment and hatred has to be confessed (however justified), because if you cannot forgive those who have hurt you, you won't get better. It is all too easy in therapy for the patient to begin to realise how much he has been hurt – this is the first stage. But for a patient to get stuck there is disastrous.

There can be a lot of things that you need to learn to forgive: the bully at school; the sadistic housemaster; the driver of the car that killed your son; the person who introduced your daughter to drugs; even your husband for dying on you and leaving you to face the world alone.

It can take a long time to learn to forgive; it's essentially an internal process, because you may well not know where any of these people are, if indeed they are still alive. And obviously, as with the wife who can't forgive her husband for dying, some of them aren't. Again, the principle is the same – offer the situation to God, confess your anger, ask Him to help you forgive the person who's hurt you, and ask Him to bless them.

As an adjunct to this it may help to hold an imaginary conversation (out loud, in your own room) with that person. Imagine he's there in the room with you. Tell him out loud what he's done to you. Imagine his reply – perhaps he will say he's sorry, he didn't intend to do any damage (such as the drunken driver who killed your son), in which case you can then offer him your forgiveness, out loud. Remember, he'll be cut up about the situation too, and he'll need your blessing, so give it.

It's not so easy when the memories involve someone who deliberately tried to do you down. Perhaps here you have to hate the sin but love (and forgive) the sinner. So forgive *him,* and bless him too – he'll need it even more if he's not repentant.

Having forgiven those who have offended you, you can now 'close the book'. This memory is in Jesus' hands, and He can deal with it from now on. As with the exercises regarding your own sins (Chapters 3 and 7), learn *consciously* now to leave this memory alone.

EXERCISE

There are so many exercises in this chapter that to add an extra one on the end is almost superfluous – but this one can be a great help in unlocking that stiff upper lip!

It is important to realise that depression can be an *emotional* mental problem rather than a *logical* one. One of the effects of depression is that the emotional responses get dulled. Not only can you not be happy, but you also can't be sad – at least, not to any degree. Part of the cure is to pay attention to your emotions by feeding them. You will get rich rewards.

How do you feed your emotions? Use anything that is essentially a non-logical emotional activity – music is a prime example. Music refreshes the parts logic cannot reach, because it bypasses the logic circuits and addresses the emotions directly.

Unfortunately most of us use music as a background, to keep silence at bay – musical wallpaper. So, concentrate on it instead. Turn down the lights, shut off the TV, put a favourite record on and *really listen* to it. Concentrate on it – at least, as much as you can concentrate on anything. It doesn't matter if your mind wanders because the music sends you off on an old memory trace – let it. Concentrate on what the music is trying to say, whether it be happy or sad. Be prepared to dance or cry if you want to. (Incidentally, dancing is a very great releaser of emotion – it's an emotional activity *and* physical exercise as well. It also gets you involved in a curious sort of way that makes you feel more a part of the rest of the world, instead of separated from it.)

When you have flattened emotions it is sometimes easier to restore the normal emotional response by listening to *sad* music rather than happy music. (This is because some depressions occur because we are scared of the depth of sadness we perceive in the world and in ourselves.) So it may be helpful for you to put an unbearably sad record on, and have a good cry. Whatever type of music you choose, concentrate on it – on the emotion it brings. It really doesn't matter what type of music you pick – classical, pop, jazz, so long as the music *means* something to you.

Nor does it have to be music – any art form will do so long as it means something to you emotionally. For me, music is the royal road to the emotions: for others films, plays, art or scrapbooks and photo albums can do the trick.

15

ANGER

What is it in your life or your life style that makes you depressed? What can you do to stop it happening?

You can't will yourself out of a depression – it just doesn't work like that. Unfortunately, those who have never suffered from depression find this difficult to understand, and although they may pay lip-service to this idea, in practice their attitude often indicates that they think you're a drip for going under so easily, and that with a bit of effort on your part you'd be out of the gloom in no time.

Not a bit of it! People like this do more damage than good. Ignore them, and if necessary, avoid them. You will find their advice, though well meant, is useless. You cannot 'pull yourself up by your bootstraps', so you may as well stop trying and save what energy you have for *really* helping yourself.

The reason why you are in a pickle is that you are trying to change the wrong thing: you are attempting to alter the *effect* of something, whereas you really ought to be getting at the *cause*. It's as if you were trying to push the car to get the engine started when the spark plugs are disconnected.

So what do you try and change? And just where does this wretched depression come from?

There are a lot of answers – almost as many as there are people suffering from depression. The type of problem that causes your depression may not be a problem to someone else with depression. They may not have your husband/wife/mother-in-law/exam results/ house/income (or lack of it) etc. and even if they did, they might not be so worried by it. There are however a number of generalisations which may be of help. The most useful one is: Depression is related to ANGER.

But you're not angry, are you? How many times in the past week, day even, have you 'turned the other cheek'? Ten? Twenty? You're always doing it, aren't you? But the anger you feel doesn't go away – it just goes deep inside you, boiling away – and it turns itself inwards, onto you.

If ever there was a psychological truism, it is this:

> *Depression is inturned aggression.*

Does this strike you as odd? Think about it for a moment and you'll begin to see what really happens when you cover up anger. Picture a situation – you're in a queue at the supermarket, and already fifteen minutes behind time, when someone pushes in murmuring, "You don't mind, do you?" and proceeds to hold you up for another few minutes. What do you do? What do you say? Many Christians would smile sweetly and say, "No, that's all right" (which is a lie), and fume inwardly. When they come out of the supermarket they are angry, but they can't express their anger because the cause of it has disappeared into the distance in a puff of exhaust smoke. Three things can happen now – the anger can dissipate of its own accord (unlikely); it can be diverted (so you shout at the children – the 'kick the cat' syndrome); or it can bury itself deep in your mind so that you ruminate on it on the way home, lips tight, hands shaking, thinking of all the things that you'd like to do to Mr Smart-Alec, but didn't (and, if the process were repeated, wouldn't anyway). So the anger burns inside you. You forget about it eventually, replacing it with further anger with yourself for being so late, plus guilt for getting so angry.

Next day you're at work and the boss comes in, says something critical (and untrue) about your work. So you bite your lip again, and the same process goes on... and on... and on....

That Sunday, you hear another sermon in the perpetual series 'Wonderful Christians in Russia/Africa/the Inner City/etc. who turn the other cheek and millions are converted as a result'. Alternatively, it's on 'Christian love', 'Christians and war', etc. This reinforces your feeling that you did do the right thing in not creating a scene. Unfortunately the level of anger inside you is giving you ulcers, putting up your blood pressure, stopping you sleeping properly and making you short-tempered with the children.

Then you wonder why you are feeling depressed. You're being a 'good' Christian – meek and mild. In fact, you'd never say boo to a goose. Then you see evil men gaining the upper hand in society (and sometimes even in the church) and yet you feel it's unchristian to stop them by force. So you get more and more furious at the wrongs in the world, and less and less capable of doing anything about it – because at heart you are not prepared to get tough because you think it's unchristian.

Am I describing you? Funny how I knew, isn't it!

I have recently been taught very forcibly that Christians have got to stand up and be counted, and have to learn to get angry on the *right* occasion with the *right* things in the *right* way. It is *not* Christian to stand by while evil occurs. Unfortunately many of us have been brought up on the 'gentle Jesus meek and mild' version of Christianity, and unless we are careful, we tend to think that this is the sum total of Christian behaviour.

If Jesus were *only* gentle, meek and mild, then where does the cleansing of the temple fit in? Jesus found His Father's house profaned by tricksters and bent officials. The problem was not just that people were buying and selling in the temple, but the reasons behind it. Ordinary people had to bring animals for sacrifice, but according to the law only perfect animals could be brought: it was not acceptable to sacrifice a sick or dying animal. God had to have the best, not the leftovers. However, the temple officials saw that they could be on to a good thing; they managed to find fault with all the animals the people brought, so the people were unable to sacrifice their own produce. Instead, they could buy animals reared by the temple authorities – at a price. In addition, they were not allowed to buy with ordinary money which was 'unclean' – they had to use temple shekels instead, so there was a good trade in exchanging ordinary money for temple money, at a fat profit for the moneychangers.

In other words, that simple and meaningful ceremony of bringing the best to be sacrificed was being thwarted by those who were supposed to be the teachers of the law, and these same people were profiteering by the whole system.

Jesus was *furious* (and rightly so). Persuasion wasn't going to help – the temple authorities weren't going to listen. So He made a whip, and drove everyone out, overturning the tables of the moneylenders. Hardly 'gentle Jesus, meek and mild'! But it was *right,* it was *appropriate,* and it was *the only thing to do* to get rid of the evil that was being perpetrated.

Look again at what Jesus, this 'gentle Jesus', said to those who were out to get at Him. There is surely no more stinging condemnation of anyone than in Matthew 23, where Jesus takes the Pharisees to task for blocking the way to heaven for others, but not going in themselves. Read the chapter, then see if you think He (a) was correct, (b) was right to say it, (c) could have done anything different. 'Gentle Jesus'?

Yet that same man refused to allow Peter to fight for Him when the soldiers came to arrest Him in Gethsemane, and healed the man whose ear Peter had just cut off. Gentle Jesus indeed.

Yes, Jesus was indeed gentle, but He also knew how and when to be firm and/or angry when appropriate. We don't always remember this when describing the nature of Jesus: it's not so easy to fit in with our preconceptions.

So when is a Christian permitted to get angry? It's a very difficult question, and different people will give different answers. May I suggest that instead of 'getting angry' you think of it as 'becoming firmer, more resolute'. It is a less violent response: more like turning the other cheek (as far as the insults go), and not causing *unnecessary* conflict; but still standing firm because truth, decency, order or justice are at stake.

Now let us go back to our two hypothetical situations, the one at the supermarket, the other at work. What should you as a Christian *really* do?

Well, you should be honest, for a start. It wasn't truthful to say, "No, I don't mind", was it? "Why don't you ride roughshod over everyone and become even more of a boor?" is what you really thought. Therefore say it – gently. "We have all been waiting for some time, but if you really are in more of a hurry, then please go before me." That's what you feel, isn't it? If there *really* is a desperate need you will *want* to help. But *his* need has to be balanced against *your* needs (and, perhaps more importantly, those of the other people in the queue). Maybe you've got a train to catch too, in which case you have to say, "No, I'm sorry, I do mind – I'm very pressed for time as it is."

At first it's not easy to talk like this. It may feel odd for a bit – but it is in fact more Christian. If nothing else, you are being truthful. We don't hear many sermons about truth in this sort of context: love – yes, truth – no. Yet both are equal aspects of Godly living. We don't follow the Christian way if we are loving but untruthful. Nor do we follow the Christian way if we are truthful but unloving. We *do* do the right thing when we merge the two together.

The results can be surprising! First and foremost, you don't go away thinking, "What a little so-and-so that man was." You've told him the truth. You've done the right thing – if his need was greater than yours then you let him go first; and if yours was greater than his, you made him wait – which is good for his sense of order and gives him a gentle reminder not to be so selfish next time! But you don't hate him, or what he's done, because it's been resolved appropriately. And *you don't hate yourself for giving in, or telling a lie.*

It requires bravery to talk like this. There are many who refuse to start or continue an argument on the grounds of turning the other cheek, when in fact they aren't prepared to do battle out of sheer cowardice. I used to do it for years. Christians are seldom taught how to deal with conflict, and therefore don't always pick the right course of action. Being appropriately firm at the outset often causes less conflict in the long run.

There is another side to this – the man who is terrified of his own aggressiveness: that if he did 'let go' he might kill someone (literally). Again, telling the *truth* is important – not blowing things up out of all proportion. Expressing your feelings *to the correct degree* is just as important a consideration.

What about the boss who criticises you unfairly? I'm sure you can see what to do. Correct him as to fact; disagree politely with him if he has got your motives wrong; if necessary ask him what he wanted you to do differently – and remind him of the other things that would have been left unfinished had you done what he suggested.

In other words, stand up for yourself but do it fairly. *Be honest.* Jesus said, "Love your neighbour as yourself." It works the other way round, too. Loving your neighbour as yourself implies *loving yourself as you would your neighbour.* You wouldn't dream of criticising your boss unfairly (at least, I hope you wouldn't). Well then, be honest with your own reputation as well. If you don't love yourself enough to care about your own reputation and be honest with those who criticise you unfairly, then eventually you will find it difficult to love your neighbour very much (because you love other people as little as you love yourself; and you dislike yourself for what you allow other people to do to you).

What if it's fair criticism? Some people find it hard to accept blame. In just the same way that a small child will injure his hand on a door and then turn round and kick the door, saying "naughty door", so many adults will do anything other than accept blame. Favourite ploys include: "She made me do it"; "*I* can't help it if we've run out of..."; "You make me angry" (the correct psychological interpretation of this last one is, "I allow myself to be made angry by what you do"); "It's my parents' fault – they brought me up wrongly"; "You never told me" (which often should be stated more correctly as, "I should have worked it out for myself").

Try saying, "I'm sorry. I'll try to get it right next time. Thank you for telling me."

Unfortunately the loss of face that this engenders can pose a real threat, especially if you are an insecure person. But denying faults will in the long run make things worse, as your critics will just turn up the volume – which will make it even harder to accept, because the loss of face will be that much greater.

So be truthful about your anger; you will help yourself and others in the process.

ANGRY WITH GOD?

Sometimes it isn't possible to deal with anger in quite this way, particularly when there is a real source for your anger that can't go away – like the death of a relative or child, or the terminal illness of a close friend or relative. At these times there is often a tendency to get angry with God for allowing the situation to happen.

Don't worry about getting angry with God! He understands. When faced with a similar situation (outside the grave of Lazarus), Jesus Himself wept. Why did He weep? He was about to raise him from the dead, so it couldn't be weeping for Lazarus. No, Jesus wept because of the damage and destruction that sin and the Devil brought into the beautiful world God had made.

If you are angry with God about sickness or death, then your anger is misplaced. God is angry and sad about it too. He loathes the sin that makes the world the way it is, but He still loves the sinner. In the same way, when you are faced with death or decay make sure you are angry with the right thing. By all means be cross about the sin that ultimately is the root cause of the unhappiness and evil that has come into your surroundings – but try to avoid blaming God for it because it isn't His fault! (Why God has *allowed* something unpleasant to happen to you is of course a different problem, and one that I haven't space to go into here. If you need help in this area, try reading *The Problem of Pain* by C.S. Lewis, published by Fontana.)

So what do you do in these circumstances? Just get angry? Yes, by all means. Be angry with sin itself, the sin that brought the world to its knees. Focus your anger onto that, onto the right place, and you will find, again, that being truthful is a very refreshing experience. Take God's side in being angry about the evil itself.

When confronted with an overwhelmingly intense problem, where sadness, anger and despair are very immediate (such as the death of a child) even when you have logically traced the *source* of the situation to the right person (i.e. the Devil), you may still be left with physical feelings of intense emotion and anger. To help rid yourself of these feelings, try exercise – the more exhausting the better (within the normal limits for your age and state of fitness, of course). Chop wood, have a bonfire, swim *hard,* go for a run: tire yourself out physically. Stress and anger are often dissipated quite well by this sort of activity. I've used this technique on a number of occasions when I've come home having had to deal with a particularly distressing medical event – and it works well.

EXERCISE

1. Make a list of those things that make you angry. Now ask yourself, "Do I face up to these situations or do I chicken out instead?" In the future, how can you face up to these problems more appropriately, more firmly, more bravely?

2. You'll probably get in at least one situation today where you start to feel angry. Go through the following routine:

Firstly – is your anger justified? If it *is,* then don't try to squash it – you'll only hurt yourself by driving it inwards. You won't get rid of the anger by denying it: you will just drive it underground where it will do more damage. Only if your anger is *not* justified should you stop. If you are angry because you have been quite fairly criticised for something you've done wrong, then accept the blame, say you're sorry, and try to do better next time.

Assuming your anger *is* justified, teach yourself to react properly to it. *Tell* the person who makes you angry just how you feel – *gently* but firmly. Just say, simply, "Do you realise how you hurt me when you say/do that?" or something similar. Often people have no idea that they have hurt another, and it gives them a chance to apologise, and to remember not to do it again.

Is this unchristian? Not a bit of it. We are urged to 'speak the truth in love'. It is not surprising that failing to speak the *truth* sours up relationships.

What about the person who *doesn't* accept that he is in the wrong when he's made you angry? Should you get louder, tougher, angrier? Isn't the Christian gospel all about turning the other cheek?

Well, it isn't always. So what do you do next? That's right – *you may need to get firmer.* Ephesians 4:26 says, "Be angry – but do not sin. And don't let the sun go down on your anger" – in other words, don't nurse your anger until it explodes, but instead use it correctly. Righteous anger is the privilege of the Christian and in no way minimises the idea of the gospel of peace. But don't overreact or enjoy getting angry, because that would be wrong.

So, is someone still bugging you? Tell them, politely, firmly, *in private, to their face,* that what they say or do is, in your opinion, *wrong,* and that you do not accept their version of events.

Have you done it? Don't you feel better for it? Hasn't it got rid of the anger that you felt, and got rid of it in the correct way? *And don't you feel closer to them as a result?* Sycophants praise all the time, but a true friend is one who is not afraid to criticise *when it is appropriate.*

So where does 'turning the other cheek' fit in? I suspect that it should be used more for those situations where you have been bringing *the Christian gospel* to someone, and he has thrown it in your face. *Then* you turn the other cheek – and try again ... and again ... and again. Or someone insults you but you know that they are in need of help: so you correct them as to fact and keep going back to them again ... and again ... and again ...

3. Of all the emotions, anger is the most difficult to handle properly. If you are still having problems with it, then I recommend you read *Counselling for Anger,* by Mark Cosgrove (published by Word as part of their *Resources for Christian Counselling* series). Don't be put off by the title, which is the only fuddy-duddy part of the book! Although primarily aimed at counsellors, this book is extremely easy to read, even for those with no background in either counselling or psychiatry.

16

ASSERTIVENESS TRAINING

People who are depressed often feel that they are not in control of their lives. They may feel they get used as a punchball, a go-between, or as a person who has to bear the responsibility for everything that goes wrong but somehow never has the opportunity to change things for the better. It's an emotional version of 'taxation without representation'! People in this situation get depressed because they feel they are held to be responsible for things over which they cannot exert any control. It's an invidious position to be in.

It is easy to get depressed with the frustration of being unable to change events around you. Yet there *are* things that you can do – lots of them. The whole topic of 'making things happen' and 'changing things' goes under the heading of Assertiveness Training.

Unfortunately Christians often feel that they should *not* be assertive, but this is to misunderstand Christian doctrine. Christians are required to be *very* assertive over certain things – 'hold fast to that which is good', 'give a good account of your faith', 'hold firm'. And it is important to get into the habit of being properly assertive over what you believe to be right. It is the opposite to being a pushover; and Christian pushovers are not 'turning the other cheek', they are just weak.

I've already touched on assertiveness training when talking about the problem of anger (see Chapter 15). Dealing with your anger, getting to grips with somebody who rubs you up the wrong way, and doing it *properly* without causing unnecessary offence (yet sticking to your position and point of view) are really specific examples of the techniques used in assertiveness training.

So how do you assert yourself in the Christian sense? Let us begin by making clear *what* you are trying to assert and how. You are *not* trying to steamroller the opposition. You are *not* trying to become a dictator in the home, office or shop. You *are* trying to ensure that your point of view is expressed appropriately, and therefore stands a chance of being listened to and acted upon – or at the very least, not ignored as much as it seems to be at the moment!

There are three points to get across, *in order:*

1. Show that you listen and understand the other person's points of view. To jump in first may give the impression of having a closed mind at the outset.

2. Now say what *you* think or feel.

3. Then say what you'd like to *happen*.

Whole books and seminars have been dedicated to assertiveness training, and I can do no more here than give a quick appraisal of its basic techniques. They are most illuminating and their application will pay dividends immediately.

The golden rules of asking for things are:

1. Know what you want.

2. Ask for it *directly*.

3. Don't be deviated from your intended course of action.

1. Know what you want.

There is no point in asking for something if you're not sure even yourself what you're asking for. If you're in a restaurant and your meal has been served burnt to a frazzle, then don't call the waiter across and say, "It's not very good." Instead, say specifically, "Waiter, this meal is burnt." Anything less than the direct line leaves the opportunity for the waiter to come back with, "It looks perfectly all right to me, Sir", whereas if you're pointing to an incinerated bit and saying something about burnt offerings at the same time, he can hardly fail to take the point!

2. Ask firmly and directly for what you want.

How often do you apologise for saying something? "Excuse me waiter ... I'm sorry to trouble you (grovel, grovel), but I'm afraid (grovel) that my meal has been burnt ... if you don't mind me saying so (grovel, grovel)." This immediately puts the waiter in a position of total assertiveness over you, with the ability to use even a minor rebuff of your request to stem any further complaint. You're behaving as though you don't have a right to complain that somebody has short-changed you on what you are paying for! Instead, ask directly – "Waiter! My food is burnt. I would like you to replace it with a properly cooked meal. Thank you." This is polite, firm, direct, to the point, and does not allow of any interpretation other than that you have been short-changed and that you are politely but firmly requesting that it be put right.

3. Don't be deviated.

So often we are taught to be 'humble' and this 'humility' turns us into people who wouldn't say boo to a goose. We are taught, by implication, that argument is wrong for a Christian. Don't believe it (look at what Christ said to the Pharisees, for a kick-off !). *Don't be deviated*. If the waiter argues with you, then be firm, be polite, repeat your request, and if necessary send for the manager. You have a *right*. Don't think that being firm is a denial of your Christian beliefs. It is not. In fact it will probably help your evangelising ability in the long run, because people are not going to listen to a wimp! If they see somebody who is secure, confident, who obviously knows where he's going, who is in control of his life, who is both courteous but firm and uncompromising where it matters, they are much more likely to listen to him when he's talking about his beliefs. In being in control of his earthly life he is demonstrating the value and application of his spiritual beliefs, and earning the right to speak.

Just as it is important to say what you want, so it is also important to say what you *don't* want. The ability to say "No" can be very important. There is a principle here that we in the West tend to forget. Because of our scientific Western upbringing we tend to think that we must seek a reason for everything. We don't have to. The reason why you don't like a particular colour or a particular pattern may not be easy to work out logically – but you don't like it, and that's all there is to it. *That you don't like it* is the important thing, not the reasons behind it. Therefore when you are trying to say "Yes" or "No" don't be deviated into believing that you *shouldn't* be thinking that way. "But *why* don't you like that colour? It matches with the rest of the room perfectly well, it's a nice colour: why don't you like it?" There isn't an answer to this – except for a repetition, firmly, of the fact that you don't like it ... and that's all there is to it. *You* do not like it. It is true that you don't like it. There may not be an obvious reason for it, but it is very true that you don't like it.

The same can be said for actions. "Why don't you want to go swimming today?"; "Why do you want to go camping for your holiday this year?" etc. The answer may well just be: "Because I don't want to".

Obviously if there are scientific, logical or moral reasons behind your decision then these should be stated as well, but don't make the mistake of mixing up what you want with the reasons you might have for not wanting it – especially if those reasons are not particularly valid. If you say that you don't want to go swimming because it's too cold, the rejoinder will be, "It's a heated pool, it's no worse than it was yesterday; why don't you want to come?" Be honest, the answer is that you don't want to: you don't feel like it. Don't lie or hide behind any 'scientific' pretext – *you don't want to*. So say so. And if there is any rejoinder, then say it again. *You don't want to*.

Insisting upon your rights, and saying "No" to people, are really two sides of the same coin – it's all about being firm and truthful about your own wishes and feelings. Some people find it very difficult to say "No" for fear of causing offence, then hate themselves afterwards for forever being led into things that they don't want to be involved with. It is much better to say "No" with a clear conscience, knowing that the long-term consequences will be correct.

When you say "No" make sure you really do give the right reasons. If it is something that offends your faith or your beliefs, say so. "No, I don't want to do that because it is against my personal beliefs." You don't have to ram the 'Christianity' bit down people's throats, and it may well be the wrong time to do so. But people are generally sensible about not treading on other people's dearly held beliefs (of whatever nature) and a simple statement like that will often suffice to close the conversation. If there are logical reasons why you don't want to do a particular thing, then that may be sufficient. ("No, I don't want to go for a walk on the moors because I'm only just getting over a heavy cold and I think it will be too much for me.") And, as I've said, if there is no logical reason to your desires then make it clear that your desires are, even so, very important.

One very instructive exercise is to pair trainees off. Trainee A has to say "Yes" to Trainee B, and trainee B has to reply by saying "No". This goes on for two or three minutes, with each of them learning to say "Yes" and "No" to each other with increasing firmness. Doesn't it sound ridiculous!... that is, until you actually try it yourself when you suddenly realise how difficult it is to continue saying "Yes" when the person opposite you is saying "No" to your face and looking you directly in the eyes. I've seen people break down in tears doing this exercise – which shows just how difficult they find continuing to hold their particular line in the face of opposition.

Being able to say "Yes" or "No" appropriately, firmly, and without being deviated, is a very important principle. Another method used in assertiveness training is for trainees to act out particular situations – as in the example above where you have to complain to a waiter about a burnt meal. This 'acting out' of the way that you deal with situations can be very instructive; especially if guided by a good group leader, you begin to see the ways in which you undermine your own case – by the way you stand, by the hesitant way in which you approach people, or by the insecure and ineffectual manner in which you put across what you're trying to say.

Earlier I talked about depression being inturned aggression, and how dealing with the cause of the irritation *at source* helps the situation and prevents you driving your own anger inwards. Dealing with anger in this way is much the same as assertiveness training. It essentially consists of identifying the problem and refusing to take "No" for an answer if you feel that somebody else is being unfair either to you or to other people. I must reiterate yet again the fact that this *is* a Christian way to behave. Over and over in the Bible we read that God is a God of justice, who hates oppression, who desires justice for the poor, the needy and the widowed. If anything, in the Old Testament there is more emphasis on morality in terms of justice than there ever is on morality in terms of sexuality. Yet how often do we in the church think of the sexual sins as being the worst possible sort and relegate injustice to a much more lowly position in the league table? I will say it again – God *hates* injustice. And your role as a Christian is at least in part to counter injustice wherever you see it. This may mean sticking up for what you believe in, and not letting the other fellow get away with something he should not (not out of indignation or desire for vengeance, but because if you don't stop him now he'll do it to someone else – and he'll find it much easier to do it the second time and the third time and the fourth time ...).

Which brings me on to the way you issue an ultimatum. It may be necessary (as a Christian) to lay down a threat. Again, this is not unchristian provided it is done in the appropriate place, at the appropriate time and in the appropriate way. For example, consider the woman who has got a small child. He needs to be disciplined: "If you do that again I will ..." is a threat. We may need to do this in adult life: "If you behave in this manner once more then I will resign and you will have to get another treasurer/secretary/minister."

Make sure, if you do have to issue an ultimatum, that you take note of five points.

1. **The ultimatum must be in response to a misdemeanour.** You mustn't threaten if it's *you* that is in the wrong!

2. **It must be appropriate.** There is no point in threatening "to knock your block off" for a minor misdemeanour – especially with children! If you do threaten like this, it makes you look foolish and devalues the threat that you are making. The punishment must fit the crime.

3. **It must be well timed.** This applies particularly to the disciplining of children, but is equally appropriate for adults. If you *delay* threatening somebody you will build up further problems for yourself. If somebody is doing something wrong against you (and others) then you have to act relatively quickly. If your boss is asking you to do something which is illegal – such as falsifying papers, then tell him *the first time,* not the fifteenth.

4. **It should be made in private.** It goes without saying that it should be done on a one-to-one basis. If you see someone face-to-face in private and issue an ultimatum, then you are respecting them and their integrity by not making the problem public. In addition it is more likely that your wishes will be carried out, because the person you are threatening is not going to lose as much

face as if he had to apologise or change his approach in front of others. It's also the Biblical way. Only if a private ultimatum fails should the problem be made more public, and then only by degrees.

5. **Lastly, whenever you issue an ultimatum you *must* be prepared to carry out your threat.**   If you don't, then you will never again be able to issue an ultimatum and have it taken seriously. If you threaten to resign if something does not get changed, then if nothing changes you *must* resign. This principle applies particularly to the disciplining of children. "If you aren't in bed by eight o'clock, then you are not going to watch television tomorrow ..." is all very well, but if your son or daughter pops his head round the door at five past eight and you *don't* ban the television tomorrow, then your child knows that your threats are not worth anything. On the other hand, if retribution follows as surely as night follows day, then when next you say, "If ...", your child knows that he had jolly well better obey or otherwise there will be trouble! Again, this goes back to the first point, which is that the punishment must be appropriate − if you threaten something which is totally inappropriate then you will not be able to carry it out. "If you're not in bed by eight o'clock, then you won't watch television for the next six months ..." is an invitation to disaster. In exactly the same category are threats that you couldn't carry out even if you tried − "If you don't do ... then I'll knock your block off " is a daft threat, will be seen as such, and will probably be ignored.

The corollary to this is very simple − everybody knows that if *you* issue a threat you *will* carry it out, which will give a great sense of awe to any ultimatum in the future, I can tell you! I don't need to issue ultimata very often, but when I do, others *know* that I *will* carry out my threat − so they've got to take me seriously.

I must emphasise that I am not talking about threatening people to get my own way, but issuing an ultimatum *to prevent them from doing something which I believe to be wrong*. Sometimes the threat has to be at the level of a personal sacrifice − "If you do this again then I will resign from my position." At other times it has to be a more obvious threat − "If you (who are supposed to be in a position of responsibility) don't do something about this within two weeks, then I *will* ..." It should go without saying that issuing an ultimatum like this should not be done without a great deal of thought, consideration, prayer and often advice from other Christian colleagues.

Behaving in a firm way like this does sound terribly unchristian, doesn't it? Can I leave you to work out what will happen if you *don't* issue an ultimatum over something which is very important? You issue an ultimatum over something which is very important? You will find that your wishes, your authority (if relevant), your point of view, beliefs, integrity and honour may all end up in the dustbin, followed shortly afterwards by your happiness and even your sanity. There are times when it is important to say firmly, "I will not allow this to go any further." Christianity is not about compromise – you cannot compromise justice in the name of love; you cannot compromise your basic Christian beliefs. In short, you have to stand up for what you believe in. It is not Christian to do anything else.

EXERCISE

With a friend, try out the "Yes"/"No" and "Waiter, my meal is burned" exercises. Isn't it difficult at first! But fluency comes with practice and you'll soon get the hang of it. Then you'll be ready to do it in real life! .....gently, but firmly.

17

FEAR IN CHRISTIANS

I find it extremely sad that certain parts of the Christian church seem to thrive by instilling fear and depression into their members.

Do these terms come up a lot in your church?

"Are you 'broken'...?"

"We are nothing in the eyes of God...."

"All your righteousness is as filthy rags..."

"We are nothing but channels for God."

"We can do nothing good of ourselves."

If so, then you may well be listening to 'worm theology' – the repression of the listener by the presentation of the gospel in such a way as to make him feel smaller than he did when he came in.

'Worm theology' is a very subtle heresy – in fact it is so near the truth that it is probably not fair to call it a heresy at all (and I don't doubt the sincere Christian beliefs of those who deliver it). It is very difficult to argue against it because it is so nearly true and there are so many Bible verses that appear to back it up. The error it falls into is in thinking that the way in which God makes judgements upon Christians and non-Christians is the same, whereas in fact it is not.

As with all heresies, the changes are very slight – it is the emphasis which has subtly shifted. All the verses and principles I quoted earlier are true *for certain applications*: they apply particularly to the actions of non-Christians who can *never* buy their own salvation, or attain forgiveness by being better in the future and doing good works, any more than you can achieve an average of thirty mph over a two-mile course when you've taken two minutes to complete the first mile. (For the non-mathematicians amongst us, in order to achieve an average speed of thirty mph over two miles, you must complete the distance in two minutes: however, at first it looks as though you could complete the task by doing the second mile at ninety mph. It's a good analogy!)

The point at which these sentences and phrases become part of worm theology depends principally on (a) who they are applied to, and (b) who they are used *against*. Worm theology tries to use these passages about *Christians,* and sadly, some practitioners of worm theology do it because of their own inferiority complexes: worm theology is convenient because it allows a subtle put-down of other

Christians – "You think you're good – boy, do you need breaking." And if in fact you *don't* think you're good, "Brother, what's wrong with you if you don't have joy in your heart?" It is in fact a sanitised version of judging your fellow Christian. It sounds saintly. Judge it by its effects: if you go out of church feeling smaller than when you came in, you're on the receiving end of worm theology.

Make no mistake about it, God loves you, whatever your current state. If you are not already a Christian, He offers forgiveness to you *free*, now – all you have to do is ask. If you are a Christian, then believe you me, you are the apple of His eye! You are *not* a bundle of filthy rags, because you have been forgiven by Jesus, and whenever God looks on you He can't see your sins any longer because they are 'covered up by the white garment of forgiveness' given you by Jesus. He really *can't* see forgiven sins. He only sees what's left – the positive things. If God can't see old, forgiven sins it's not for you to dredge them up again and again, thinking that you'll be forgiven better for confessing them the more. As we said earlier, "When God takes your sin, He throws it into the deepest ocean – then puts up a sign saying 'No Fishing'!"

You could imagine the following conversation between a worried, depressed Christian, whom we'll call Christopher (it means lover of Christ, if you didn't know) and God.

Christopher starts praying. Only this time, we can 'hear' God answering.

"Hello, Lord."

"Hello, Christopher."

"I'm sorry, Lord, I've done it again. I really can't look You in the face. I'm sorry."

"That's OK, I understand. You're forgiven, Christopher: of course you're forgiven. Thank you for saying you're sorry."

"I really am sorry. I'm always doing it. Do You remember last week when I did it?"

"No, Christopher, I don't."

"Oh, You must remember – Monday afternoon ..."

"No – I don't remember it at all...."

For the Christian, when God forgives He *forgets* – the sin, at least: He does of course remember the events, and the problems you've given yourself as a result, but as far as God is concerned the sin itself no longer exists – Christ has paid for it, and God no longer sees it.

It is easy to get muddled up about salvation, heaven, and reward for Christian service. The parables of the talents, of the sheep and the goats, the general tenor of the Old Testament (which can be summed up as 'ultimately you get what you deserve – God will reward good and punish evil'), and many statements throughout the New Testament, confirm the general principle that *after you have first become a Christian* God will reward you for the good works you do – in other words, Christianity suddenly becomes positive, not negative. It is not a matter of, "Have you confessed *all* your sins?" (though that's important for the Christian) but of Christ saying to us, as He said in the parable of the talents, "Well done, good and faithful servant." Of course all your talents ultimately come from God, because He made you – but you have the choice as to whether to use them or not!

God loves you. Now you are a Christian He loves you even more (if that were possible). You are the apple of His eye – His favourite child. He would have sent Jesus to die for you even if you had been the only person in the world to follow Him and become a Christian. He wants you to fulfil the potential He has set within you. He wants to be able to say to you, "Well done!" (Not, "What a load of filthy rags – still, I suppose I'd better forgive him.")

Unfortunately it is psychologically convenient to some people to try to make their hearers feel rotten – 'sub'.   Substandard this, substandard that. People like this are latter-day Pharisees who recite the letter of the law without understanding its spirit. Jesus didn't have much time for people like this, because at heart they thought they were *great*. ("I am more of a worm than you – therefore that makes me *better*. I am more broken than you – so five more spiritual points to me.")

It requires a certain amount of Christian maturity to accept that the job of the preacher is not to make people feel rotten inside, but to lift them up to God. In fairness it is not always easy to put across the difference between God's dislike of sin, and God's complete love for the sinner. Certainly, the initial conversion experience needs to be preceded by an understanding of our own sinfulness and the knowledge that we can't get to God on our own, but thereafter our relationship with God should be a positive, not a negative experience. It shouldn't be a matter of 'being challenged' every time we go to church – this is a twisted version of the Christian gospel and I don't believe for one second that it should be the norm.   There are, obviously, times in every Christian's life when certain things are brought to his attention by God, and it may take the form of a direct challenge. But by and large God is not there to criticise and judge us as little worms, but wants to accept our praise and call us His sons and daughters. After all, in heaven we are going to be princes and *rule*. Worms don't wear crowns!

I want so much to tell you that God loves you, depression, sin, failure, success, good things, bad things and all. *He is on your side.* Yet some people make it sound as if He were in some way against you all the time, for all the bad things you've done and the sins of omission that crowd into your life: it's as if Jesus said, "Come to Me, all who are weary and heavy-laden, and I will tell you off."

So where does this leave the depressed Christian? If you are subjected to a lot of worm theology, you will find going to church almost unbearable, being 'challenged' every service over failings of which you are acutely aware. It is no fun – and it's not what God wants to happen to you. The Bible tells us that on the day of judgement it will be *the Devil* who will be the accuser of the Christians – he will try to persuade God that individual Christians are not good enough. The Devil tries the same trick on earth, too!

So when you feel that you are continually being challenged, and that God is criticising you a lot, be warned! It may well not be God whispering in your ear. We are told that the Devil can masquerade as an angel of light. Think about it – an angel of light would say lots of 'holy' things – about self-sacrifice, being more loving, requiring forgiveness etc. The only thing wrong is that it may not be the appropriate thing to say at the time..... which is why God wasn't saying it to us in the first place. God understands our limitations, and knows we can't change everything at once, so He doesn't ask us to. He knows what we can stand and what we can't, and doesn't ask us to do the impossible.

When we are depressed it is all too easy to think that God is cross with us. We read the Bible – and the punishments stick in the mind more than the blessings. We think emotionally, "That's me – I'm like that. God is cross with me because I'm so bad / faithless / lazy. He's speaking to me through His Word, and telling me off." When you pray you find yourself confessing sins again and again and again, just because you don't feel any better. Under circumstances like these you feel terrible reading the Bible, praying, or going to church. All around you are challenges, criticism, failure, despondency, punishment, death, hell.

The final and most vicious version of this problem, faced by many Christians, is the fear that they may have committed blasphemy against the Holy Spirit – which according to Mark 3 is unforgivable. *Many* depressed Christians fear that they may have committed blasphemy against the Holy Spirit, so if you are like this, you're not alone. But I can assure you you haven't done it. It is a truism that anyone who thinks they may have committed the unforgivable sin *can't* have done, because the ultimate sin is actually rejection not of

God, but of goodness itself, to a point where you don't even *care* whether you've committed blasphemy against the Holy Spirit. So as you're worrying about it, it can't apply to you, by definition!

Blasphemy against the Holy Spirit isn't a matter of saying "Damn the Holy Spirit" (as if God would be that petty!), but rather a refusal to recognise good in *anything*. Look again at what caused Jesus to speak in this way. He had just healed a man by casting out an evil spirit. Far from being pleased, the Pharisees responded with, "He casts out devils by using the power of the Prince of devils." They couldn't even rejoice that the man was healed! If your mind is that twisted then you really are beyond the pale – but then you wouldn't be reading this book!

When you are depressed your emotions get distorted, so don't rely on them. Think back to what I said earlier about only noticing unpleasant things in a Bible passage. Find a passage: then go through it with a Christian friend and see it through *his* eyes – and I guarantee that your friend will find statements of blessing that you'd never even noticed. If you are depressed, then Bible study is probably safest if you read the passage and then make a list of the blessings and the criticisms in two separate columns. Making a list like this forces you to go through the passage in a more orderly fashion and see it in a more even light. So when you come to a passage like "the wicked shall be cast into the fiery pit", you have an entry in each column – one for the wicked – and one for the others!

If you are inclined to be fearful, then I suggest you reread the first short chapter of this book. Most of the comments in it are intended for fearful Christians such as you. I can't emphasise enough how much God loves you, how fond He is of you, and, however bad you *feel*, He *has* forgiven you and always *will* forgive you, *and He is on your side.*

Healing these fears requires the use of logic and memory rather than emotion. Don't expect to *feel* forgiven, especially if you are depressed. Understand that God has *promised* to forgive all who ask – ask, note, not beg. You *are* forgiven, whether you feel it or not. The trick is to force yourself to start behaving as though it were true: and once you realise that this is how God wants you to live, greater confidence will follow. (Your forgiveness is of course true – it's whether you *feel* it to be true that's the difficult bit!)

I think we sometimes have too staid an idea of God. Jesus has a great sense of humour: just think of the parable of the mote and the beam ('First take the plank out of your own eye, then you'll see clearly to take the speck of dust out of your brother's eye!') Instead of thinking of God as being 'out there', big and frightening, and not listening, remember He is here beside you – even when you aren't

aware of it. He loved you when you were not a Christian – how can
He possibly love you less now that you have decided to follow Him?
He *does* understand all your problems: He doesn't like the things you
do that are sinful, but He understands the pressures that drive you to
sinning, and He wants you to learn from your mistakes and gradually
progress on the road to being the person He would have you be. He's
not interested in flattening you – quite the opposite. He's trying to
build you up. The only ones God uses the flattening technique on
are those who feel they're the bee's knees – but *they* wouldn't be
grieving over their mistakes! Sledgehammers are for squashing hard
nuts. Those with soft centres get the kid-glove treatment!

Therefore if you are plagued with guilt feelings, do the following:

- If you are not a Christian and you are prepared to spend the rest
  of your life following Jesus, ask for forgiveness in Jesus' name and
  it will be given instantly.

- If you are a Christian, then God is seeking to bless you and build
  you up. Your present depression is *not* occurring because God
  has got it in for you, but because He is preparing you for better
  things. If you feel condemned at the end of every church service,
  then you may be too depressed to see the promise of good things
  – in which case you probably need a lot of love, support and
  reassurance from loving Christian friends; but if *they* too are feeling
  perpetually criticised from the pulpit, then the church you are in
  teaches worm theology, and you ought to get out of that
  fellowship, quickly. If you feel criticised through your Bible
  study, then use a good commentary – in reading the passage
  through another's eyes you will probably get a more balanced
  view of things. Alternatively, do Bible study in a group, or with
  a friend, so that others can balance up your depressed approach.

EXERCISE

The real antidote to fear, of course, is love – "Perfect love casts out fear." If you are frightened of God Himself, then find a mature Christian in whom you can confide, and go and tell him/her how you feel. You'll find it therapeutic!

18

EARLY LIFE AND PARENTAL INFLUENCES

It was Wordsworth who coined the phrase "the child is the father of the man" – and Freud picked it up. Think about it – it's a very important concept. All adults begin as children, and bring memories from their childish years into their adult lives. Some of these memories are good, some are bad, some are in the conscious and some in the subconscious. Unfortunately we don't always realise that we have these memories until something happens to jog them. How often, in the middle of a task, have you suddenly begun thinking about an entirely unrelated event? Sometimes there are obvious connections: you may be stimulated to think about a certain event in your life when you hear a piece of music that was associated with it, or encounter a smell that brings back memories. On the other hand, you may be totally unable to work out any logical reason to account for your sudden train of thought. All of us have memories – but the trouble is that not all of these memories are conscious, and unconscious memories often drive our thoughts in inappropriate directions.

The problem lies with 'the child being the father of the man'. It wouldn't be so bad if it were the other way round – if we could take our adult appreciation of things with us into childhood. But unfortunately we can't. We take our childish understanding of things (or should I say our childish *mis*understanding of things) with us into adult life, and unless we replace these memories with more adult ones we may come a cropper. Consider the adult who is scared stiff of spiders, or who jumps onto a chair if a mouse appears. These are not logical fears – in England spiders don't kill, and mice, though capable of transmitting disease, are relatively harmless little creatures. But look back in the lives of the people who are scared by spiders or mice and you may well find that their odd behaviour is a remnant of a childish fear – at a time when, *to the child,* the creepy crawlies really would be capable of doing extremely unpleasant things, at least, in the child's imagination. Unfortunately for the adult, he or she cannot remember the original source of the worry, and so takes into adult life a deep-seated, illogical (and therefore logically unapproachable) sense of real fear of a harmless creature.

In practice things are not as cut and dried as this. Have you ever wondered why you do not like certain people, or why you go in fear or awe of others? You may find that they remind you of people from your past and that you have merely transferred the feelings you had about the past people onto the current people. This can often be the root cause where you have difficulty in relating to authority or parental figures. At school I was badly bullied by a rather large, fat boy – and from then on I have tended to regard all heavily built people with a certain suspicion. It's very difficult to erase old memories like these.

SELF IMAGE

There is another, more sinister, shadow lurking from the past – memories of attitudes people had towards you, or of attitudes you had towards yourself. It is sinister because we do not remember attitudes in the same way as we remember specific events, and we are very prone to take those attitudes as being 'the way it is'. Consider the child who grows up always feeling that he is not quite as bright as his older brother. If he is constantly nagged with, "Oh Robert, *why* don't you try harder?" or, "Robert, *when* will you learn to be neat?", then after a time Robert will think that he really is incapable of being bright, or neat, and will take these attitudes as being 'the truth about Robert'. Unless disabused of them, he will carry these attitudes almost unquestioned into his adult life. Then when he is given a task he may well feel that he can't do it – or at least, not as well as someone else. It's ingrained in him that he's 'not as good as the others'. But if he consciously puts aside his feelings and just gets on and does the job, he may be very surprised by how well he performs.

This principle doesn't just apply to children who are not as good as their brothers or sisters or peers. If the brightest boy in the class is always met with the comment, "Well, that was very good, Stephen, *but*..." then he will get the impression that whatever he does is never going to be good enough for his superiors and for those in authority. He may try harder (and probably *will*), but all the time he feels that he'll never, ever get there. There's always another, "That was very good *but*..." round the corner to greet him: "That was perfect – but couldn't you have done it faster/by last week/in colour?"

What about the self-image of the woman who in childhood who was always called 'plain'? In adult life is she going to feel relaxed, at peace with the world, knowing that her husband thinks the world of her and her neighbours admire her for whatever qualities she's got? In other words is she going to feel good? Not a bit of it. She'll be having that word 'plain' ringing around in her head like a fly in a jam jar. Whatever she does, whatever she wears, whatever make-up she uses, whatever hairstyle she picks, she will always feel 'plain'. So what will she do? If she feels she can't be beautiful, witty, dazzling, attractive, elegant, with 'clothes sense', and so on, then the best she can do is to hope that she won't stick out in a crowd as being excessively plain. In fact, she will try not to be noticed: so she'll pick a plain dress, a plain hairstyle, probably not bother with her make-up, and in short *make* herself very plain. She becomes a self-fulfilling prophecy. Because of the constant nagging of her parents she will become the very thing that they have dubbed her, and probably for no good reason at all.

Let me give you an example of this from my own experience. I was brought up just after the war when food was not easy to come by and rationing was enforced. At that time there was great emphasis on the need for eating well at whatever opportunity you got, and therefore my parents' approach was that going out to enjoy food was less important than going out to get a good square meal. It was one of the pillars of civilisation – you went out for meat and two veg. And I remember one day in the late seventies sitting in a Greek restaurant faced with the menu and thinking, "Blow it, I'm going to have a kebab." And I could (almost physically) hear my mother's voice ringing in my ears, "Now John, do eat sensibly, meat and two veg." I can assure you that it took a great effort of will to order that kebab! But it was worth it, and laid a ghost in the process. Note, my parents were *not* wrong; it was I who was wrong for taking their advice with me into adult life without questioning it. Their advice, which was very appropriate when it was first issued, was no longer appropriate for me in the seventies. Looking back, I can't see why I was so stupid as *not* to challenge it earlier, but this just shows the degree to which attitudes grab and hold you – they seem unchallengeable, absolute truth, so we *don't* subject them to logical analysis. Equally, I am sure that my parents would be horrified to find that I had taken what was meant to be general advice for sensible, normal living at that time and applied it at a time and place that they had never dreamed of.

All this goes to show just how easy it is to take attitudes learned in childhood and misapply them as an adult. It is surprisingly difficult to realise the conditioning process that a child has been through, once he's an adult. If you've always lived under certain repeated comments such as "plain", "could do better", "you are selfish", then you will find as an adult that *it is very difficult to stop yourself thinking along these lines*. We assume that these things are true of us, because they have always been said about us, and what's more they were said by our parents whom we (generally) look up to and respect.

These attributes, falsely acquired, can become our 'sweatshirt messages' (see Chapter 14) – those deeply ingrained feelings we have about ourselves that we display to the outside world. We may be acutely sensitive of what we perceive to be our faults (even though they may never have been true of us, or else only true for a short period in the past); yet we continue to believe in them and overreact to try to 'hide' them.

DEALING WITH HIDDEN INFLUENCES FROM THE PAST

Kicking childish habits presents a lot of problems. The main difficulty is to *recognise* your built-in assumptions for what they are – assumptions. Disentangling your *real* personality and attributes from what you *think* are your attributes can be difficult because of the self-fulfilling nature of your beliefs. If you were unpopular at school you will tend to assume that no one likes you, and that you will forever remain unpopular. Then you behave as though you are going to be friendless: as a result no one likes you because of your attitude! So are you popular or unpopular? Once you think of yourself as potentially likeable, all these unwanted effects drop away.

It is also common for the opposite to occur. Quite often a person who has laboured under particular ideas about himself as a child may make tremendous efforts to overcome this particular criticism and go too far in the other direction. If, as a child, you are constantly told, "Don't just sit there, *do* something!" (because you are, in fact, lazy) then as an adult you may find the word 'lazy' ringing in your ears whenever you stop working – so you try harder, and harder – but no matter how hard you try, you are never satisfied with what you've done – so you try harder and harder. In this way you can make yourself into a workaholic, a man for whom any thought of rest instantly brings guilt feelings and the reminder of the thought, "Don't just sit there, *do* something." Workaholics feel they don't do enough – their friends think they do too much, and their friends' comments are much more appropriate for the present situation. So listen to them!

But how do you recognise what *really* is the truth about yourself amongst all the odd ideas about yourself that you may have gathered? The answer is by questioning and comparing *openly* the difference between you and your fellow men/women. Study your activities over a week or two – why is it that you don't go dancing (for example)? Is it for good reasons – such as you really don't like it? Or for bad reasons – you never learned to let your hair down and relax? Or is it because you think it's unchristian? If so, why were you led to believe this? Was it your decision or someone else's that you've adopted? And if it was someone else's decision, have you adopted it correctly, or was it advice that was once appropriate because of the nature of the local disco, but is no longer appropriate now the drug-pushers have gone? The point is not, "What conclusion did you come to?", but "*Whose* conclusion was it – and why?" If you are happy with how you came to the conclusion, fine. But if you find that you've borrowed someone else's ideas without questioning whether they are still appropriate, then you need to do some more thinking until you have got *your own* answers, not borrowed ones.

What do you think of yourself? Make a list of what you see as your good and bad points, and your general beliefs about yourself – then see if these are justified by comparison with other people's ideas about you. Go and ask a wise, mature Christian for his honest assessment of your list.

So many people feel that they are incapable, by comparison with their fellow man. Yet most people are average. (They must be, if you think about it!) And what the average person can do, *you* should be able to do. In addition, many people are above average. So what these above average people can do, you also may be able to do! To some extent your ability to perform a task is related not to your intrinsic ability for that task, but on how far you believe within yourself that you are capable of carrying it out. There are some interesting people, mainly in the United States, called hustlers, who earn their living taking wagers on apparently impossible things – such as beating Billie Jean King at tennis, or Arnold Palmer at golf. The hustler's mentality works like this – "If I throw a ball to you, you will probably catch it. If I say, 'There's five pounds for you if you catch this ball', you might just drop it. If I say to you, 'Here is five hundred pounds if you catch the ball', then you have a greater chance of dropping it because you have become more self-aware of the possibility of dropping it and of losing the money. And if there is ten thousand pounds on your catching it, you will become so nervous that you fumble and drop it." On the other hand, the hustler has learned to become so self-confident (or unselfconscious, if you like) that he sees no reason why he *shouldn't* be able to catch that ball. So he takes wagers on it – and being cool, calm and collected, wins more often than he loses. This is how hustlers earn money!

It's really rather like stage fright. A pleasurable and relatively easy activity – such as talking or playing the piano in private – becomes a nightmare full of forgotten words, stumbled lines, missed notes and general mayhem when you have to do it in front of an audience. What's the difference? Well, there is only one – you are so self-aware of what you are doing that you force yourself into making mistakes.

If you become truly unselfconscious, unaware of yourself, and just get on with whatever task is in hand at the moment, you will probably find that you can do very much better than ever you thought you could. Your first thoughts *should* be, "Why *shouldn't* I be able to do this? There are others who can do it – why shouldn't *I* be able to do it as well?" This attitude can carry you forward in situations where you may have only a little talent; but it enables you to concentrate what talent you have in the best possible way.

If somebody wants you to give a short talk, why shouldn't *you* be able to do it? You can talk to other people can't you? You talk to your parents, your wife, your children, your friends? Why *shouldn't* you be able to do it? You may not be a Charles Haddon Spurgeon or a John Wesley – but then, how many of us are? So get on and do it. You've been asked to run a fete? Why shouldn't *you* be able to? You organise your house, your business, the family holiday – why shouldn't you be able to organise that fete?

So look again at your own talents. How far are you queering your own pitch by adopting an attitude of mock humility towards the talents that God gave you? The prime thought should be, "Why *shouldn't* I?" As God said to Joshua when he was about to lead the children of Israel into the Promised Land, "Be strong, be confident, for I the Lord am with you." It's not a statement, it's a command! – "Be strong". It's backed up by a promise – "For I the Lord am with you" – but it's still a command. If you are a Christian, then the Lord is with you always – He promised He would be. So, for *you*, "Be strong, be confident" – for God is with you.

There is another aspect to this. The more self-conscious you are, the more uneasy you will appear to others, and this uneasiness will get in the way of establishing an easy, friendly, relationship. The less you are aware of yourself and your possible feelings, the more time and energy you have to spend on the other person's needs, which can only be good for him, and beneficial to your relationship. You will appear to be more truly a friend, more of a helper, more able to cope if your own insecurities and doubts aren't allowed to intrude.

SPIRITUAL PROBLEMS EMANATING FROM CHILDHOOD

Spiritually orientated problems can stem from childhood, too. God is our Father. How can we establish a good relationship with God as Father if our relationship with our earthly father has been marred? How can we encourage a man to know and love God as his heavenly Father when his earthly father beat him (physically or verbally)? If we feel that we can never please our earthly father, how much more do we feel that we will never be able to satisfy our heavenly Father, whose standards we see as being even higher, and therefore even more unattainable? If we never felt loved or appreciated by our earthly father, how can we learn to feel appreciated by our heavenly Father?

The converse of this is that when talking with a person who has difficulty believing or trusting in God, we must be aware that his expectations of God and his sense of security with Him may be clouded by what has happened to him in the past. We should expect a man who has difficulty making relationships with people whom he can see and touch to find it even more difficult to establish a relationship with God, whom he can't touch – and we mustn't judge him for being like this.

God as a perfect Father is not going to criticise us incorrectly or unfairly, nor inappropriately. There is a glorious passage in the prophecy of Isaiah about the coming of Christ where it says "a bruised reed He will not break" – in other words however battered and bruised the individual Christian is, Jesus is never going to do anything that will destroy or break asunder an already bruised and battered personality. Jesus's actions are to build up, help, edify and fulfil the person and the personality that God made and whom (remember) He made in His own image.

EXERCISE

Have a go at identifying the 'attitude' words (such as "could do better") that were used about you when you were a child by parents, friends, teachers, etc. Make out a list of them. Include as many of your own attitudes to yourself as possible – such as "not very likeable". Now go down the list and tick off those items that you still feel apply to you now. Then ask a few close friends to create their own lists about you and see how many of the attributes actually coincide! You may get a shock.

Once you've got these two lists you are in a position to do something to help yourself. Learn to ignore your feelings about yourself that are no longer appropriate. Consciously realise, consciously bring to mind the fact that they *aren't* appropriate any more. The more you realise that those words are there, goading you, the more you will know what to do to overcome them.

Then start to appropriate to yourself the good words that people use about you. If someone describes you as being reliable, hold your head up and praise God for making you reliable in the eyes of other people. *Then consciously stop thinking of yourself as unreliable.*

What about the unpleasant attributes that others wrote down in their list? Don't worry about these at the moment. Often these attributes are present because you are trying too hard to deal with what *you* see to be a problem, but no one else does. Once you've learned to deal with your own perception of yourself, and can accept other people's compliments and good criticisms of you, go back to them, ask them for a new list of your attributes, and *only then* start to deal with any bad points. You may well find that a lot of your previous bad attributes have vanished, now that you are no longer overcompensating for what you originally incorrectly perceived to be your own faults.

Learn also to *accept compliments*. It's often hard. If you are someone who sees criticism at fifteen miles, but doesn't recognise a compliment even if it hits you in the face, then relearn your attitude to compliments! Learn, when praised, to *accept* the compliment. Say "Thank you". Don't try to apologise for having a virtue, as so many do ("Oh, it was nothing"; "Oh no, it wasn't good at all, I should have done it much better..."). Look them in the eye, and say, "Thank you very much". Got it?

19

CHRISTIANS, DEPRESSION AND SEX

Sex is a very sensitive issue in our society, particularly in Christian circles. It's a powerful and intense drive within us, and coping (or not coping) with it can cause considerable stress.

There are three distinct problems for the Christian. These are:

1. Dealing with the intensity of sexuality itself – in other words, coming to terms with being both normally sexual and a Christian.

2. Dealing with sexual sin and the problems it brings in its wake.

3. *Knowing the difference!*

In many ways the third causes the most problems! The church has often leant towards making sex *itself* into a sin, hence causing people to feel guilty about just being sexual. Then, having made them feel guilty, it prevents discussion of sexual issues in anything but condemnatory terms – which makes Christians feel their sexuality (and hence their very personality) is unchristian, dirty, unclean, unfaithful. Hence many Christians have been given the wholly un-biblical idea that sex is *in itself* unclean, and as a result have become uptight about being normal.

There is a lot to undo here. Badly thought-out approaches to sexuality harm people very deeply and sow the seeds for profound upset and emotional anguish. Because there has been so much confusion, misunderstanding and sheer blind prejudice about the subject, I want to start right at the beginning and establish the Biblical point of view on sexuality. Only when we understand the good use of sex can we begin to discuss sexual problems in any meaningful way.

A warning – by the very nature of its subject, this has to be a very frank and explicit chapter: the more so because many Christians find it difficult and embarrassing to talk about sex. This reluctance to approach the subject creates even more difficulties for Christians experiencing sex-related problems. But there is no point in denying that problems exist. Healing only comes when problems are brought out into the open.

Unless you have been called to celibacy, the Bible wants you to be a sexual Christian. (Doesn't it sound odd, talking like this! Yes, a sexual Christian. There is no contradiction in terms.) But many, if not most, Christians are afraid or ashamed of being and feeling sexual. Depression can occur simply because of this – shame of being normal! Because depression and guilt can also occur following sexual misdemeanours, it is important to distinguish carefully between the two situations. Sex is fine. Misuse of it is not.

BODIES

Let's start by talking about our bodies in general terms. We often don't have a very Biblical attitude to our bodies, and tend to think of them (for no good reason) as unclean.

In some ways this is a hangover from the old pagan Greek ideas about ourselves, and the Gnostic heresy, both of which said that we are made up of body and mind; the mind is pure but the body is dirty. This is emphatically *not* a Christian concept, yet it hangs about us like an all-pervasive smell. The church in general doesn't approve of the use of our bodies; we don't use dance much in worship (even though David danced before the Ark of the Lord with all his might) and many churches disapprove of dance both as recreation and as a secular performing art.

Probably a lot of these attitudes are cultural in origin. We English are so scared of our bodies that we don't even use them for touching, except in a ritualised way such as shaking hands. How different things are in other cultures! Putting a hidden camera into cafés in various parts of the world showed that in an hour, unrelated South Americans talking together would touch many times, Americans rather fewer times – and the British never! *We* even apologise if we touch someone inadvertently.

Did you know you can kill a child by not touching it? If a child receives no physical contact at all, he can go into a decline and die of 'emotional malnutrition'. By contrast, have you ever seen a cow elephant and its calf? The elephant's trunk is all over the place, tweaking the calf back towards the cow, touching it, reassuring it, saying *physically,* "I'm here."

All people (and especially depressed people) are greatly helped by being touched. The hand on the arm, the arm round the shoulder – these say so much more about friendship than mere words. Touching is good for us, and it's time we learned to do it more appropriately. When Jesus healed people He often touched them; and in the New Testament the laying on of hands was both the means of cure for disease and the 'mode of transfer' of the Holy Spirit.

If we British are guilty about touching people in a non-sexual way, how much more do we become inhibited about sexual expression? If touching non-sexually is virtually taboo, what does it implant in our minds about sexual contact (even of the mildest form, such as a kiss or a cuddle)? The more taboo we make our bodies, the more we teach that 'bodies are unclean'. We learn mainly by example – so if parents don't exhibit any sexually orientated contact such as a peck on the cheek (never mind a full-blown kiss and a cuddle!) then their children are likely to grow up thinking that their bodies are vile, and sexual things viler still – things to be done in the dark, behind closed doors, in secret, furtively.

We don't help by our negative attitudes towards naming parts of the body or discussing sexual matters openly (in appropriate circumstances, of course). As a doctor I am accustomed to talking about intimate parts of the body to complete strangers, so you would expect that I would be without inhibitions. In fact, outside the realms of medicine, I seem to have just as many hang-ups as everyone else. This was brought home to me in no uncertain terms when my elder son was at the stage of finding out about himself. "Shoulder, Daddy!" "Wrist, Daddy!" Then he looked down at himself in the bath and said, "Little wiggly worm".

Oh dear, I thought, I've not told him what a penis is called. I'm not as broad-minded as I thought ...

That simple act of not giving my son a name by which to call his penis meant that for him it was (literally) an unmentionable subject – he couldn't mention it because he had nothing to mention it by. It is easy to see how subsequently the penis could adopt a certain mystique of its own – because you can't name it you can't talk about it; if you can't talk about it it's unmentionable and because it's unmentionable it's evil. The progression is simple and swift.

Mind you, things soon changed with my son – he had to have a circumcision just about the time he started his first writing book at school, and the first entry was all about his operation (complete with drawing!) I bet the teacher had fun with the class that day! I can just imagine her desperately trying not to cause offence to the other children. But there need be no shame, no upset. Things like this are a fact of life – they're mentioned in the Bible; they're not obscene; it's just that our society has turned them into taboo subjects.

Obviously I'm not suggesting that we go overboard and start discussing intimate matters as a matter of course, over cocktails. There is a time and a place for everything. But we do need to be aware, particularly in Britain, of how much we have falsely assumed that our bodies are evil *in themselves,* and their sexual aspects more so.

We need to become less uptight about the proper and wholesome use of our bodies. Both church and society need to relearn the blessings of touching one another non-sexually. We must consciously abandon attitudes that imply that our bodies are basically sinful, firstly because such attitudes are non-Christian, and secondly because taking that point of view makes sexual problems that much harder to deal with.

SEXUALITY

Although Christianity preaches a gospel of forgiveness, freely offered by a loving God, there are times when this doctrine seems to be wearing a little thin. Although it is not what the Bible teaches, Christians often unconsciously demonstrate that they believe in a hierarchy of sins, some of which are relatively trifling, and some of which are really heinous. There are even some sins which it is 'good' to confess to. How often at prayer meetings have you heard people praying, "Forgive us our lack of love / lack of devotion to Thee / our pride / our selfishness"? Such confession of sin is almost made into a virtue.

But have you ever been at a prayer meeting when somebody has prayed, "Oh Lord, forgive me for my lust"; "Lord, forgive me for my adultery"? Yet sexual temptations affect Christians just as much as other people, and adultery is not unknown in Christian circles. If the sexual sins are so common, then why are they not confessed, and the problem *shared* more often? Are the sexual sins the great unmentionables of the church, and by being unmentionable thereby given the status of being unforgivable, or forgivable only after great penance? Unfortunately many Christians think that the worst sins of all are sexual (and if they don't consciously think it, they unconsciously behave and talk as if it were the case – which is worse, because unconscious prejudices are harder to correct than conscious ones).

The Bible doesn't treat sexual sins as being worse than any other: in fact, I can't think of any Biblical characters whose sexual misdemeanours caused their ultimate downfall! On the other hand, pride, arrogance and turning deliberately away from God are three things which, in the Bible, God punished most firmly. The sexual sins are noted as sins, and as being wrong, but there is no sense in which they are considered worthy of *extra* punishment.

Yet for Christians, even sex properly used is often the great unmentionable. Have you ever heard a sermon or a prayer in which God is praised for having created it? Or thanks given to Him for all the rich blessings that it can give? For the beauty of woman? For the manliness of man? It's unlikely. Sex is the thing we don't talk about in the Christian church – it's unmentionable, dirty, and sexual sins are forgivable only with difficulty. Just *being* sexual is a sin, in some people's eyes.   As a result, if you have sexual problems you immediately feel that your problem is much worse than any other. You will be embarrassed even to mention it to other Christian friends. You feel you have to keep any sexual problems to yourself, so it's only you that feels despicable, dirty and depraved. Are you therefore not one of the damned, the unforgiven, the unredeemed, the unredeemable? What is to save you from these, the *real* sins (unlike pride and lack of Christian love which are 'good' sins to confess to)?

This attitude is not a true reflection of what the Bible says about sex; but it demonstrates that Christians often don't have a balanced approach when dealing with sexual problems, which of necessity need handling in a sensitive and loving fashion. Christians often have a hang-up about sex (of any sort) and in some ways this hang-up is more of a sin than the evils it condemns.

To be fair, the church isn't solely to blame, because in most religions and social groups sex tends to be a taboo subject. I suspect this is because the Devil always wants to taint and destroy the nicest things that God has given us, and as there are so many good things about sexuality the Devil wants even more to destroy it.

In developing their ideas of Christian sexuality, many Christians use less than the whole Bible. These same people would object, quite rightly, if bits were deliberately cut out of the Bible. If the Book of Revelation were removed there would be an outcry – "God has given us the whole Bible – cut part of it out and you alter the balance of the whole thing."   In practice, however, we often ignore or eliminate large portions of the Bible without realising it. When did you last hear the Song of Songs read out in church as one of the Sunday readings? Or hear a sermon based upon it? Or study it at home or in a housegroup?

Let's be positive. Why is sex so important to God that He gave us such strict rules about it? The answer is surprisingly simple – God made us so that sex within marriage would be very good, between people who in expressing their love, care and respect for one another become, as the Bible puts it, 'one flesh'. Sex is a very intimate thing. It changes people. It is not for nothing that the Bible says that a man and woman shall leave their families and join to one another, becoming 'one flesh'. Being 'one flesh' is a very intense situation! It's very precious, it's very delicate, and God is so concerned that this situation should be treasured that He gave us a lot of rules to make sure we keep it that way.

How can we develop a Christian approach to a subject as potentially sensitive and difficult as sex if we never listen to the whole sweep of what the Bible *really* has to say about it? How can we begin to appreciate sexuality as being good if we only hear bad reports of it? We talk about the evils of sex, but not the blessings; we quote excerpts from Paul's letters on some of the problems of sexuality, but we never follow up with a full-blooded description of how God really intended us to use it. He gave us a whole *book* of the Bible devoted to the emotional and sexual relationship between husband and wife. That's how important God thinks it is. How can we, how *dare* we, try to talk about a Christian attitude to sexual attraction and sexual love if we haven't assimilated what God has said positively about it?

So try studying the Song of Songs and get a bit more in balance. What's all this about "your breasts are clusters of dates. I will climb the palm tree and pick its fruit"? If such a statement seems vulgar, profane, or just plain pornographic then think again. It's part of Holy Scripture. God inspired it. This is what *He* really thinks about sexuality. He made it, for us, and He wants us to use His precious creation rightly, and get joy, comfort, fun, love, pleasure, togetherness and oneness out of it. If the Song of Songs seems 'off' to you, then maybe you'd better rethink your own attitudes to sex – after all, God inspired the Song of Songs just as much as He inspired "For God so loved the world that he gave his only begotten Son."

What was the attitude of Jesus towards sex? Isn't it nice that the first miracle He performed took place at a wedding – and, as the marriage service says, "He sanctified the whole state of marriage by His presence there."

His reaction to sexual sin is also interesting. When the woman who had been caught in adultery was brought to Him, His reaction was not to go and stone her (which the Levitical laws said was the punishment), but to say to the onlookers, *"Your hypocrisy is just as bad as her adultery."* Then, very quietly, when everybody had gone away, He turned to the woman and said, "Don't do it again." I'm sure He was saddened by the lack of trust that had developed within that woman's marriage, and the barriers that had come between husband and wife (because by then her adultery had become common knowledge). He didn't condone the adultery – but He was not prepared to let others make her sin into something special. Their hypocrisy was just as bad and no worse.

Jesus had no second thoughts about associating with those who had transgressed sexually (whilst at the same time not condoning their actions). Mary Magdalene was once a prostitute; the woman at the well had had five husbands. He didn't consider people like this to be beyond the pale. On the other hand, He was quite prepared to take the Pharisees to task over their lustful thoughts, and told them that lingering over the thought of adultery was exactly the same as physically committing adultery. So, on the one hand (in the Song of Songs), God is saying sexual attraction is good. On the other hand, the Ten Commandments and the statements of Jesus and Paul all say, "Handle with care, and obey the Maker's instructions."

If sexuality is so important to God because it gives such great benefits to those who are married, then it is likely that He will give us laws to protect us from using it incorrectly, to make sure that we don't make mistakes that destroy the best that He has to give us. But we must not confuse the negative side of those laws with a negative attitude by God towards sexuality itself. It's *because* God knows that sex is so precious to us that He has circumscribed it with rules.

At this stage there is an important point that needs clarifying. The Bible uses the very intimate 'one flesh' concept not only as relating to man and wife but also as an expression of the intimacy of the relationship between man and God (the church is the bride of Christ, for example). This is why, when God's people neglected Him, the Bible talks about them "whoring after false gods", because this implies the opposite, a most intimate relationship of a carnal nature.

Many of the statements in the Bible about Israel and Judah's falling away from God are given in statements with a sexual background – e.g. Judah "behaving like a prostitute towards Egypt". Please understand that this sexual background is there precisely because there is such a parallel between the sanctity of good sexuality, and the sanctity of the man-God relationship: the effects of destabilising this sanctity are similarly traumatic. These statements are *not* intended to draw a parallel between falling away from God and sex *itself;* only the *abuse* of sex is included in this parallel. If you don't understand this you may find yourself drawing the wrong conclusions about sexuality.

In the Bible, sex and sexuality are *always* good. God made them, and they are good. In the Song of Songs there is no talk about desiring one another merely in order to have children. The sexual desire of the two lovers for each other is central to the whole book, which is unashamedly direct in naming the physical attributes of each partner which are most sensually attractive to the other.

In other words, it is perfectly in order to be a sexual, sensual Christian. There is no contradiction. There is no shame. God made sex and it is *good*. It is only the misuse of sex that is a problem.

So you have God's permission – encouragement, even – to be a sexual person! Thank Him for it, enjoy it, use it appropriately. It is one of His gifts to you.

Sexuality within Marriage

I have only one comment to make on this – WHOOPEE! That's what it's there for, folks. Enjoy it, it's good for you.

Some people feel guilty about contraception. The Romans had sheaths, so the practical side of contraception has been possible for ages, if not very widespread. Until the twentieth century, however, it was common to find that you could have twelve or sixteen children, of whom only one or two would survive into adult life. All this has changed, with the advent of antibiotics, vaccines, better living conditions and better nutrition, and it is unusual in the developed world for a child *not* to reach adulthood.

In Genesis God gave mankind the commission to go out and subdue the world. We can't be selective about it. If we feel that we have a God-given right to subdue smallpox, diphtheria, scarlet fever, tuberculosis, malnutrition, and infantile gastroenteritis, then we cannot at the same time say that we should not subdue the consequent tendency to overpopulate the earth – which is what happens when you've managed to cure a lot of disease and are still producing children at the rate of sixteen per marriage. This is what happens in some of the developing countries and the net result is starvation. I hardly see it as God's way.

Therefore I think it perfectly normal and moral for a Christian family to decide under God how many children they would like to have. However, in some ways the pendulum has swung too far, from families which are too big to families which are too small. We may well find that having three or four children, rather than just one or two, makes for a better family group. It allows a greater sense of 'family', with collective responsibility for the actions of the whole family, rather than the sense of unopposed individualism which tends to be created in an only child, or one of two.

There is no mention of contraception in the Bible, either for or against, and, as in similar cases, I can only conclude that situation ethics apply – in other words you find out the Christian approach by looking at the situation and deciding what is best for everybody. At a time when only one or two children out of a whole family might reach maturity, it made obvious sense not to have contraception – otherwise mankind would die out. But at a time when scientific advances have made it almost certain that any child born will reach maturity, it makes Christian sense to limit the family in order to avoid overpopulation and mass starvation.

Routine use of contraception can give rise to singular problems – in the old days it was not a matter of *when* to stop having a family, but *could* you. Now it's a matter of when to *start* – and how much time between pregnancies – and when to stop permanently. The responsibilities of choosing when to start a family are in many ways greater than the responsibilities of 'just seeing what happens' when no contraceptives are either available or used.

This whole subject has its own guilts and problems attached. Many women have a massive hunger to be pregnant: some find they only really have a sexual drive when they have a chance of getting pregnant. Personally, I think that Christian sexuality is about a lot more than just making babies. We are after all the only animals that copulate face to face: I'm sure there is something very deeply significant in this. We're humans – and we don't just copulate, we make love: we are not just better-developed animals. And I suspect, therefore, that the female thirst for continuing pregnancy (which does occur in some people) may be more of an animal and less of a human attribute – perhaps akin to the man who wants to sow his wild oats and doesn't really care whom he gets pregnant in the process. In this sense male and female sexuality can both be seen as being not entirely Christian, even though they are very 'natural'.

(As a passing comment to this, I am very wary of this word 'natural'. There is a current vogue for 'natural' things, as though 'natural' equates with 'good'. What can be more *un*natural than ascorbic acid made in a chemical plant? Actually it's vitamin C and it's good for you. And berries? They're 'natural' so they must be good for you, mustn't they? How about Deadly Nightshade, then? 'Natural' does not necessarily mean 'good', and 'natural' *certainly* doesn't necessarily mean 'Christian'.)

If we as Christians only consider sexuality in a biological sense, so that we only think of it in terms of starting off a new human being, then I think we miss out on the fact that we are made higher than the animals. We also miss out on the 'one flesh' aspects. Our sexuality is a subtle and beautiful way of making two people very, very close. It's very difficult to continue arguing when you've made love. It *is* quite easy to lie back afterwards and start talking about your plans for the future, contented and relaxed in the arms of your spouse. I see the expression of sexual intimacy between a man and a woman as the absolute centre of the marriage from which everything else fans out, and I am sure that this intimacy is the basis of the 'one flesh' about whose sanctity God is so concerned. *This* is the real reason why fornication and adultery are not good. *This* is the reason why pre-marital sex is not advisable – it spoils what is to come. It's like giving someone a birthday cake with a piece taken out. Sexuality is central to marriage, beautiful, lovely, and made by God – so enjoy it!

⋆   ⋆   ⋆

Let's move on to the areas of sexuality that can cause difficulties for the Christian. In considering these it is *vital* to keep our sense of proportion and our sense of logic. Just because a sin is sexually orientated doesn't mean that all sex is sinful, merely that this particular use of it is wrong.

For example, how many times have you heard Christians criticise pin-up pictures as being totally unchristian, and in terms which imply that any expression of sexuality is wrong? Yet I suspect that what God wants us to say is, "Praise God for such a beautiful person, praise God for her sexuality, but please forgive her and us for abusing that sexuality and using it and displaying it in a way for which it was not intended" – for the benefit of a lot of other people, not for the pleasure of, and intimate relationship with, her husband. In this way we distinguish between good and bad in sexual matters. It is all too easy to castigate the *sexuality* of the woman in the pin-up rather than the *use* of her sexuality. The two are not the same thing. Sexuality is good. Its use may not be.

*   *   *

Sex is very, very nice, and a very deep drive within us. Because of this it's easy to be tempted to use it in the wrong way. But by the same token, sexual sins are very understandable and in many ways easier to fall into than other sins, such as greed, pride and jealousy, which are much more deliberate and vindictive in nature.

There are two equal and opposite points to be made as a result. Firstly, because it is relatively easy to fall into the trap of sexual sins, you should not feel that they are worse than all the others put together. They are so near to our normal expression of sexuality that it is all too easy to go too far. This doesn't mean that the sin is any less of a sin! – but it is just another sin, and *not* especially terrible in comparison with any other. Sexual sins are *not* worse than other sins, and in the Bible are never treated in this way. (The Bible never regards sexual sins as 'the last straw'.) Therefore don't feel you are in any way unforgivable, or have to atone for your misdeeds in some *special* way if you commit one. Asking (just once) for forgiveness is quite sufficient.

Secondly, it is *because* the sexual drive is so basic, and in order to help us not to make a mess of things, that God has surrounded sexuality with quite a number of instructions to guide us. The number of laws is testimony to the importance of using our sexuality correctly, not an indication that sex *itself* is wrong.

SEX AND DEPRESSION

It is important to understand that problems with sex are often just the tip of an iceberg. Rarely do sexual problems mean anything on their own - you have to look for a deeper problem which is driving the sexual problem onwards. For example, sexual problems within marriage are often related more to the problems of the *interpersonal* relationship between husband and wife than to the *sexual* relationship between them.

Impotence and Loss of Libido

Depression and sexuality are often quite intimately related, though not necessarily in any particular order. It may be the depression that is causing problems with sex, or problems with sex that are causing the depression. This is very true of the next subject that we need to look at – the person whose sexual drive has been greatly reduced, or whose ability to take part in physical sex has been curtailed – particularly in the case of a man who is no longer able to achieve an erection. The technical words for these two conditions are **loss of libido** – which means loss of interest in being sexual – and **impotence** – which means loss of the physical ability to take part.

Impotence

There are many causes of impotence, some physical, some psychological. Inability to get an erection can sometimes occur as a result of a depression, or severe anxiety about sex in general. It is also moderately common as a side-effect of antidepressant drugs, and also from diabetes. If you are getting impotent and are on medicines from your doctor, then *it is very important that you go and tell him because he can switch you on to an alternative drug.* With impotence arising from depression, improving the depression will cause the impotence to disappear. Do consult your doctor *whatever* the possible cause.

Loss of libido

In depression interest in sex is often very much reduced, as is the interest in just about everything. This can have two apparently opposite effects. The reduction in interest in 'normal' sex can be replaced by an increased use of masturbation. The reason is quite simple – having 'normal' intercourse requires a certain amount of mental energy which the depressed person hasn't always got; therefore he or she turns to masturbation as comforting, and relatively undemanding.

Secondly, to engage in normal sexual intercourse you have to like yourself a bit – and if (as many depressed people do) you loathe yourself, you may fear that your husband or wife will reject you for the horrible person you are, and because you fear such a rejection you don't want to start the preliminary flirtation before making love, simply because you fear a rebuff. Alternatively, you may hate yourself so much that you despise your spouse for thinking that you are interesting /attractive. Couple these feelings with a little bit of guilt from too strict a Christian upbringing (the sort of guilt that says that sex is really not very nice), and you end up with a completely turned-off sexual drive. This is particularly sad, because when you're depressed the closeness and intimacy of sexual intercourse can be a great help in making you better.

'Normal' sex requires a certain amount of self-confidence. If as a woman you are happy with your body, confident that your husband finds you attractive, and that you can turn him on sexually, then this is good, Christian, and normal. But to attain this level of feeling about yourself requires a considerable amount of confidence, which involves acceptance *of* yourself *by* yourself. ("Me – attractive?") Likewise, for the man, if he is depressed, lethargic, perhaps out of work, and generally feeling low, similar things will be happening. He may not have the energy to take the initiative in starting lovemaking (and of course it is more often the man who initiates the foreplay leading to intercourse). He too may fear rejection – rejection not for what he looks like but for what he is – no longer the he-man macho person that he may think a husband ought to be. So instead of starting that traumatic, revealing exercise called intercourse, he rolls over and tries to go to sleep.

In these circumstances it is up to the partner to help, and a great deal can be done. If your spouse is not very interested in lovemaking, then it is up to you as the non-depressed person to take the initiative and make the running. Lovemaking is important for both of you, for the non-depressed member of the partnership just as much as your depressed partner. It isn't just a matter of selfish demand – the amount of good that you can do your partner by continuing intercourse is immense. Intercourse is *encouraging!* It encourages the depressed person to feel that he or she really is loved and cared for. It says in a very emotive way, "I love you as you are, I accept you as you are, and I want to be near *you* even if at the moment you are depressed." It's very encouraging to be told this and to have it demonstrated physically!

Often with loss of libido it is only the *beginning* of making love that you have problems with. Once the initial arousal has started you may well find it most interesting and pleasurable to continue. (In many ways it's rather like going swimming when you're depressed – you can't be bothered making the effort to gather the swimming things together, but once you've actually got into the water it's good fun.) *Because* the benefits of intercourse are so great, I think it very important that as a depressed person you should be aware of the duty both to you and to your spouse of continuing with regular love-making.

It is important to you because of the effect it has on you, and it is also important to your spouse because he or she is going through a period of great strain in trying to deal with you in your depressed state. If at the same time you deny him or her physical closeness and intimacy, then this is one of the quickest ways to get him or her angry and frustrated and also one of the quickest ways to begin to cause a marriage rift. ("She's changed – she doesn't want me any more. I don't understand her.") A spouse subjected to this sort of pressure for any length of time is eventually likely to cave in, and as love turns to frustration may well reach out in another direction and have an affair.

Therefore, to keep your marriage healthy when one of you is depressed, remember your marriage vows – "With my body I thee worship..."; "To have and to hold..." Even if you don't particularly want to be bothered but your partner would like to make love, then please respond, if only as a duty. It will benefit you both and I believe it to be the Christian thing to do. You will probably start enjoying it once you get going anyway. And if your partner is the one who normally takes the initiative in these things and he or she is no longer interested, then perhaps it's time for you to take the initiative and effectively say to your partner, "Come on, I love you so much that I'm not going to let you do this to yourself."

Do you think it sounds unpleasant that I am suggesting that a couple should make love when one of the partners is not really that interested? I'm not suggesting that you force yourself upon your partner, but instead encourage him or her to continue to bring out that aspect of your marriage which is still there (even though probably covered up under layers of depression) and which is all the better for being expressed. In some ways it's not unlike a person who has had a smash in the car and who is now terrified to drive – you do them a service, not a disservice, if you insist that they take the keys and drive home. This way confidence comes.

EXTRAMARITAL SEX

Millions do it. And that includes Christians. If you've read the section on sexuality within marriage, you will appreciate that the reason why God says premarital and extramarital sex are wrong is not so much because it hurts *Him* as because it hurts *us*. Premarital sex destroys the *uniqueness* of the marriage relationship, and extramarital sex destoys the *sanctity* of the marriage relationship. Both of those dilute the benefits of the 'one flesh' ideal. In the old days (and still today) there was also the problem of pregnancy, which could ruin a girl for life and make her unmarriageable, give a child a family without a father, or totally destroy an existing marriage; to say nothing of the venereal diseases which always could, and still can, kill and permanently maim. It is impossible to get any of the venereal diseases if neither of you have intercourse outside your marriage, and again I see the restrictions laid down by God as being a way of preventing His people from damaging themselves and/or their offspring as a result.

However, the central theme of marriage is the 'one flesh' arrangement, and all the physical problems of pregnancy, VD, etc. are merely peripheral (though important) issues. The lack of trust that can be involved in one single act of adultery can destroy a marriage. It happened to one of my friends – 'something' just disappeared from within their marriage, a totally inexpressible 'something' that just vanished into thin air. The marriage was never the same again and ultimately it broke up. Adultery doesn't have to produce a child, nor cause VD, in order to wreck a relationship totally and completely.

So what if you're a Christian and in the middle of an affair? For your own sake, God would prefer you to stop. If you don't, you'll hurt yourself more. But it isn't easy, particularly if there are problems at home (which there almost certainly are if you're having an affair). Extricating yourself may not be without emotional trauma.

That's for the present. But what about the hundreds of thousands of Christians who have, in the past, had an affair or had to marry because the woman was pregnant; or those who had a sexual partner or partners before they were married? I'm sure by now that you don't need me to tell you that God loves you as you are, and that the degree of purity/debauchery of your previous life has no bearing on the matter whatsoever! If your extramarital or premarital affairs are a source of guilt to you, remember what I said in Chapter 3 about writing out your prayer of forgiveness and then secreting it somewhere. If you have asked, just the once, for God to forgive you then *He has done so*. There is no point in dredging up your past life again, ruminating on it and kicking yourself for it. God has already forgiven you, and really doesn't want to hear any more about it because the sins are dead and buried.

On the other hand, the *problems* from that phase of your life may still be with you – you may have had an illegitimate child, or contracted herpes or AIDS, and living with this is the problem that you have now to face. As before, God is interested in you as you are now and is not concerned with what you might have been had you not done what you did. The last thing God wants you to do is to mope around thinking to yourself, "If only, if only, if only..." Don't goad yourself with problems from the past. Live your life as from now.

ABORTION

Exactly the same is true of abortion. I think that, except possibly in a very few cases, abortion is totally wrong. It results in the destruction of a human life. What do you do if you've already had an abortion and now feel that it was wrong? The answer is very, very simple – and at the same time extremely difficult to do. You tell God about it, you ask His forgiveness, *and then you accept His forgiveness*. The third thing is the hardest! There is a very great tendency to kick yourself for the next five years (if not the rest of your life). The feeling that you have murdered your own child is enough to give anybody a depression. Instead, give the problem to God. He loves you just as you are. He might well have preferred you to have the baby and maybe get it adopted, but what is done is done, the sin has been committed, it has been forgiven, Jesus has paid for it and He would have gone to the cross to pay for your sin had you been the only person in the world, and if that had been the only sin that you had ever committed. It is not a terrible, unforgivable sin, it is a sin like any other, and being a sin is capable of being forgiven.

The difficult bit is accepting that you are worthy to receive forgiveness. Well actually, you're not! Nobody is worthy to receive forgiveness. This is what grace is all about – grace is all about being *un*worthy to receive forgiveness, and yet being given it. We have this terrible tendency to think of sins as being on a scale from nought to infinity with little white lies at the bottom, and murder, adultery and abortion up at the top. A sin is a sin is a sin. Perfection in God's eyes is like whether you can jump across a ravine. It doesn't matter whether you miss by half an inch or twenty yards, you still go down. And in God's eyes a big sin and a little sin are the same. Where 'big' sins and 'little' sins *do* differ is in the degree to which you yourself are affected by the sin, and the degree to which you feel that you have really tried to commit a sin deliberately, rather than half-involuntarily. You have to do more accepting of *yourself* over the more deliberate ones.

God understands, God cares, and God has the life of that unborn child safely settled with Him. Leave it with Him and stop thinking about the things that might have been if you had done something different. God loves you as you are: you are no worse having had an abortion than you are if you had told a deliberate lie. Remember Paul? He was actually a murderer (by association at least). And what's more, he was a murderer of one of the apostles. Who knows what Stephen would have done had he not been martyred? Maybe he would have written another gospel, perhaps there would have been letters of Stephen to the various churches – who can tell? But asking questions like these is not necessarily appropriate. We accept quite easily that the events of the New Testament were ordained by God, that it was part of God's plan that Stephen should die and that Saul should have been looking on. It doesn't mean that God couldn't deal with the situation, nor that He enjoyed watching Stephen suffer. In exactly the same way if you have had an abortion then maybe it was the wrong thing, but God can deal with the situation, and even use it to advantage, *provided you will let Him*. The difficulty is whether you are going to allow yourself to accept the forgiveness that He wants to offer you. This forgiveness is not dependent upon your earning it. You don't have to try harder, make yourself better, pray harder, get forgiven more. Just accept. Perhaps the prayer you need more than anything else is, "God please forgive me, and give me the grace to accept your forgiveness."

HOMOSEXUALITY

You might be surprised to learn that, in Britain, as many as 1 in 10 people have some degree of homosexual orientation, so the homosexual tendency is surprisingly common. On the other hand, overt genital homosexuality is much rarer.

There is no question about it, homosexuality is uniformly criticised in both Old and New Testaments as being an incorrect use of sexuality. However, the Bible says quite specifically that it is the *practice* of homosexuality that is wrong, not the fact that you may have sexually leanings in that direction.

All adolescents go through a phase of 'having a crush' on someone else of the same sex – usually a slightly older hero or heroine figure at school. This is *normal* and *natural* development, and is not related to homosexuality. If you are like this you are not gay, and not likely to become gay. It is a phase, and soon your attentions will automatically start switching to the attractions of the opposite sex – very much so!

However, adolescents at this point are vulnerable, and it is possible to keep them at this same-sex-crush stage by introducing a physical homosexual relationship: for example, taking a boy at this stage in his development and initiating him into genital homosexual activity. This is why it is so pernicious to start discussing choice of sexual orientation with adolescents. If allowed to mature unhindered, most adolescents will naturally grow through this stage and become fully heterosexual. On the other hand, by introducing doubt, or the sense of choice into a young person's mind, especially if coupled with physical homosexual experience, it is possible to delay or prevent him (or her) from developing towards full heterosexuality.

For the most part, homosexuality seems to be a very psychologically orientated disease. Looked at from any angle it seems unnatural – biologically, evolutionarily (if you believe in evolution), and socially. It is probably a learned deviation initially triggered by an abnormality of the mother/son relationship (though there is also a suggestion that homosexuality might also be related to different levels of certain hormones at critical times before birth). Psychologically, at least part of the problem is that men and women alike need to have their own developing sexuality affirmed by their parents, otherwise it is likely to become distorted.

Whatever the cause, the practice of homosexuality is frequently associated with very deep-seated guilt, even amongst those who think they have 'come out' and declared that they are 'gay'. This is demonstrated by the guilt reactions so many 'liberated' gay people display when they find out they have contracted AIDS.   Their 'liberation' often proves to be all too superficial.

If you are gay I would remind you (as always) that God loves you as you are. (But as with everyone, He would like certain things changed.) Do make sure that you get appropriate help – from your pastor, your GP, from other Christians. It's not always easy, because there is still a tremendous stigma attached to homosexuality in some professional circles, and especially in Christian ones.

Don't be misled by the "Gay Christian" movement. They may think they are being helpful, but I believe them to be totally wrong. I don't believe that it is appropriate to be a both a Christian and a practising homosexual who has not the least intention of trying to change his orientation.

Remember that Christ was quite happy to be in the company of 'prostitutes and sinners'. We've read this so often that its impact is lost on us. It's interesting to speculate where Christ would be found if He came to London now? St Paul's? Westminster Abbey? My guess is that at least some of the time He'd be found in Soho, talking to those who frequent the gay bars and clubs. (Maybe if He'd been crucified on Tower Hill in the 1990s, instead of in Jerusalem in AD 30, His first resurrection appearance would have been to a former rent boy. That's the male equivalent of what Mary Magdalene once was.)

It doesn't matter to Jesus what you've done, or what you've been. He's interested in what you can become once He's forgiven you.

Jesus is not put off by *anybody,* whether or not the society of the day finds their behaviour acceptable or unacceptable. If you're gay, Jesus still loves you. He wants you to develop from where you are into the person you were originally designed to be. Relax. Accept yourself (Jesus has accepted you), and get appropriate professional guidance.

Clinically speaking, sexual medicine at this level is deep and difficult, and to go into the problems and solutions for the homosexually orientated Christian is beyond the scope of this book. Do however look at *The Broken Image* and *Crisis in Masculinity,* published by Kingsway, both written by Leanne Payne, who is a Christian counsellor with considerable experience of dealing with homosexual problems. Her testimony is that homosexuals are in an arrested state of emotional development, at least partly because their 'biologically correct' sexual orientation has not been truly affirmed by their parents.

Don't feel especially guilty if you are homosexually orientated. Homosexual sins are just the same as other sins – no more and no less. Hiding your problem, being ashamed of it, is a quick recipe for disaster, because the fact that you can't (daren't?) talk about it testifies to the guilt you feel about it and the fear of being ostracised by the church (and, by implication, ostracised by God).

God loves you *now.* He accepts you, even if you don't accept yourself! Learn to accept that He loves you *now,* as you are, and it will give you greater confidence to face whatever changes may be needed in the future.

MASTURBATION

It is confidently reckoned that 105% of all adolescent males and 99% of all females masturbate at some time in their lives, especially during adolescence. (You're not odd. So there.)

Guilt over masturbation is widespread amongst Christians, which is unfortunate and unnecessary. The Bible never refers to masturbation *at all* – which is odd (to say the least) if masturbation itself is a sin. Unfortunately, our understanding of Biblical sexuality is not all that Biblical! We have to cut away the social pressure of the last century which tried to deny the very existence of sexuality, and made out that any sexual thought was, by definition, impure. The Bible doesn't say this at all!

The result of trying to deny your sexuality is a very perverted existence indeed. (You can see this in the way some Christians go on and on and on about the sexual sins that *other people* commit. They've obviously not come to terms with their own sexual feelings and have to externalise them onto other people/activities/publications.)

As with our previous discussion about the relationship of Christianity and sexuality, let's go back to the Bible and see what it *actually* says on the subject.

As I've just said, nowhere in the Bible does it say that masturbation is wrong. There are only two circumstances in which the emission of semen is even mentioned. The first is the sin of Onan. Onan refused to impregnate his dead brother's wife, as was expected by the customs of the day: instead he practised coitus interruptus (which is withdrawing just at the time of ejaculation so that the semen is ejected outside the woman's body). There are two ways of viewing this – either that coitus interruptus is wrong, or that Onan was being unfair to his brother and his brother's wife in refusing to do what was at that time plainly his duty. Personally, I think that bearing in mind the context, the latter approach is more likely to be correct.

The second time that we hear about the emission of semen is in relation to ceremonial cleanliness – priests were not allowed to perform their duties if they had had a penile discharge in the last seven days (and a 'discharge' could also include venereal disease). A penile discharge was only one of *many* other factors involved in ceremonial cleanliness. In this respect there are more frequent references to contact with blood, dead bodies and disease, and the prohibitions over eating pork.

Ritual cleanliness was at one time important. The Old Testament laws were there to give the Jews some ideas about holiness (and its opposite, sinfulness), and payment for the sin by sacrifice. Without in any way wishing to minimise their importance at the time, I think it helps to think of these ceremonial laws as being 'practice' laws – getting the Jews to a position where they could begin to understand the awesome perfection and holiness of God by starting off with a few concrete examples. (Concrete examples are a great help in this – what are the parables if not practical examples of spiritual points?)

Jesus Himself confirmed this when He agreed with the actions of David in using the ceremonial bread to feed himself and his men when no other was available. This special bread (called the Bread of the Presence) was used in the tabernacle, in the worship of God, and according to Old Testament law, could only be eaten by priests. David and his men were hungry, and no other food was available, so they asked the priests if they could have the ceremonial bread, and were given it. Jesus confirmed that this was perfectly acceptable, even though it was against the ceremonial law.

Once the Jews had learned the principles of *ceremonial* cleanliness (i.e. ritually clean actions), the next step was to consider a *truly* cleansed life, in the New Testament fashion. The need for ceremonial cleanliness ('practice laws') had gone, just as adults no longer need to recite their alphabet. Nowhere in the New Testament is there any reference to a need for *ceremonial* cleanliness. In fact Paul says that even circumcision is not to be carried out any longer – it is not even neutral, it's actually *un*christian to ask for it to be done because it is harking back to the Old Covenant. The old laws have been fulfilled in Christ, and the ceremonial laws no longer apply. Hence we eat bacon and eggs for breakfast, and don't prohibit doctors and undertakers from attending church (because of their 'uncleanliness' having touched dead bodies).

We can therefore dispense completely with the idea of 'uncleanliness' associated with the emission of semen (for whatever reason): the concept is entirely ceremonial, and nothing to do with the New Testament.

What about the act of masturbation, though? What does the New Testament say about this?

The actual act of masturbation is not mentioned in the Bible, so it is not likely to be wrong in itself. However, masturbation is usually accompanied by sexual fantasies. This obviously leads on to a different problem, which is: how far is it related to lust? Jesus said that if a person looked at a woman in such a way that he *thought* about committing adultery with her, then it was just as if he *had* actually committed adultery – the thought about the sin, and the sin itself, are one and the same thing.

However, that was for adultery, not fornication, and remember, adultery (by thought or deed) is a transgression of the 'one-flesh' state of marriage. Fornication is somewhat different, being intercourse before marriage. The difference is very important. Firstly, adultery undermines the 'one-flesh' state of an established marriage; and secondly, there should be no reason for a married person to commit adultery – your sexual drive has a legitimate outlet, and it requires a certain effort of will to direct it elsewhere.

On the other hand, fornication is having intercourse before you are married. Whilst the act of fornication is obviously wrong, in an unmarried person is the *thought* of sexual activity necessarily 'impure'? Is thinking sexually about someone else when you are single (and searching for a mate) not altogether different? I find it very hard to believe that the adolescent Christian is expected to have no sexual thoughts whatsoever. Is he (or she) supposed to find his mate purely cerebrally and not feel even the slightest physical attraction to *anyone* until he is married to her? Not feel even the faintest beginnings of that sexual tingle which is part and parcel of the overall attraction of man and woman?   And then the minute that they are married suddenly get madly and passionately sexual?   I can't really imagine that there is intended to be a sharp divide between the two.

Secondly, what did Jesus mean by "look at a woman lustfully"? The more I think about it, the more I feel that Christians have jumped in too quickly and defined lust in terms which were never intended by Jesus.   I don't think that admiring a pretty woman's face (or her legs, or her figure) is lust. I think lust in the sense that Jesus intended it would be better applied to the person who is running through the actual action of adultery in his mind, "First we'd do ... and then *I'd do ...* and *she'd do...*" *That* is lust. *That* is what I believe Jesus meant.

Sexual experience was primarily designed to be shared between two people, so masturbation can never be the be-all and end-all. And it can slip into difficulties when it becomes overwhelmingly frequent, where there is involvement with hard-core, deviant pornography or when it is done in same-sex groups.

Whatever the rights and wrongs of the situation, I am sure that God doesn't want us to get worried about it. If it *is* a sin it's a very 'natural' one! Don't think of it as especially terrible. It is, however, difficult if you are not yet attached and also feel masturbation is wrong. Sexual appetites don't go away, and sexuality when you are young is like food – it's hard to do without it for any length of time.

Many Christians find it so hard to deal with the problem that, however much they want not to masturbate, they find after a few days that their sexual drive is up in fourth gear again – and it is the repetitive nature of masturbation that causes so much distress: in some cases, the feeling that however hard you try, you know you will fail in the end.

God loves you *as you are*. If your age, your intended course of study, or financial constraints mean you can't marry for some time, it doesn't mean your sexual drive automatically goes away! God understands. He is probably more concerned that *you are upset* about the situation.

I don't claim to have any direct hot line to God on this, so feel free to disagree with me if you want. All I know is that too dogmatic and legalistic an attitude towards masturbation has caused misery to many thousands of adolescents – and taught them as a by-product that sex itself is something that you worry about, have anxieties and guilt feelings over and that sex is intrinsically 'not nice' and certainly not Christian. And you can't get away from the fact that the Bible never mentions masturbation, *not even once*.

*　　　　　*　　　　　*

If you *do* feel that masturbation is wrong, what do you do about it?

As I said before, often it is a symptom of and a pointer to a different problem – usually deep insecurity. You won't be able to surmount it simply by trying not to masturbate or trying not to look at the opposite sex. (This is especially true for adolescents where the sexual drive and hormones are at their strongest, and at a time when they are beginning to choose their sexual partner for life.) Almost certainly you will fail, and in failing you will kick yourself twice as hard.

As usual with depressions and guilt feelings, the treatment is not to attack the problem head-on but to find out what the underlying problem is and deal with that. It's almost certainly loneliness or insecurity, and that's the area that you have to deal with first.

As I've said over and over again, and it's all the more relevant here, God loves you, as you are, including your sexuality. After all, He made it. It may be that you should use your sexuality in a different way, but you're not going to earn His love by 'being good', and you will probably go backwards emotionally if you repress your sexuality (as opposed to constraining it), in just the same way that if you repress anger you often end up with a depression. The very fact that you worry about masturbation is likely to make you masturbate more, out of sheer insecurity.

There is, however, one way that may prove helpful. It doesn't help to repress your sexuality: it doesn't get rid of it – it just drives it underground. What can help is to sublimate it – in other words, use its energy, but in a different form. Sexual energy can be redirected in this fashion, often to such a degree that the sexual need itself no longer remains unfulfilled. In practical terms this means getting very involved in alternative activities which are fulfilling, creative and exhausting. Redirecting your energies in this way has three effects. Firstly, it gives you extra energy for the things you are actually doing. Secondly, it fulfils your sexual drive through changing it slightly. Thirdly, because it is a more outward-looking existence, it takes your mind off yourself and your own problems. On the other hand, the sublimation of sexual energy is not necessarily easy (especially if you're an insecure teenager).

★   ★   ★

There are three groups of people who have problems with masturbation. The first group comprises the adolescents and the unmarried. The second includes those who are married, but are either unhappy in their marriage in one way or another, or else have not been able to come to terms with full-blown adult sexuality (almost like a child who hasn't progressed from nursery food). The third group consists of those who have been widowed, separated or divorced, yet still retain their sexual drive, now unfulfilled.

It is so easy to make all these groups feel guilty about their sexual feelings – they are all vulnerable people with sensitive emotions. It is all too easy to pontificate (from a position of security, being happily married) about the intense emotional struggles and upheavals that afflict people when they try to sort out the Christian response to their sexual drive. Let's see instead if we can look at the situation gently, carefully and lovingly.

1. In Adolescence

Adolescence has a tendency to hit people with the momentum of an express train and with about as much sensitivity. Suddenly, at puberty, from being relatively asexual beings, adolescents become painfully aware of their altering shape and their awakening sexuality. There is no real warning of what is to happen, and for the young man or woman who may be a new Christian it can be very tough, both trying to lead a Christian life as well as coping with the intensity of the sexual drive (especially in a church that doesn't like to acknowledge the existence of sex, except in deprecatory terms). Add to this the emotional insecurity that comes with adolescence, the gradual and developing independence from parents, peer pressures, often glandular fever (which depresses and exhausts), and an awareness that you have now left childhood – and you have the recipe for a very strung-up kid indeed. It's a very exhausting, worrying, exhilarating, depressing, contradictory time. However rebellious or suave a teenager seems to be on the outside, inside he's usually churning away.

Not only is this a very worrying time in social terms, but the teenager also has to cope with his emerging sexual drive. And it's some drive! It peaks in intensity only a few years after it's begun – and yet an adolescent may have many years to go before he or she has any chance of getting married. The age of puberty is dropping steadily, so twelve- and thirteen-year-olds are experiencing sexual urges; compare this with the situation a few centuries ago when puberty could be as late as eighteen or twenty – in fact, very near to the time of marriage.

This total upsetting of a previously settled life style means that adolescents are very much more likely to masturbate as a source of comfort, and as a method of release of these pent-up sexual feelings for which, as yet, there is no orthodox outlet.

Sadly, the Christian response has often been insensitive. Often there is just condemnation that it is wrong, lustful, sinful and to be avoided at all costs – but we are not talking of automatons with no feelings, we're talking about ex-children, who, however much they may try to ignore it, have still got a very strong sexual desire to cope with. The trouble is that the more the Christian adolescent thinks that masturbation is wrong, the worse he or she feels about him- or herself – which just adds to his or her sense of insecurity. The worse he feels about himself, the more he will want to masturbate for immediate relief of his sexual hunger, and for gratification of his emotional insecurity.

Masturbation may well be the first practical effect that sex has on teenagers – and if they are made to feel guilty about it, they can extend this guilt onto the whole of their sexuality, until they come to the position where all of sex is perceived to be unchristian. Then, in order to feel 'good' or 'saved', the adolescent Christian has to try in some way to deny the existence of his or her sexual feelings. But sex is so basic that they will find this very difficult – about as difficult as persuading themselves that they don't feel hungry when consistently deprived of food.

Guilt over masturbation can cause a great deal of anguish, particularly to the Christian adolescent brought up in a relatively strait-laced church. Can I remind you once again that the Bible doesn't even mention the subject?

2. In Marriage

The second group of people to have difficulties with masturbation are those who are married, but who find 'normal' sex threatening or unfulfilling. It often happens! If this is you, you're not alone. Because our society, and the church, is so often uptight about sex, individuals get similarly uptight, unable to relax enough to feel happy and guiltless about enjoying it. In addition to this unease, there can also be added a difficulty in forming adult relationships. Masturbation carried on into marriage is merely demonstrating the presence of a hurt person, scared to 'open up'; in other words, a fragile, injured personality. We don't help such a person by saying, "You're *wrong.*" We help them most by asking, "What is it about masturbation that is fulfilling your innermost needs? Why can you not feel fulfilled and satisfied with your spouse?" Is it comfort, solitude, the need to fantasise about being caressed? What is it about 'normal' sex that is so threatening? Or is it a symptom of a deeper hurt, within the marriage itself, where the two members are no longer seeing eye to eye, and perhaps are no longer in love?

People in this state may need to be taught the beauties of true sexuality so that they no longer fear it; so that they learn not to feel guilty about sex itself and realise that God made it and it is *good*. (They may also need a little discreet tuition on physical lovemaking.) They may need to get help over the 'mental' aspects of marriage, so that emotionally they become more truly one with their partner – true marriage guidance. (When people say 'marriage guidance' they usually imply 'marriage-on-the-rocks guidance' – but I don't mean it in this sense here.)

If you're in this situation, relax. Try to work out why 'normal' sex is unfulfilling and/or threatening, and then work on what you've discovered. Begin to sort out the relationship with your spouse, if appropriate. Learn again that God made sex, and it is *good*.

3. Widowed, Divorced and Separated

The third group of those who may have problems with masturbation are those who are widowed, divorced or separated. Just because the spouse has gone doesn't mean the sexual drive has gone as well. Often a recently widowed person will have thoughts about his/her dead spouse that are frankly sexual in nature. And why not? Sex was as important a part of the marriage as was the companionship. Would you stop a widow thinking about the previous companionship of her husband? Well then, don't imply she shouldn't be thinking of what the sexual side of their relationship was like.

And for the separated or divorced? Again, these are fragile people, who never felt called to the single life. They still have sexual feelings. In many ways, their problems are similar to those of the adolescent, and coming to terms with their new situation with its extra stresses and strains (especially if they have to look after the children as well) brings its own insecurities. Physical lovemaking may well be sorely missed, and masturbation is one way of at least partially relieving the sexual urges, the sense of loneliness and the feelings of insecure exhaustion. As with all other reasons for masturbation, it helps to see things in a wide context: if you are in this situation and feel that masturbation is wrong for you, then don't try to attack it head-on instead, recognise those sources of tension and frustration that are leading you in that direction and deal with *those* instead.

EXERCISE

Read the Song of Songs in the Old Testament. It's a love poem which is considered chaste by Eastern standards. This is what God really thinks about sexuality! (It's also an allegory about Christ and the church.)

20

WHY CHRISTIANS GO OFF THE RAILS

From time to time we hear of Christians who appear to have gone off the rails completely: active, practising Christians who have at the same time been involved with very unchristian activities. The list of involvements is long – alcoholism, involvement with prostitutes, wife beating, affairs, fraud, child molestation – you name it, it's been done by Christians. But why? Why should practising Christians, who obviously ought to know better, allow themselves to become involved in such things?

For every one caught in the act there must be many more who are secretly involved in similar activities. You may be one. If you are, it's almost certain that you will be suffering great stress as a result. But – and here's the important point – your *real* problem is almost certainly *not* at the point where you perceive it to be.

Let's try to work out why Christians might behave in this way. Firstly, let's look at the unchristian activity itself. What function does it have in the lives of the Christians concerned? What is its most immediate effect?

If you look at the list of items (and maybe add your own problem in there as well) you will find that there is a common thread to all of them – they all offer immediate emotional relief.

- **Alcoholism:** going on a binge numbs the pain of living and blots out the problems – for the moment.

- **Having an affair:** relieves the crushing sense of isolation of the person trapped in an unhappy marriage.

- **Going on a spending spree:** gives an immediate uplift through pampering yourself.

- **Involvement with pornography/prostitutes:** offers release of emotional and sexual tension.

The results are all *immediate*. And they are all what I would term 'escape mechanisms' – where emotional pressure is relieved (but wrongly or inappropriately).

It's rather like a garden hose which doesn't fit very well on the tap, so it dribbles at the connection. If you put your thumb over the other end of the hose, the pressure inside rises, and the dribble becomes a leak. Push your thumb down even more firmly, and the resulting rise in pressure may even push the hose off the tap.

There are three ways you can stop the leak. You could wrap a piece of cloth round the junction of tap and hose. This works for a bit – then the cloth becomes sodden and the leak starts again. You could push the hose on more tightly – but without a leak the pressure will rise even more, and as the connection is ill-fitting the increased pressure will start up the leak again.

Or you could reduce the pressure in the system by taking your thumb off the end of the hose, and *as the pressure inside the hose reduces, the leak stops*.

The analogy with the 'escape mechanism' sin is precise. *Escape mechanisms occur when the pressure inside the system is too high and the system fails at its weakest point*. For 'physical pressure' in the hose, read 'emotional pressure' in the individual. Escape phenomena occur when the emotional pressure inside the individual rises to such a pitch that something, somewhere, has to give. But the point at which it 'gives' is not necessarily the point where the pressure is being applied. It's much more likely that the individual will escape from the pressure at his weakest point – his 'besetting sin'. The escape mechanism provides immediate relief of tension – but that tension has probably been been generated in a completely different area to the 'subject area' of the escape mechanism sin. In other words, a Christian may hit the children because he can't cope with the stresses at work: that same Christian may do the same thing if he has a marital row, or gets into money problems. In other words, whilst the causes of pressure may vary, in any one individual the chosen escape route usually remains the same.

The sort of person who has problems with escape behaviour is *not* the bad Christian, the one who isn't trying, but the one who is *trying too hard,* and it's because he *is* trying too hard that the escape route is necessary. The bottom line is that his internal emotional pressure is too high. Often it hits the Christian who has 'buttoned himself up' too tightly (especially in religious areas) and has no adequate release for his inner feelings, guilt and emotions. If stressed too much he may find that he cannot contain his feelings any longer and he has to reduce the emotional pressure somehow.

This is why it's the 'good' Christian who gets problems of this sort, and why an individual Christian is more vulnerable as a leader than as an ordinary member of the congregation, because of the extra pressure of church responsibility. Unfortunately, Christian leaders who 'go off the rails' are perceived by the outside world as hypocrites, when in reality they are nothing of the sort. Almost certainly each and every one rues and regrets what he finds himself doing, but can't find any other escape for the pressures building up within him.

Whether or not anyone else finds out about them, the repetitive nature of his 'escape sins' drives the Christian involved to distraction. He finds he can't stop doing them, which makes him doubt whether he means it when he asks for forgiveness, knowing that he'll be in the same position again next week. The reason he can't stop these sins is not obvious *to him*. *We* can see why – the escape sins are the result of pressure produced elsewhere in the system, and not of pressure in the escape mechanism area.

What does he do in response to his own escape phenomenon? *He hates himself*. He hates the sins that he commits and yet finds he cannot avoid committing them. And his response? – to try harder. It's *always* to try harder! Unfortunately, in trying harder to avoid committing those selfsame sins, he puts even more emotional pressure on himself. After a time he can stand it no longer and back he goes to his old escape route again. He gets drunk; or he beats his wife; or he goes on a spending or eating spree; or he finds a prostitute.

He will see the escape phenomenon itself – the alcohol, the battering, etc. – as his besetting sin, and will try harder to get this aspect of his life under control. But the more he tries the worse things get, simply because *he's trying to attack the wrong problem*. Go back to the hose – the reason the water leaks out at the tap is because the pressure inside the hose is too high. If you try to seal up the connection you aren't attacking the root cause of the problem: you're actually making it worse, because now the pressure in the hose can get even higher. In exactly the same way, the Christian who is trying to deal with his own escape phenomenon is trying to deal with the wrong thing. He won't help himself much by trying to deal with the escape sin directly, because this just stops the release of emotional pressure, and may actually make things worse. Instead, what he should look at are the reasons why he needs an escape – in other words, he needs to find out what is raising the pressure so much.

At least we now know what is going on. And I'm sure you will appreciate that a Christian who has this on/off approach to Christian living is going to be very unhappy indeed – ripe for a depression based on really good 'facts': "I am a lousy Christian because I so often sin and do ..." – whatever his escape phenomenon is. The more he tries to get rid of the problem, the worse it gets, which makes him feel even more terrible; in fact it may make him suicidal because he feels the problem itself is totally out of control. Maybe he's not really a Christian, he thinks, and produces as evidence the fact that he can't control his escape mechanism. The power of God is certainly not working in him (he thinks) because he can't get rid of the problem. He may even wonder if he's possessed......

(Escape behaviour is much the same as the Achilles-heel sins we discussed in Chapter 4, and all the comments there apply here.)

Christians get *very* distressed by their 'escape mechanism'; they are often aware that they are walking a tightrope. Because of the type of sin, and its repetitive nature, they often find it difficult, if not impossible, to talk about it to other Christians. What would the deacons say if they knew their minister did....? What would the others think if a Sunday School teacher confessed to...? So they shut up, and keep their terrible secret to themselves – which piles the pressure on even more. What if someone in the church finds out? Worse – what if the papers find out? Tighter and tighter go the screws – and the more the internal pressure rises, the more the escape mechanism is used.

Christians in this position also feel they are walking a tightrope as far as God is concerned: they know their behaviour is wrong, yet they do it again and again. God forgave them last time, but will He this? At what point will God throw up His hands in horror and bring retribution down? (Worrying about this makes those screws go on tighter and tighter...)

God doesn't work like this. "How many times should I forgive my brother? Seven? Seventy?", came the question. "Seventy times seven (i.e. infinitely)," said Jesus, "and how much more will God forgive you?"

DON'T TRY HARDER – TRY DIFFERENTLY!

If you're a victim of escape mechanisms, take heart! God loves you. Yes, God really loves you. No, He doesn't like your escape mechanism, whatever that is, but your escape sin will never stop Him loving you – and in any case, He knows that the escape mechanism is there because you're trying in the wrong way, not because you aren't trying at all. He loves you; and you are His; and all He wants you to do is let go of the *cause* of the internal pressure.

This degree of pressure inside is usually caused by trying to be perfect all on your own. It's a sort of Christian pride. At heart you feel, "I'm not yet good enough to be forgiven. I must try harder." And you can use any number of verses in the Bible to 'prove' your point – for example, " 'Be ye perfect, as I am perfect,' says the Lord." There are many others: the exhortations in the New Testament letters, the condemnations of the prophets. It's backed up by proponents of worm theology (see Chapter 17) who like to 'lay it on their congregation' and convince one and all that they are even worse than they thought.

Nor is it helped by the unconscious hypocrisy of church members, (the Sunday lie-in, as Peter Meadows calls it). In this, by refusing to discuss our problems we unwittingly give the impression that we are better than we really are. This makes for a climate in which no one can discuss their weaknesses, temptations and failures without feeling really unchristian.

Consider a typical church after a Sunday service:

"And how are you, Fred?"

"Fine, thanks." ("No I'm not. I got blind drunk last Wednesday night. Secretly.")

"How are you?"

"Fine, thanks." ("No I'm not. I can't stand the pressure at work any longer and I'm seriously thinking about ending it all.")

"How are you getting on, Mary?"

"Not too bad, thanks." ("No I'm not. I've put on another half stone from binge eating, then I took it out on the kids.")

But you couldn't tell them what you really mean, could you? It would be all over the town in next to no time. People wouldn't understand. They wouldn't be sympathetic. They'd treat you as though you'd got leprosy and had suddenly become untouchable. Christians are not supposed to do things like that. Therefore *anyone who does things like this cannot be a Christian.* Oh no, you can only confess 'good' things here – a generalised lack of love, a failure to pray as hard as one ought to, and a failure to read the Bible as much as one should. Generalised problems. Acceptable problems. *Unreal* problems.

And meanwhile, emotionally you're bleeding to death, trampled on by the apparent goodness of everybody else (*"They* don't have problems, do they? – they just told me so."), unable to come to terms with your own problems, loathing yourself for the frequency with which you fail, and absolutely certain that God is going to have it in for you in a big way when you get to the pearly gates.

God loves you. He really loves you. He loves you when you're trying so hard to be a Christian, even if you're going about it completely the wrong way! So start off by realising that He loves you *unconditionally;* that even if you repeated your escape phenomenon every day for the next six thousand years, He would still love you dearly. What He really wants you to do is to stop trying to attack your own escape phenomenon, and instead look at why you have such increased internal emotional pressure.

There may well be a lot of external pressures in your life – illness, money problems, marriage problems, family problems, and these may be enough to raise your internal pressure to bursting point. But there are also *internal* pressures, particularly when you are a victim of Old Testament legalism: the idea that once you have committed a sin you are sinful, unlovable, no longer a friend to God. The Old Testament approach to sin was, "I've committed a sin – O hell (literally)." And you stay in hell until you expiate your crime by presenting an offering – making a sacrifice. Then all is right until the next sin comes along – and you have to make another sacrifice, another offering. And so it goes on, day after weary day.

Jesus came to save us from this. Paul said that the law kills – because as sinful people we can *never* obey it fully. This side of heaven we can never be in perfect communion with God – *so don't expect it. Don't try to make yourself perfect*.

However, as well as saying, "the law kills," Paul also said, "but Jesus came to give us life."

The New Testament approach to sin is quite different: "I've sinned. There's a penalty for my sin – but it's already been paid. Hallelujah! Thank You Jesus for taking it away from me. Help me to be nearer You in the future." No self-abasement; no self-flagellation; no kicking yourself for three days just to prove to God that you feel bad enough about it to prove you mean it when you ask for forgiveness.

Because it's freely available, forgiveness is, in a way, almost too good to be true. And because it's so easy, a lot of people think that they *haven't* had it, and then they think that they don't *merit* it, and then they think they ought to *make* themselves merit it. "I must prove to God that I deserve forgiveness."

When you say it like this it sounds stupid. But believe you me, if you have that sort of temperament it is *easy* to fall into the trap of 'must try harder'. Yes, of course we must try harder, but *not* to obtain forgiveness. Forgiveness is instantaneous, unbelievably so, and absolutely free. Your most repetitive sin is instantaneously forgiven, not because of what you are but because of the One in Whom you are trusting. You have given your life to Jesus – He, in His turn, has promised that He will forgive you *for everything*. You don't have to beg, plead, or grovel. Yes, He wants you to try harder, but probably in a completely different direction. He wants you to be perfect, but being perfect is not something that *you* can do. It's something that Jesus does through you. Being perfect is enjoying walking in Jesus' footsteps.

Ah, I hear you say, but I try so hard to be perfect and then I sin again. So what? – it's all forgiven. And the very fact that you've asked that question just illustrates that you haven't grasped the point at issue – that being a Christian is not a matter of slavishly obeying the law in order to get forgiven, but of being a new person in Christ so that you are now free to make mistakes with impunity (not that you want to!) The French philosopher Voltaire put it rather cynically when he said, "God will forgive – that's His business." I don't agree with his attitude, but he has a good point! It *is* the business of God to forgive. He loves to do it and *it saddens Him when Christians don't allow Him room to forgive them.* He hates it when Christians try to earn forgiveness by being better. What He wants you to learn is to accept yourself, *as you are,* knowing that *He* in turn has accepted you, *as you are,* and that He wants to use you, *as you are,* to do things for Him. You don't have to struggle to achieve forgiveness – you've already got it, if only you realised!

So, go on from here. Don't worry about the difficulties of curbing your escape behaviour *directly* – you'll find that the need for escape behaviour becomes much less as you reduce the emotional tension within yourself.

Taking steps like this is not easy. It goes against the grain for those who have been brought up in a legalistic fundamentalist tradition. But it is the Biblical way.

So if, as a Christian, the escape phenomenon is your particular problem, rethink where you stand in the eyes of God. He doesn't think of you as a worm, but as a forgiven friend. It doesn't minimise or excuse those things you do that are wrong; it just enables you to start off from where you are and be positive about your life instead of negative about it. Learn to accept His forgiveness and gratefully – gleefully – get on with the business of living positively from now on, confessing your sins and immediately afterwards ignoring them. In other words, don't bother about sin! Take the pressure off yourself (and it's your own pressure on yourself, not God's). Maybe God isn't asking you to do half the things that you think He's requesting. Make sure that you're not trying to earn your own salvation (back to the works again!). He loves you as you are. Trust Him, and live by it.

EXERCISE

List the sources of stress in your life. How many of them can be contained/reduced/ eliminated?

PART 3

WHY ME, LORD?

21

THE SPIRITUAL GYMNASIUM

We have now discovered what depression is, physically and emotionally. However, just because we know *how* something happens doesn't mean we have established quite *why*. So why has God allowed this? Why have you been singled out? What makes you different from other Christians? How could God be so callous as to put you into a situation which is the nearest thing emotionally to hell on earth?

We've already touched on some of the answers in earlier chapters. Let's rephrase the question. Given that God loves you so very much, what is it about depression that makes it imperative that you should go through it?

Part of the answer is tied up with the ineffective way in which so many people treat depression: "But you've no reason to be depressed"; "Pull yourself together"; "Snap out of it"; "It's only your monthlies"; "You'll be all right, just have a bit of exercise and get to bed early – you'll be fine by the weekend." These and hundreds of other quotes are the product of insensitive people who have never been through it themselves.

In contrast, think of the people who have helped you. Almost certainly they will themselves have been through some form of emotional upheaval in the past – which is why they are much better equipped to help you. *They* understand at first hand what you're going through – they are the ones who have the ability to say those comforting words, "I've been there before you. I know what it feels like – so don't worry, you'll get through it eventually." True empathy like this is so much more valuable than mere sympathy, and someone who can say these words can become a much closer friend of the depressed or anxious person. When you've fallen in the water you don't want somebody on the bank demonstrating the breast stroke, you need him there in the water with you, swimming beside you, supporting you; or at the very least you need somebody who has been there quite recently and knows what it's like to try to swim with boots on.

The only way to be able to give practical help like this is through having experienced the problem at first hand yourself. Therefore *if you are depressed, consider yourself privileged because God has some important work for you.* You may eventually become a lifeline for others who are depressed, anxious or emotionally upset, and you will be equipped to help them, not by shoving platitudes down their throats, *but by befriending them, showing you understand them, and supporting them emotionally*.

The type of people who can really help others are the ones who know their way around depression from the inside, the ones who learned to deal with their own depression and have really allowed themselves to be sorted out. Do you want to be one of their number and be able to help other people in a way that many other people cannot do, because they just do not have the wherewithal to do it? If so, you first have to go through your own emotional upheaval and sort *yourself* out before you can be of help to others.

Begin therefore to appreciate that *God* wants you to have your depression. He wants you to go through it because you will learn from it – about yourself, about other people, about Himself. It will deepen your Christian and your secular life – it will make you much better balanced, more sensitive, more mature and probably more creative. In short, it will help you to realise the full potential that God has placed within you. And I can assure you that once you begin to think about your depression positively like this, rather than negatively, you will be halfway to recovery.

God wants to use you: but He can't if your abilities haven't been properly honed. He wants to develop you, to get the best out of you.

If you want to develop a man physically you make him exercise – perhaps in the gymnasium or on the running track. He exercises and exercises until, slowly at first, his muscles are built up and his coordination is honed to perfection. No one ever became an athlete just by sitting in a chair and thinking about it. In order to have his moment of glory on track and field an athlete needs to put in hour upon hour of punishing physical activity, training, and practising.

Exactly the same is true of mental problems. Those who want to be of use to God in helping others with their emotional problems will never become prepared just by sitting and thinking about it in an abstract, theoretical way, nor just by praying about it either. Even though God is there to guide you, you need to complete your part of the work – you need to be put into training, dirty your hands, gain real experience. This training involves lots of spiritual exercise, which is why I like to refer to Christians in a state of emotional upheaval as being 'in the spiritual gymnasium'. It's where you get put through your paces – and God won't let you out until your spiritual muscles are bulging and under good control. But when you're out... just think of what God can do through you!

So don't think of your time of depression as being wasted – it is anything but. You have to learn things at first hand – actively not passively. It won't work any other way. (See the section in Chapter 24, under the heading 'Lay Psychiatry', about the way cats learn mazes for a more detailed appreciation of why learning at first hand is so important.)

You are in the spiritual gymnasium for very positive reasons. And as with a physical gymnasium, when you've just had a hard work-out you end up tired. You wouldn't criticise an athlete for being a weakling just because he was exhausted at the end of a three-hour training session in the gym; nor should you say to a depressed Christian that he is a spiritual weakling when *he's* been in the spiritual gymnasium. Being there tires you out – but once you've recovered, the end product is something that is stronger, more resilient, more useful than the unfit and untested person that went in.

Where does faith come in all this? Shouldn't you, as a Christian, try to 'exert more faith' and get out of your troubles that way? Emphatically not. If you attempt to use faith as a cop-out to avoid the hard work of sorting out your problems, you will end up falling between two stools. The problems won't get sorted out, because you've not knuckled down to solving them. And your faith is likely to become castles-in-the-air, head-in-the-sand stuff, where your faith is working against reality instead of with it. You will be hiding behind it instead of leading off with it. Instead of, "Lord, I believe – help Thou my unbelief," your prayer will tend to be, "Lord, I *don't* believe: help Thou ...." which isn't the same thing at all.

You are actually exerting a lot of faith just through gritting your teeth, *staying* in the gymnasium and getting on with the job God has given you. It takes a lot of *real* faith to let God sort you out in this way, and don't let anyone persuade you otherwise.

Faith is not a substitute for knowledge or experience. If you gloss over your problems then they remain unsolved, and deep inside you will know it. If they remain unsolved they are likely to return at just the wrong moments – when you are brought low for other reasons.

Therefore, for your faith's sake, tackle your problems head-on. In the long run it is by far the most painless way of sorting them out. And don't worry about losing your faith in the process; maybe you'll have a rocky time, for a bit. But God won't get cross, or blame you, or let you down. He understands. (After all, He's the one who is testing you out.)

My own experience in the spiritual gymnasium was long, painful and hard: when I was at medical school I was quite severely depressed for about a year and a half, and moderately depressed for another four or five. During that time I was led to test just about every aspect of my life and beliefs. I did a lot of honest doubting. But I can honestly say this: God has never *ever* punished me for doubts I've had while I've been asking and facing these hard questions. He has let me face the problems; and gently guided me towards the answers. God never rejects an honest questioner; so don't be afraid to be one if necessary, in order that you can fully sort out your problems. God will honour you for doing this, and in the long run your faith will become more secure, as a result of the answers you find.

I am sure that I needed to go through the spiritual gymnasium. Being there taught me a lot about sensitivity, and what it feels like to be anxious and depressed (useful for a budding doctor!). All the same, it was a ghastly time – an experience I wouldn't wish on anyone. But now, looking back, I know that I've gained much from it that I couldn't have acquired in any other way. Without it I'm sure I would been much less of a person, much less of doctor and much less of a Christian. A lot of things got sorted out in those six troublesome years!

My faith benefited also. I went into the gymnasium believing in a fervent, but a shallow way. I came out with a faith that *at the time* felt much less secure and vulnerable – but was in fact based on a more solid foundation, and from that base it then slowly developed and matured. Had I not gone into the gymnasium I think it would have remained shallow and undeveloped to this day.

But for all that it wasn't a pleasant time, and it took many years before I was able to go back to the place where I trained without fearing the memories it brought back.

If God wants you in His spiritual gymnasium, be grateful, and thank Him for it. It means that you are going to be trained to help others in ways that you otherwise couldn't. It means that God is going to sort you out! If you are brave and face your problems head on you will get out more quickly! Don't lose sight of the fact that *God* wants you there: He wants to hone you to perfection, ready for action. So praise Him for what He has in store for you. Praise Him for how He's going to be able ultimately to use you. Praise Him that He's confident enough about your character to put you in this position and test you out. Thank Him for the increased sensitivity and maturity that you will eventually acquire.

And if anyone criticises you for being a spiritual weakling, look him straight in the eye and say, "God wants me here" (which implies, "Who are *you* to argue with *Him*"!). It doesn't half boost your confidence! It also makes your Christian friends realise that they have to rethink their ways of helping you, and learn to pull *with* you, instead of against you.

Happy exercising!

EXERCISE

1. Workers need rest and recreation (i.e. re-creation). Unfortunately, a lot of people who are depressed feel that they don't deserve a break – they feel they haven't earned it.

   Don't forget that you're in the spiritual gym, so you *need* that mental relaxation. Spoil yourself. Give yourself a treat. Do something slightly out of the ordinary, perhaps just a little extravagant, that you wouldn't normally do – like buy that book you've wanted for ages; or have a meal at that restaurant. You'll appreciate it, you'll remember it with joy, and it will relax you.

2. Stones can trip you up, or act as stepping-stones or cornerstones. The same stone can do all three jobs at various times. Meditate upon the fact that your present stumbling block will eventually become a stepping-stone both for you and for others, and a cornerstone for your life. Thank God for the opportunity it presents, and ask Him for the courage to go on and face the trials ahead, in the knowledge that (a) it is His will and (b) it is ultimately going to help you serve Him better.

If you're depressed, you probably have a more or less constant sense of guilt. However, guilt comes in two forms: true guilt, where you really have done something wrong; and guilt feelings, when you just *feel* guilty, irrespective of whether you are truly guilty or not. Unfortunately many depressed people can't tell the difference. *You* may be suffering from guilt; or guilt feelings (unrelated to any real sin); or a mixture of the two.

True guilt is related to sins – of omission or commission. There is only one remedy – repentance and confession. However, it's not always easy to accept that you've made a mistake, and many Christians make themselves unnecessarily unhappy for weeks, months or even years by refusing to accept their faults. Confession is a humbling exercise, and a particularly difficult one if your self-esteem is low for other reasons.

Real guilt is important, because it gets between us and God. However, *most depressed Christians aren't suffering from real guilt at all –* instead they're the victims of **guilt feelings,** which are quite different. Most depressed people overemphasise their faults, and feel very guilty over failings that others would consider trifling. It is common for depressed Christians to confess their sins over and over again because they don't feel any better afterwards, and don't feel forgiven. Note that word 'feel' – there is all the difference in the world between the person who hasn't been forgiven, and one who has, but doesn't *feel* as though he has.

Guilt *feelings* come from six sources:

1. There is **guilt over the mistakes and sins that you feel you have made,** especially those you feel have contributed to your present depressed state; the depressive tends to ruminate on these mistakes far more than the mistakes themselves justify.

2. There is a **generalised feeling of being 'sub',** in an ill-defined way. You begin to be aware of an underlying all-pervasive sense of rottenness; uncleanness; incompetence. You feel unlikeable and unlovable. And the more that you think about it, the worse it gets: the more you realise how low you feel, the worse you become. Then, because you're feeling low, you do something to make yourself feel a bit better; under these conditions people usually do something which is illegal, immoral or fattening, so immediately

after your little pick-me-up you feel worse because there really *is* something now to feel guilty about! Then the whole cycle starts again – feeling terrible, giving yourself the wrong sort of pick-me-up, feeling worse, etc.

3. **Anxiety in Christians often manifests itself as guilt:** "Have I done the right thing?"; "Were my motives pure (I bet they weren't, I'm sure they weren't....)"; "What will the others say....?"; "I hashed that up, didn't I....?"

4. In addition to anxiety about specific events or problems, there is also a general sense of anxiety. Doctors have a specific name for it – **floating anxiety.** Floating anxiety doesn't remain floating for very long – it soon finds something to attach itself to. Initially when you feel guilty or anxious about a specific event, your anxieties about it overshadow your feelings about other things. When the specific worry passes away (you pass your driving test, or get that job), you might think your worries would disappear: not a bit of it. You may get a couple of hours' respite – and then you begin to worry with the same intensity about something else, such as whether you've booked the right holiday .... Your floating anxiety has attached itself to this new ('real') source of concern, and will remain there until displaced onto some other 'real' problem. (They are always 'real' problems, blown up out of proportion by the addition of the floating anxiety.)

In Christians, floating anxiety can cause grave problems over guidance. Because depressed Christians can easily be made to feel guilty, and because their floating anxiety quickly attaches itself to any verse or sermon, often all the depressed Christian receives from Bible study is a sense of further condemnation. He prays for guidance; then reads, "I will always be with you.... Be determined, ... confident; and make sure you obey the whole Law.... Do not neglect any part of it and you will succeed wherever you go."[1] This is actually a tremendous promise (with a condition attached); but the depressed Christian will let his anxiety attach to the verse so he perceives it as, "If you don't do what I say, down to the last jot and tittle, then I won't let you succeed." Granted, the passage implies this to some extent, but the *point* of the passage, its whole thrust, starts not with man but with God. *"I will be with you..."*

As a result depressed Christians often find that reading the Bible is a very threatening activity indeed – "All those prophecies of doom or gloom if the Israelites don't follow God...... they must apply to me.... I'm sure the Lord wouldn't be bringing this verse to my attention if He didn't have a message there for me... oh

---

[1]Joshua 1: 5,7 (GNB)

woe..." And in doing so they miss the *main* point of the passage.

For this reason I am most cautious about quoting individual verses to depressed Christians – it is so easy to take them the wrong way round and read into them things that either are not there, or are faint by comparison with the main point of the verse. For the depressed Christian (and often for the non-depressed one as well) it may be better to quote a summary of the passage, so that the person can see the underlying principle, rather than getting enmeshed in the individual words.

So, rather than quoting, "Do not neglect the law.....", I would want to talk about the *whole of the first half* of Joshua 1, where Joshua is given God's commission to lead the Israelites into the Promised Land. The emphasis in the whole passage is undeniably positive: God is commissioning Joshua to lead the Israelites into the Promised Land. The Lord tells him *three times* to be determined and be confident (but only *twice* to be obedient!) because He will be with him. The real thrust of the passage is the emphasis on 'God being with you', but also that we are *commanded* to be determined and confident, because God *will* be with us....

Seeing a passage in a broad sweep like this gives much less ground for anxiety: it's much harder to adopt an anxiety-ridden approach to a passage when you're looking at it in an overall manner. It's like looking at a picture in a newspaper – if you concentrate too much on a small piece of detail you may only see a lot of hazy dots; but if you stand back you will see how it fits into the picture as a whole.

5. **Many Christians feel guilty about being depressed,** thinking (wrongly) that their depression is a condemnation of their belief and life. This sense of guilt can be intense, and is frequently made much worse by the unhelpful attitude of other Christians. In the worst cases depression is treated as a sin. (See Chapters 26 and 28.) This is usually far from the truth, yet at first it seems a very plausible argument, easy to adopt if you don't understand depression properly.

The depressed Christian feels guilty enough; and his sense of guilt is only increased by such an approach. If you're depressed you will find it all too easy to agree with criticism directed at you: your general sense of being 'sub' will see to that. Therefore, you will all too easily accept the other Christian's (incorrect) verdict of, "You ought to look at your faith because there must be something wrong if you're feeling like this." It's the wrong diagnosis, but the depressed Christian finds it easy to accept (because he feels so guilty anyway). So he goes away and tries to confess more, believe more, be a better Christian. It doesn't work. (It can't work, because that isn't his real problem.) Then he finds it doesn't help – which makes him doubly unhappy because he now feels that not only is he truly sinful in the eyes of God, but even when he tries to do something about it, nothing happens. Maybe God isn't listening..... Or perhaps He doesn't exist....... Or maybe He's so angry with him that He's not going to forgive.... And on goes *another* layer of anxiety, stress and depression. (We'll talk about this further in Chapter 26.)

All these sources of guilt leave you with such an overwhelming burden over events real, imagined, or just blown up out of all proportion, that you end up not knowing where to put yourself. You get driven down even more, made to feel more and more guilty – and what is worse, possibly 'not a proper Christian'. So you try in vain to be a 'proper Christian' and things get worse (because by now you have become so self-aware and self-critical that you would need to feel one hundred per cent perfect in order to think that there was any improvement at all). The end product is a Christian who feels outcast, substandard, guilty beyond redemption, unlovable, unloved, lonely, and a fool for being like this (yet unable to change).

It is such a pity that this happens, because it's so unnecessary. *If there is a sin involved in being depressed it's a refusal to accept forgiveness, not a failure to seek it, nor a failure of faith.* Above all, the depressed Christian feels that he is unworthy to be forgiven by God; that God has lost patience with him because of his misdeeds; and that his depression is a sign of God's anger directed against him.

Again, and again, I will repeat it – God loves you *as you are*. It is only by realising *how much* God loves you that you can really begin to get healed. The fact is, quite simply, that it is impossible for you to fall out of God's hands. Impossible! I defy you to do it! He loves you far too much, whatever you've done, whoever you are. How sad it is that we have managed to turn Christianity so completely upside down – that the privilege of being totally unworthy, a total failure and *still* dearly cherished by a loving, heavenly Father has been changed into the idea that you have to obey the rules, otherwise God will take it out on you.

6. Finally, **tiredness, sleeplessness and emotional exhaustion** (all common features of depression) **serve to magnify minor guilt feelings into major events.** I am aware of how much more anxious/guilty I tend to become over events (real or imagined) during the day after I've had my sleep disturbed through being called out in the middle of the night. *Tiredness multiplies guilt feelings.* This is why 'looking at things in the cold light of day' can make such a difference to anxieties you have when it's late and you're

overtired. The remedy is simple – defer making critical judgements when you know you're tired: sleep on it first!

DEALING WITH GUILT

For the depressed Christian, guilt *feelings* are more likely to cause trouble than true guilt; and as we've just discovered, if there is a sin in Christian depression, it's when the Christian refuses to *accept* forgiveness, not a refusal to *seek* it. So let's tackle the whole problem of removing guilt and guilt feelings.

We *must* start off by considering true guilt. There is no point in trying to remove guilt feelings if they relate to true guilt which is as yet unconfessed.

We've already looked at ways of dealing with true guilt (see the exercise at the end of Chapter 3, where you write out your prayer of confession, then keep it locked away, unopened, as a testimony to your forgiveness.) Once you have confessed your sins they are *gone*. You have to ask for forgiveness once, and once only, and then they are *gone*.

There is nothing more to say about true guilt.

Any problems which remain after confession relate to guilt *feelings*.

However if, after asking for forgiveness, you still *feel* guilty, it may be appropriate to confess your sins to another Christian (preferably a mature one). It's amazingly therapeutic to do this – rather like the old adage of 'a trouble shared is a trouble halved'. The Bible recommends it (see James 5:16): however, it's not a *requirement* for forgiveness, but so that we can allow ourselves to accept forgiveness more easily. I don't agree with mandatory *ritual* confession as a prerequisite for forgiveness (as in High Church Anglican or Catholic practice), but I do recommend confession as *appropriate* for those sins which you find are preying on your mind. It's also useful if you find you are dealing with *recurrent* problems – not that you should feel required to confess to another person every time you sin, but instead confess the fact that you are having persistent trouble in this area. (And if you are having persistent problems with one particular sin, do look at the section on 'escape phenomena' in Chapter 20, because it may well be that you are trying to attack the wrong thing, which is why nothing is improving.)

As we've already discovered, it is *impossible* for you to fall out of God's hands. But maybe you're afraid you've done so already and committed the (so-called) 'unforgivable sin'. Let's look at this in detail. You will recall[1] that Jesus had just cast out an evil spirit when the Jews accused Him of being in league with the Devil: "You cast out devils by using the power of the Devil." Jesus turned on them and said, "Man can be forgiven for everything except blasphemy against the Holy Spirit." What did He mean? The Pharisees hadn't said anything about the Holy Spirit, had they?

As with so many things in the Bible, the real significance of the passage is not immediately obvious; you have to work at it a little to find its underlying implications. The Pharisees were saying that even though Jesus had done something good, they were not prepared to recognise it as such: instead they thought of it as evil, coming from the Devil. In saying this they showed that they had mixed up good and evil so completely that they couldn't recognise good when it stared them in the face (literally!). In this incident, Jesus was saying, "You can misunderstand Me, you can misunderstand God – and you can be forgiven for it: but the minute you start misunderstanding and rejecting *good itself* then you're really in trouble."

Once a person is at the point where he confuses good and evil deliberately and completely, then he *doesn't bother* about what is good and what is evil, he *doesn't bother* about any offence that is given, he *doesn't care*. So if you are *worried* that you have committed blasphemy against the Holy Spirit, by definition you *cannot* have done so. The very fact that you are worried that you might have offended God this much is in itself totally sufficient evidence to prove that you can't have done it!

Nevertheless, if you are worrying that you have committed some terrible unforgivable sin, ask for forgiveness and *ask for God's grace to accept the forgiveness* that He offers. This is the hard bit! Depressed people often have difficulty in accepting good things that are free, mainly because they feel so unworthy of receiving them. Even as committed Christians we still have this curious idea within us that we can in some way earn forgiveness, and that forgiveness will not be given until God sees that we are suitably reformed (by praying harder, or abstaining from a besetting sin, or reading the Bible more). God just doesn't work like this!

Although we cannot earn forgiveness, we are given it by the bucketful! 'Grace' means just that. We couldn't earn forgiveness, nor earn the right to be forgiven, even if we tried. The whole point of 'grace' is that it is entirely *un*conditional. In spite of this, many depressed people feel so low, so unclean, that they no longer believe in themselves and no longer like themselves much, if at all, grace or no grace. They loathe themselves for requiring God's grace so often.

---

[1]Matthew 12:22-30

How Do You Start To Like Yourself?

The Bible says that we are to love our neighbours as ourselves – but to many a guilt-ridden Christian the problem is more cogently stated as, "Learn to treat *yourself* as you would your neighbour." This is not easy to do, particularly when you don't think that you're worth anything. To the Christian who is depressed, looking after himself seems a very selfish concept: everything in him screams against it being the right course of action. It seems selfish, and anyway, he feels he doesn't deserve it.

We're back to earning our own forgiveness again, aren't we? ("You can't be forgiven until you prove you're worth it.") This is not God's way. He still wants to give you good things when you *don't* deserve it. Even more, He wants to give you good things to help you get better, develop, and mature into the much happier, much more sorted-out person He would have you be.

There's another way of looking at the situation, this time on a purely cerebral level. God loves you. It is quite wrong to hate something that God loves. So you'd better get on and start loving yourself!

All this is easy to say, but emotionally very difficult to carry out, simply because of the way you feel about yourself. In practical terms, how do you go about it?

In general, go easy on yourself. Think what you would advise if it were your neighbour who was depressed, rather than you – then take your own advice! Feed yourself properly, get enough sleep, allow yourself time and money for recreation, so that you really can begin to enjoy life. If God loves you, then who are you to take it out on yourself? You must learn to behave appropriately towards yourself – and that means learn to give yourself treats! When was the last time you did something just for yourself? It doesn't have to be anything expensive – it could be going to the cinema; sitting and watching the ducks playing in the local pond; walking round the Botanical Gardens; spending a day in a museum; going to a disco; or buying a record or book for yourself. It needn't cost the earth – but what you must do is learn to love yourself enough to be prepared to give yourself gifts.

It may not be physical things you need – *time for yourself* is just as important. It's so easy to say, "I don't deserve a holiday/break", especially if you are behind with your work. But this answers the wrong question. It's not what you deserve, it's what you *need* that counts. (It's also cost-effective – though this shouldn't be why you do it. In giving yourself that (so-called) undeserved break you will be resting yourself so that you are better fitted for the next job you have to do. Giving yourself what you need may in fact be very much more productive than giving yourself what you think you deserve.)

But it isn't easy to look after yourself and to give yourself treats when you hate yourself so much. You'll do it once or twice but after a time you may well give up, because you still think you're not worth it. It's strange how we have so little patience with ourselves, yet if someone else were to have the same problem we would expend a great deal more energy on helping them, and feel it only right and Christian that we should do so. It requires real dedication and guts to start doing it to yourself ! But it is important because *you are the only one who can do this to yourself* – no one else can.

It's not always just a matter of receiving the gifts that is important, but who is the giver. It's not just that you receive a book, or a record, or a trip round the local stately home, it's the fact that *you* are giving it *to yourself*. It's all about letting yourself off the hook, encouraging and helping yourself by giving yourself enough to make you feel that you are at long last moderately friends with yourself.

It sounds daft talking like this, doesn't it? But a lot of people who are depressed really loathe themselves. We must get into the habit of thinking of ourselves as God's children, precious to Him, and of treating ourselves as other Christians would treat us – with dignity, with respect, with love and with care.

In some ways, depression is a disease of being too selfish, and in other ways of not being selfish enough. It is a disease of selfishness in that you can become inordinately self-aware at times when you should forget about yourself, yet on other occasions you have to *make* yourself self-orientated enough really to care for yourself. You are the only one who can do it. You are the only one who can make yourself go to bed at the right time, or get enough of the right sort of food, or go for an evening out. Think of looking after yourself as a Christian duty. It's not something you can take or leave, but something that you *must* do as part of your Christian life.

Do You Know Where to Stop?

One problem that can arise as a result of anxiety and obsessional states (which are common associates of depression) is the difficulty of knowing where to stop. There is *infinite* need in the world, for money, for material assistance, for time and for involvement. It is all too easy to look at a problem – say, giving to famine relief – and think, "If I give a pound, shouldn't I be giving two? And if I give two, shouldn't I be giving three? Where do I stop? " Attitudes like this, if taken to extreme, destroy the giver; he finds it impossible to spend on himself through guilt/anxiety about others who could be receiving his money.

Problems with time are similar. There are always meetings that you could attend, things that you could do for other people (like cutting their lawn); all these take away from the time you have available for yourself. Again, taken to extremes, you end up with no time for yourself. Where do you stop? Isn't it Christian to think of others first?

To the non-depressed Christian, questions like this can often be quite challenging. To the depressed person they can be destructive. The amount of guilt that you acquire through not giving that extra pound, or not going to that meeting, has to be experienced to be believed. The trouble is, it doesn't stop there. Next time, you'll be feeling that you should give another pound as well as the extra one you've already given. And not only should you go to that extra meeting regularly from now on, but there's an extra 'extra' meeting you've heard about as well......

Well-meaning Christians can grind themselves into the dust in this manner. The unqualified insistence that the Christian should 'give everything to God' is all very well for the person who is whole, but inappropriate and impossible for the broken-up one. For a start, 'giving everything to God' is a concept which requires maturity and balance to understand, because it implies quite clearly that what we have should be *made available* to God .... who may well give much of it back to us again, because we need it. However, the Christian who is broken up will see it only as God asking him to give away what little he has left....

So what do we do to counter this sort of obsessional/guilty thinking?

Firstly, recognise it for what it is – not a challenge from God (in most cases), but an expression of your current problems. At the heart are two assumptions:

1. that you are not worthy to receive anything, you don't deserve anything, and should give away what you've got to others (who obviously *are* deserving), and

2. that God will do you in if you don't display Christian charity.

   We're back to earning our own salvation again, aren't we.....?

Secondly, look at Jesus. How did He respond to stresses? There was infinite demand for His abilities, especially as a healer, yet He limited His ministry to three short years. He regularly 'got away' to be alone, to pray, to recuperate. He knew what His area of ministry was, and didn't try to do things outside it. He knew that within His human body He had finite resources, finite strength, and finite time; and because in His earthly body He had temporarily lost His omnipresence, He could only interact with and influence those immediately around

Him. So He recognised His limitations, and worked within them. He did *not* go round like a whirling dervish, trying to evangelise all the Jews *and* the Romans *and* the Samaritans, *and*.....He picked His targets (after prayer and communion with God), and went after them specifically.

We must do the same. We are similarly constrained by time and space: we can't do everything. We can't single-handedly feed the whole of Africa and simultaneously evangelise all of Britain on our own. We need to develop two things: an awareness of the areas that God would have us work in – the really central things He wants us to spend our time and money on; and an awareness of the fact that we are human, that we have our own needs, and that God wants to bless us, not criticise us.

God never works in a stingy way. 'Good measure, pressed down and running over' is what God wants to give us. (The simile is about measuring out corn in the marketplace by volume in a standard-sized measuring container. If it's pressed down, more goes in per given volume. And if it's piled high and running over, you get even more....) God delights in treating us like this. He does not *demand* things from you before He will deign to give you anything: He loves to give you good things. And most emphatically, He will not demand from you what you do not possess: so He will not want you to give back so much time or money that it leaves you a pauper.

EXERCISE

1. Get out your diary and plan some treats for yourself for the next four months. At least one a week, please. They don't have to be expensive – just regular, and for you.

2. Still feeling guilty? Remind yourself constantly that this is a *feeling*, not the truth. If you have asked for forgiveness you *are* forgiven, whether or not you *feel* forgiven. Therefore, act as if you are forgiven: believe it to be true. If you do this consistently and frequently you will help to remove those incorrect guilt feelings.

It may help to re-enact the exercise in Chapter 7.

23

CONSCIENCE

I wonder if you've considered just where your conscience comes from? Have you ever thought that your conscience might *not* be coming directly from God? And did you know that in the Bible a person with an apparently 'strong' conscience (in secular terms) is actually referred to as 'weak in the faith'? (See 1 Corinthians 8.) It is even possible for your conscience to be *opposed* to God!

You probably think that your conscience is God-given, accurate and incontravertible: some people refer to their conscience as the 'voice of God within' – and many Christians imagine that if God speaks to us *directly,* He does it through the conscience.

Unfortunately, things aren't quite as simple as this. If you were to define conscience solely as 'the pricking bit' – the uncomfortable feeling itself – I might well agree with you; but we usually use the word 'conscience' to imply a great deal more. What we refer to as 'our conscience' also includes ideas of *what* is right and wrong, as well as the uncomfortable feeling we get when we go against what we feel we should be doing.

At first this may seem like splitting hairs, but it certainly isn't, as we shall see. The truth is that what we think of as 'our conscience' is made up of a number of separate items. Part of it is the memory of what we did in the past; of how our parents reacted and how they taught us to react. Another part is recollection of how the Bible tells us to react. Yet another part is emotion. Finally, there is the 'pricking bit' – that part which compares what we think we ought to do with what we are actually doing – and makes us feel uncomfortable if there's a difference!

This distinction is important, because it greatly affects the way we think about our conscience. In particular, when God 'awakens your conscience', He does it almost exclusively by stimulating the 'pricking bit' into action. What He *doesn't* usually do is alter the memory banks this pricking bit uses when trying to work out what is right and what is wrong. Changes to this come later, and from a different source.

As as rough rule of thumb, it is worth considering the conscience as being *the memory that we have of parental, religious, ethical and moral influences,* using the word 'parental' in its widest possible sense, *as well as* the part of us that makes us feel uncomfortable when we go against these memories.

Your conscience is therefore not entirely the supernatural thing you perhaps thought it might be. (Were our consciences entirely supernatural, Christians would all think in *exactly* the same way.) There *are* times when people have their consciences directly sharpened up by the activity of the Holy Spirit (especially at conversion, and usually through activating the 'pricking bit'), but sharpening up the conscience in the course of the ongoing Christian life usually occurs through the reorganisation of the mind's memories as new Christian teaching is assimilated. The Christian's conscience is changed for the better when, through Bible study or teaching, he *consciously* realises that a particular course of action is appropriate for a Christian. His conscience then refers later on (perhaps even unconsciously) to memories of these new ideas. Thus the Christian has re-educated his conscience – not so much the 'pricking bit', but the memory banks this pricking bit refers to.

In this book you will meet many examples of this rethinking process – in effect, where permission is given for you to change your attitudes to a particular subject (such as sexuality): this has a knock-on effect in that it also re-educates the way your conscience performs.

Consider anger, for example. The young Christian (and unfortunately quite a lot of older ones too) often thinks that the Christian response to anger is simply 'don't exhibit it'. But it is a lot more complex than this (see Chapter 15) and if you simply and routinely turn the other cheek you may actually be doing what is wrong (in certain situations). Even so, the young Christian may feel his conscience pricking him when he displays anger, *even though he may be completely right to be angry on this particular occasion*. It can take a long time before a new Christian understands the proper use of righteous anger; once he does understand how to use anger correctly he will be able to display it appropriately without his conscience troubling him.

In other words, because the Christian has deepened his understanding, his conscience no longer pricks him in the same way as it did before. Once, logically, you begin to understand how to react better, your conscience will remind you only if you go against this new teaching, provided it has fully supplanted the old methods. (However, if you have deeply ingrained memories, especially in areas where you have relatively little recent clear-cut guidance, you may well find your conscience defaulting back to the old way of doing things.)

Think of your conscience as a very dynamic thing, especially the memory banks that it uses to operate. Some of these memories are undoubtedly derived from patental influences and it is important for you to think back over your own chldhood, and the parental influences you had then, in order to see if you now consciously agree with the way in which your parents brought you up and the precepts they gave you. If they did it well, then remember it. If they did it badly, or from a non-Christian viewpoint, or there were aspects of it that weren't so successful, then consciously work out why it was that it didn't work, and consciously reorientate your ways of thinking to account for this.

In this way you will be a better person, a better Christian (and in turn a much better parent) – and have a more truly Christian conscience.

This re-education of the conscience is included in the concept of 'the renewal of the Christian mind'. I cannot emphasise enough how much your conscience is related to memories of 'example figures' from the past. Your conscience is not a purely supernatural thing under God's control – the Bible never says this, nor does it imply it.

Having said that let us look in more detail at what the Bible does say about the conscience: the results are surprising. 1 Corinthians 8 talks particularly about those people who have a conscience which is *too* active (and therefore in Christian terms 'weak'). The subject at issues was whether it was right for Christians in Corinth to eat meat that had been sacrificed to idols. At the time it was impossible to buy meat unless it had first been sacrificed in this way. Some Christians, however, said that their consciences were telling them that this was wrong, that they should not eat meat and should therefore confine themselves to eating vegetables. Paul says that, as idols are only bits of metal and stone, and the gods they were thought to represent don't actually exist, then it is not a sin for the Christian to eat meat that has been sacrificed in this way.

In other words, those with the less active consciences were *theologically* the more correct. Nevertheless, Paul was anxious to point out that the Christian who has a tender conscience (and therefore only eats vegetables) is just as much a Christian as a person who doesn't have a conscience about it and is therefore happy to eat sacrificed meat. He also points out that the strong Christian whose conscience is not tender shouldn't look down critically upon a weaker Christian (who has a too-active conscience).

Christians are generally of these two sorts – ones with over-sensitive consciences and ones with the (doctrinally) correct consciences. The ones with the over-sensitive consciences tend to be legalistic, very much aware of 'doctrine', treating any deviation from doctrine or lapse in carrying out the details of doctrinal requirements as being a sin akin to heresy; in particular they look at those with less tender consciences as being too free-and-easy. The ones with the more correct consciences, whom Paul describes as 'strong in the faith', regard those with the very extreme consciences as being too disciplinarian, too rigid and too dictatorial.

It is very interesting to see how those who are commended by Paul as being strong in the faith are actually the ones with "*less* of a conscience" – these people have a robustness of personality which allows them to know when to be flexible. Being flexible (within limits) is one of the marks of maturity. The strong Christian doesn't have too tender a conscience: he doesn't have to worry about keeping the letter of the law, because he knows that this would be going back to Old Testament morality, turning him into a legalistic Christian – or in other words a latter-day Pharisee. Yet he does know where he should "draw the line", and does so firmly, and with courteous conviction.

On the other hand, the weak Christian (with the 'strong' conscience) can't see the wood for the trees: in applying great attention to detail, he may well miss the overall point of the spiritual law at issue.

Consciences mature when their owners mature! A person with a tender conscience (i.e., weak in the faith, according to Paul) will benefit from becoming a wiser, more mature Christian, because in the process he will re-educate himself and his conscience so that he worries less about the minutiae of the law and instead sees more of its *underlying* importance. Christian maturity is quite a complex concept, and I've devoted the whole of Chapter 30 to it – you may want to read that chapter in conjunction with this one.

Let's see what happens if your knowledge *isn't* mature and you misapply the Christian laws. For example, consider the person who can't work out when to apply the two concepts of God – i.e. both infinitely loving and infinitely just. To illustrate this, there is a pithy, if slightly unfair, joke called 'The social worker's version of the parable of the Good Samaritan'. It runs as follows:

> "On the way from Jerusalem to Jericho a man was mugged. Two social workers passed by and one observed to the other, 'We really must do something about those poor robbers.' "

Well, perhaps they should, but that wasn't the point. If you apply this sort of topsy-turvy logic, you end up in a mess. If, when you should be thinking about God acting in a loving fashion, you substitute the concept of God as a judge, then when you need mercy you will feel that you will be given justice (i.e. you will be condemned). And when you do it other way round, and apply the principle of a God of love when you should be using the concept of a God of justice, you end up with no justice and a wishy-washy God who will tolerate anything. By simply *mis*applying these two laws about God – that He is both perfectly just and perfectly loving – you have made a mockery of the Christian image of God, yet it seems logical (up to a point). Then if you try to live by that image of God, you will have on your back all the time a vengeful, abusive tyrant who is vindictive towards you when you sin, and totally unjust to boot because everybody else is let off far too lightly – a most unpleasant 'God' to depict inside your mind.

Unfortunately a lot of people go round with this idea of God stuck firmly in their brain. It isn't what God is like, needless to say, but it is important that people who think of God like this get disabused of the idea as quickly as possible. If you have been taught in the past to think of God as being only a God of justice, a vengeful God, a God who cannot stand sin, and you apply those ideas across the board, then no wonder you're depressed! You will never match up to your idea of what you think God wants you to be, and you will forever feel that you are at the bottom of a very deep pit indeed. On the other hand, if you re-educate yourself so that you are no longer afraid of God, nor afraid of being damned by Him for your failings, then you will become more liberated, more mature, and a far better Christian because you will be more relaxed. It's what God wants you to be.

Legalists are, at heart, scared of God. They think that by making sure that they obey every little part of the law, they will escape the wrath of God. They toady to God. On the other hand, the liberated Christian knows that he need not fear that God will punish him in this (unfair) way – in other words, he knows that God is on his side, and that God will always treat him lovingly, kindly, firmly and graciously, and always forgive him unconditionally when he confesses his sins. Legalistic Christians fear God. Liberated Christians respect Him (and love Him the more because they know He is not vengeful).

Think, if you will, of the situation the Pharisees were in. They were correct intellectually, but not morally. They had the interpretation of the law down to a fine art and in doing so missed the point altogether. It is so easy when you are depressed and a Christian, (particularly an evangelical Christian), to fall into the trap of becoming like a Pharisee and thinking that obedience to the *detail* of the law is the important thing. In doing this you will almost certainly miss the overall plan of God, the overall reason for the law and the overall great law behind the little ones. As Jesus said to the Pharisees, "You pay tithes of dill and mint and cumin but you neglect the weightier aspects of the law." (At that time people were supposed to pay in tithes a tenth of all they produced. They were correct down to the finest detail – and in doing so missed the point entirely.)

Our consciences can get dulled by constant exposure to the wrong things. It's not that the 'pricking bit' has changed, but that the memory bank it uses for reference has slowly been changed for the worse. Constant wearing away at the conscience can make Christians tolerate things they would never have dreamed of in earlier years. It's so easy – you start off with a clear idea that stealing is wrong ; but at work you use the office phone for the occasional urgent personal call; then the non-urgent personal call... and so on. Eventually what would never have been countenanced a few years earlier is done without a thought, and certainly without any sense of conscience .... until you're up before the boss or the police get involved. It is so *easy* to dull your conscience in this way. ("It's all right, we always do it like this.") Constant exposure to the wrong influences dulls the conscience; custom and practice can wear away at the toughest people.

Previous experiences change the conscience, too. One of my friends was converted from a background of what can only be described as pure hedonism: and it's interesting to see how this, even now, affects the way his conscience works. Some things he does make me wince – yet on other occasions he has great 'consciences', agonising over things that to me seem quite trivial. (And who's to say I'm right and he's wrong? Maybe my conscience has become far too tender as a result of *my* background?)

Re-educating your conscience isn't always easy. It can be very painful emotionally if, for very logical Christian reasons, you have quite deliberately to go against the pattern of events that were laid down in your conscience in the past. Recently, one of my Christian friends had to act extremely firmly in the handling of a problem within his local church, and in the process had to get justly angry with people in positions of authority. His actions were taken after a lot of heart-searching and prayer, and he needed to be totally unwavering in requesting that a particular person should either change his attitude or step down from the position that he was holding. As he said to me afterwards, it was exceedingly difficult to do this because this kind of firm, unwavering, *apparently* uncompromising approach seems to go against the grain of the Christian ethos. It doesn't in fact, but it *feels* wrong when you have been brought up in the 'gentle Jesus meek and mild' tradition. He had to re-educate his conscience to understand that Christian love sometimes has to be tough.

★   ★   ★

Can I digress slightly onto a form of psychiatry called family therapy? There is a most interesting book by Robin Skynner and John Cleese called *Families and How to Survive Them* (published by Mandarin), a very readable book for lay people about a branch of the mind sciences called family psychiatry. Although I don't agree with all their conclusions, nevertheless family therapy contains some very good ideas. One of them is that in your childhood, either consciously or unconsciously, you put certain ways of behaving into a sort of walled-off area of your psyche – you hide them away from the rest of the world. In their terminology you 'put them behind a screen'. If a family has a problem dealing with anger, (and therefore for them anger is a taboo subject), then when a child is angry his parents treat him in such a way as to make him feel very upset at being angry. Because he feels so upset by what happens to him, he soon learns to put his anger 'behind the screen' so it's out of reach; therefore he finds it difficult to become angry, but by the same token, he doesn't know what to do with his angry feelings and this makes him uneasy in a different way. In particular, he is likely to be all or nothing: he'll be an obvious peacemaker – until he explodes! Because he doesn't understand how to cope with his anger he doesn't show it, but bottles it up until he can't stand it any longer.

Everybody has different things 'behind the screen' in various combinations: some people have anger there, some have *all* emotion there, some people have sex there, some have joy there, and so on. These subjects, therefore, become taboo feelings that your family teach you *by example* not to express. Unfortunately, this also prevents you from using these emotions correctly. There *is* a proper use for anger, emotion, sex and joy. If you have any of them behind the screen, then you will not be able to bring them out and use them correctly when appropriate.

This brings two conclusions: the first is that those things that are 'behind the screen' form quite a large part of your conscience – the childhood memory of the taboo subject. In these cases, the conscience is therefore misguided because these subjects should not be behind the screen: they should be available for *appropriate* usage. Therefore this person's conscience is warped. Even if he is a Christian, he still has a warped conscience.

The second conclusion is that whenever you attempt to bring out an emotion from behind the screen, you will experience intense feelings of guilt. If you're learning to bring your anger out appropriately, (i.e. learning to express your anger in the right way), you may feel very uneasy and guilty as a result of your childhood conditioning. This is difficult enough to deal with if you are *not* a Christian. But if you feel that in learning to express your anger, you are transgressing not only against your family's conscience, but also against Almighty God's dictates, then you are in a real pickle. In this sense it is genuinely harder for a Christian to get better than for a non-Christian, because a Christian has the additional fear of offending God. On the other hand, the Christian has the clearer guidance as to the rules and regulations, (and the promise of forgiveness if he breaks them).

However, he doesn't always know how to apply the rules properly – which is why he has the problem in the first place.

There is therefore a double problem for the Christian trying to 'bring things out from behind the screen' and get in touch with those emotions which he has screened off incorrectly. It is very dangerous for him *not* to try, because otherwise he will continue as an immature person with all the hang-ups that the screened-off emotions bestow upon him. On the other hand he may find it immensely difficult to go against his 'family conscience' (and what he may also see as against God) in trying to sort out some of his more mixed-up emotions. I see this as a very real problem for Christians, because it is all too easy to try to bring something out from behind the screen, get a guilt feeling (note, not *true* guilt) over some aspect of it which went wrong, and immediately retire into your shell, feel very guilty and then not try again.

It is especially difficult where there is a very fine line between the unnatural repression of feelings and correct Christian control. This is particularly true of sexuality. The mature Christian will happily accept that he is a sexual being, but will know where and where *not* to use that sexuality. A repressed Christian is not properly in touch with his sexuality, but the danger is that in trying to become more open about it he may go overboard, use it unwisely and then truly be guilty, not just have guilt feelings. For example, there is one school of psychiatry (with which I heartily disagree) which treats sexual problems by showing patients blue movies, etc. This might make them less repressed but will lead on to an awful lot of other problems. It may be an exaggerated way of looking at it, but I see a lot of the problems that Christians face as a microcosm of that problem: of not going too far, but yet needing to go far enough.

How then do you bring your problems out from behind the screen? The answer, I think, is *gently* – one piece at a time. If you do things gradually then you will become more comfortable over the stance you have adopted, whereas if you take things too quickly you may find that the guilt feelings that ensue are enough to put you off trying again for quite some time. It also has to be done appropriately. For example, it should go without saying that coming to terms with one's sexuality should be done within one's family, not outside it.

On the other hand, by definition it can be more difficult to get things out from behind the screen in the presence of your immediate family – especially your parents – *because it was they who taught you to put them behind the screen in the first place!* Any attempt to change your approach to the feared subject will almost inevitably invite disapproving noises from your relatives. This doubles your sense of unease at approaching the feared subject, and may even cause you to put it back behind the screen again.

Exactly the same problem occurs when dealing with your spiritual family – in other words, the church. If you've grown up in a church that cannot handle sexuality, or anger, or the use of money, then any attempt by you to treat those subjects in a different way will be regarded with disapproval and discouragement.

The answer to pressure like this from family or church is to ensure that the advice you get, and the emotional support you seek, is from a more impartial source: in the case of family pressure, seek help and counsel from *unrelated* mature Christians; in the case of the church, read what other Christians have to say, and perhaps seek advice from Christians who are not members of your home church.

Just as you have had things placed behind the screen for you by your parents and family, so you too can influence your children in the same way. It is important to have a positive approach to your children's consciences, and allow them to develop *appropriately*. For example, there is a place for allowing toddlers to play doctors and nurses and find out about all the various bits of themselves. If they do this innocently, without guilt, then they will become far more at one with themselves and not have hang-ups about their anatomy at a later date. (On the other hand, one would not suggest that your children do it when they are with other families!) And although they may do this at an early stage while they're finding out about themselves, there has to be a progressive, gentle and appropriate warning off from that area of activity as they grow up. But note, this gentle warning off is not done in a repressive fashion – the attitude is not, "Don't talk about that, it's dirty", but, "Don't talk about that at this moment because it is not *appropriate*." It is so important to teach people that emotions – particularly sexuality and anger – are perfectly good and appropriate *in the right place*.

Which brings us back to teaching and the placing of ideas into the conscience. How many people learn their Christian behaviour from a truncated Bible? How many Christians learn about sexuality without ever being taught from the Song of Songs? How many know about anger only from the gospels and not from the prophets? How many learn only about self-denial, fasting and prayer, but miss out on all the God-ordained feasts, dancing, celebration and expression of sheet exuberant emotion? The more that you study the Bible, the wider your understanding, the deeper your knowledge, then the better equipped you will be to see how everything fits together. Jesus said, "You shall know the truth and *the truth shall set you free.*" Christian truth also frees and re-educates the Christian conscience.

★　　　★　　　★

So have we got rid of the operation of the Holy Spirit by making out that our conscience is mainly a matter of memory? Not a bit of it. For a start, once we realise that the conscience is made up of two parts (the pricking bit, and the memories it operates on), we can understand that sharpening of the conscience occurs in two ways – supernaturally, on the pricking bit, and (mainly) humanly, on the memory banks.

However, many Christians think that God *guides* us directly and supernaturally via the conscience. Tell me – *where in the Bible does it say this?* The Bible says that those who refuse to listen to their consciences will have problems; but this is not the same as receiving guidance *directly* from God. 'Conscience guidance' is indirect, a matter of knowing that the Bible says that theft/adultery/drunkenness is wrong. We don't need direct supernatural guidance to tell us that.

Many Christians, quite erroneously, muddle up supernatural guidance and conscience. God doesn't guide us *supernaturally* through our conscience. Our conscience is there to provide ordinary *human* guidance – a memory of what our parents, our past experiences, and our knowledge of the Bible says we should be doing (and the whole point of the 1 Corinthians 8 passage about the too-tender conscience is to highlight the fact that a 'strong' conscience is not necessarily a more Christian thing).

Direct divine guidance is another matter altogether. Our conscience does guide us – but only in those areas where we already have clear examples, such as not passing by an old lady who's fallen over in the street. Supernatural guidance – where there is no clear moral direction, and there are many potential choices – is a different thing altogether. How do I spend today – do I mow the lawn, visit Aunt Ivy, go swimming, read a book? There may be no clear answer from the conscience (unless I *promised* to do one of these things), and doing something because I *feel* guilty about it may well not be right. (I may feel guilty about the state of the lawn, but it may be better for me to sit down and have a rest.) We're back in the realms of guilt *feelings* again....

Although God has guided me *supernaturally* many times in the past, He's never done it via my conscience. I've often looked back and seen how God has guided me by putting a thought into my head of something I *wanted* to do (like go and drop in on a friend) without any sense that I *ought* to... and I've gone there to find a problem waiting, to which I seemed to provide the solution, or a good thing there for me to receive.

Conversely, there have been many times when I've 'had a conscience' – really a manifestation of anxiety – about something, and found by following 'my conscience' that what I did was anything but appropriate, and certainly not the result of listening to the still small voice of God! *Except in extreme cases, God doesn't guide us by making us feel guilty.* When He guides, it's positive, not negative; warm, not cold; gentle, not anxiety-provoking nor fearsome. When God specifically intervenes to put thoughts into our heads, we may not even know He's done it – until we look back afterwards. I repeat – God does *not* guide supernaturally by making us feel guilty.

Having said this, the memory-banks of our conscience are very important to God, and remain an essential part of our *non*-supernatural guidance. (This may well include an indirect supernatural element: when we've been given supernatural guidance, supernatural wisdom, supernatural conviction, we remember it, and add it to our store of "wise ways to do things", which, as we've discovered, forms the basis for our conscience.)

Our conscience reminds us of things we think are right to do; so for the most part our conscience is God-orientated and 'on God's side'. But this is a far cry from the idea that our conscience represents the still small voice of God speaking to us *directly*. Our conscience may be still and small; but its voice is mostly a reminder of things learned (correctly or incorrectly) from the past.

God gave us our conscience to use much as we would a diary – it's a place where we store useful information, in this case about how we ought to be doing things. On the other hand, when God gives us supernatural guidance He does not go via the conscience – He uses other routes. I repeat: God does *not* intervene to guide us by making us feel guilty.

EXERCISE

Draw up a table with six columns. Label these: Subject; Me; Parents; Friends; Church; Bible.

In the first column, list the following subjects: Money; Sex; Power; Alcohol; Dancing; Smoking; Race; Laughter; Emotions; Fun.

In the next column, briefly fill in your own attitudes to each subject.

Then fill in each of the remaining columns according to the attitudes each group holds. Try to quote examples in the Bible column.

Now look at the results. How far do your own attitudes relate to what the Bible actually says? How far do your feelings on, say, dancing, reflect what you've been taught by your parents or your church, rather than what the Bible says?

Bearing in mind that our consciences work on what in the past we've been told is right and wrong, how far are your attitudes on these subjects governed by what the Bible really says, and how far are they derived from other sources? Looking at these lists, are there any attitudes that you should consciously start to change as a result?

PART 4

HELPING AND HEALING

24

HOW *NOT* TO HELP IN DEPRESSION

One of the sad things about depression is the ease with which people who are trying to help put their foot in it. In fact, some people only open their mouths in order to change feet. The more you understand about depression, the less likely you are to say the wrong thing, but even the most skilled psychotherapist sometimes inadvertently gives offence. Even more, therefore, should the lay helper be aware of things which can upset or hinder the recovery of the depressed person.

"Pull yourself together."

This is the worst, and unfortunately the most frequent, of all the mistakes made by helpers. The problem with depression is that you *can't* pull yourself together – the helper is assuming that you aren't trying, whereas you know yourself that you are, but it's not working for you. This gaffe hurts because it implies that you are being lazy, that it's your fault for being depressed, and that you could get out of your depression very quickly if only you were sensible and buckled down to it. To the person who is depressed, who hasn't got the energy to help himself any longer, and who has been battering his head on a brick wall for far too long, this advice comes like a dip in the Arctic Ocean – it stops him dead in his tracks and chills him to the marrow. The helper never intends it to be this way, but that's not the point.

If you are on the receiving end of this sort of 'help', tell the speaker gently but politely that his advice is not appropriate and suggest that he reads this book to find out why. Then *ignore him*. He doesn't know what he's talking about, and has no insight into your problems. Don't try to argue it out with him: you will only end up in tears, because his point of view *seems* logical: it isn't – but convincing him of this is another matter altogether.

"Don't get so emotional."

Depression is a disease of the emotions, especially when, in the past, emotion has not been expressed in the right way. The fact that the patient is able to express his emotions at last, even if they are apparently unpleasant ones, is actually a good thing rather than a bad one. To be on the receiving end of a bout of rage isn't very pleasant, but if you want to react to it, don't say, "Don't get emotional", but, "What is it that makes you *so* angry, rather than just angry?"

Depression is often the result of inturned aggression, so any outward-turning of this anger is to be encouraged. The helper should try to assist the depressed person to acknowledge the existence of his anger, and then to channel it into an acceptable, Christian outcome. (There is a great deal of difference between the person who expresses anger solely as anger and one who goes overboard and expresses his anger as rage.) Do refer to the chapter on Anger for a more detailed analysis of this subject.

Bursts of anger are sometimes the result of subduing justifiable anger: it can become like a tin whose contents have been packed in and compressed so much that eventually the lid flies off with a bang. Anger which is vented in this way is often directed against the ones that we love most, because we feel 'safe' with them. It's less threatening to explode at those we know are unlikely to hit back or leave us for good. The job of the helper in this case is to help the depressed person to learn how to express *reasonable* anger, in the *right direction* and so prevent the explosive situation developing.

"Let's jolly her along."

Well-intentioned souls who try to jolly the depressed person along don't help very much. Their approach is that depression can be healed by a shopping spree/day out at the Ideal Home Exhibition/taking the children *'away'*. Depression is a good deal more deep-seated than this! Although all these things may help, they are only the tip of the iceberg. Equally, those who say, "You should return to work"; "Think of others more"; "Be grateful for what you have"; "Take up evening classes", etc. may be right in one sense, but there is an implied criticism which says, "If you weren't so selfish you wouldn't feel so bad." Again, this is not the right way to look at somebody who is depressed. It isn't necessarily their *fault*.

In any case there is a further problem – which is that when you are in the thick of depression, you have no energy to trail around John Lewis looking at the latest in fashionable clothes: it may be all you can do just to get dressed in the morning. There is no energy for anything extra; although it may eventually be a good idea to do these additonal . activities (especially with the help and companionship of a friend), advice like this is for *much* later on when the depression is well on the way to resolution.

The 'Christian' rebuke (in love of course!)

It is very easy for a helper to think that he has been honest and

'Christian' when in practice he is actually being very critical, and a hindrance. He may have a 'logical' answer to the problem – but if it's not the correct answer he isn't helping at all, and may well make things worse. We've discussed this theme on many occasions in this book – but for a fuller discussion of this, see especially the chapter on Guilt.

It is very easy to give offence to somebody who is depressed. He will see criticism at a hundred yards, but won't notice a compliment until it hits him in the face. Simply because he is so sensitive, any implied criticism of his Christian life can be a blow below the belt.

For the helper, any criticism, and *particularly* 'Christian' criticism, must be levelled very gently indeed. If in doubt, don't do it. Included in these 'Christian' gaffes are – the implication that the whole of the depression is related to some unconfessed sin; or that the sufferer is not 'praying hard enough'; or that there is something wrong with his spiritual life in general. I can't emphasise enough that the problems with a depressed person's spiritual life are almost certainly a knock-on effect from their depression and *not* the other way round. Depression is nearly always a disease of the emotions, not the spirit.

SUICIDAL FEELINGS

There is a world of difference between true suicidal intent, and the 'suicide attempt' which is not intended to kill, but merely to draw attention to oneself. (This latter condition is now called parasuicide.) True suicides usually don't leave room for recovery – the woman who jumps off a high building, or the man who tries to hang himself are obvious examples. On the other hand, parasuicides *intend* to be discovered and stopped – the prime example is the girl who swallows a handful of pills, then rings up the ambulance. Unfortunately, the ambulance doesn't always get there in time.

True suicidal feelings are very dangerous and a medical emergency, but by definition truly suicidal people often don't give away what they're about to do. Dealing with the truly suicidal is not for the amateur – you need medical help, and quickly too.

On the other hand, the parasuicide likes (and seeks) as much attention as possible. She (or he) is trying to get love by manipulation; the sad thing is that in some people this is the only way they can relate to others in a crisis. The best response to somebody who is threatening *para*suicide is to give no extra attention whatsoever, because of the 'illegal' way in which it is being demanded. As a result she is made to feel more lonely *because* she is 'trying' to kill herself than she otherwise would.

This doesn't mean, incidentally, that you don't care about her – it's just that she mustn't feel she is getting attention. You don't give a child sweets for being naughty – and if you pander to a parasuicide then all she learns is that by being dramatic and 'illegal' she can get more attention. This brings even more problems later on.

Just as it is important not to be manipulated into giving attention by a 'suicide' attempt, it is just as important, if not more so, for helpers to give more attention when a person is *not* being manipulative. When faced with a demanding, 'suicidal' patient it is all too easy to respond only when you have to – at the time of a 'suicide' attempt – whilst being glad to let sleeping dogs lie when things have quietened down afterwards. But this type of response makes things worse, not better: if when the patient is 'good' she receives no attention, it just reinforces her idea that 'suicide' attempts get the attention she craves. So the helper must forestall this: he must pay attention to her when she's co-operating, being 'good', fitting in. This gives her positive input; then, when he ignores her during a 'suicide' attempt, she will be aware of what she's missing as a result of her behaviour. Unfortunately it is all too easy to reward bad behaviour with attention and good behaviour with indifference, and it only makes things worse.

Here comes the next problem – how do you know which is the potentially suicidal person, and which is the parasuicide? You can't always tell, though you can often hazard a good guess, based on the patient's previous behaviour. If in doubt, opt for safety and treat it as a real suicidal threat.

True suicidal feelings are usually emotional, rather than logical. It is important for helpers to understand this and not say the wrong things to a Christian who really has tried hard to kill himself. It is easy to take the logical and unhelpful view that, "Jesus died that we might have the gift of eternal life, so what right have we to throw it away?", but this comes across as a rebuke to the depressed and suicidal Christian. Or alternatively, "That was a stupid thing to try – what did you hope to achieve?" OK – so in logical terms it was stupid, but it was probably done at a time when everything seemd *emotionally* without hope, and without sufficent thought of the consequences. The thoughts of someone at the time of a suicide attempt are too emotional, confused and frightening for logical sequential thinking. While sympathy *isn't* the right treatment, condemnation is *worse*. At the time the person who is attempting suicide feels too shocked and numb, but later on the guilt is sufficient unto itself !

There is another aspect to suicide – the person who *fears* that he will do it. For example, he will be afraid to go up high buildings for fear that he will get an urge to jump off. However, *these fears are not real suicidal feelings.* The crux of the matter is that he is *afraid he might* commit suicide: people like this never do it! It's very common to have this fear of doing something to yourself: I call it 'the fear of fear'. If you don't recognise it for what it is, you can get terrified by it:

"I can't go up there, I might jump off."

"Don't leave me alone with those pills, I might take an overdose."

"I can't go on that platform, I might jump in front of the train."

Fears like these can paralyse you if you are a sufferer, because you fear that (against your will) you might on impulse do yourself in. It's a very frightening feeling – but once you recognise it for what it is, you take all the sting out of it. People with the 'fear of fear' never commit suicide. You just wouldn't be able to do it! Once you realise this, you can't torture yourself any longer with the thought that you *might.* Then, because you know it's no longer a possibility, the fear goes away.

This fear of self-destruction is like the fear that certain Christians have of doing something so monstrous that they fall out of the hands of God, lose Him, and lose their faith.

You can't do it! God is far too big for that, and once He has called you, and you are His, *nothing,* but *nothing* can take you away from Him. You couldn't get away if you tried! Again, like the 'fear of fear', once you know it's impossible to fall out of the hands of God, you won't worry any longer that you might do it – then you relax and the fears go away.

Lay Psychiatry

Psychotherapy requires skill. It is not a place for the amateur. No one in their right minds would set a layman loose with a scalpel and tell him to perform brain surgery: in exactly the same way interpretative psychotherapy is dangerous in unskilled hands. Unless you know what you're doing you can do more harm than good – and be warned: whereas physical pain cannot be remembered, mental pain can, so any further problems you create won't necessarily go away after you've left.

What do I mean by interpretative psychotherapy? I *don't* mean just talking to the patient. I *don't* mean talking through past hurts. Interpretative psychotherapy, for the purposes of this chapter, is about an analyst *interpreting back to the patient* what is going on, such as, "You are doing this because..." For a start, you may be wrong! And now you've confidently shoved the patient onto the wrong track. This is how good psychotherapists work. It is much more beneficial (and far less hazardous) to let the patient make the connection – the psychotherapist merely acts as a facilitator. "*Are* you doing this because..." is a better way of saying it. It leaves the patient open to saying, "No! – it's nothing to do with it", or alternatively gives him the chance to say, "Oh, I'd never thought of it like that ... Mmm..."

Good psychotherapists ask questions: they don't give answers. They may have a good idea of where they are going and what they are aiming for, but they'll do it in such a way as to allow the patient to get there actively, under his own steam. It also has the overriding advantage that they don't direct the patient up the garden path by mistake.

In any case, the healing that comes through psychoanalysis and psychotherapy invariably comes from within the patient – stimulated by the questions of the psychoanalyst or psychotherapist of course, but still from within the patient.

Active learning (where you work it out yourself) is much better than passive. Some years ago psychologists carried out an experiment to test this. Two cats were placed in a pair of identical mazes: one could move freely, the other was in a cradle. The apparatus was so arranged that when the one cat moved actively to explore his maze, the other cat was moved passively to an identical point in his own maze. In other words, one cat explored the maze actively; the other had the identical experience – but passively. After a time the cats were released and left to go through the maze on their own. The cat which had explored it actively got through very much more quickly than the one who had explored it passively: the seond cat didn't really know the maze at all.

Exactly the same principle applies to our own mental explorations. If *we* make the connections, we remember it well. If others make the conections for us, we may not remember it for very long. The best psychotherapists know how far they can indicate to the patient the directions he should explore, whilst at the same time allowing the *patient* to do the exploration. This is called 'non-directive counselling' – it's non-directive in that the counsellor is not telling the patient *what to think,* but it *is* directive in that the counsellor is showing the patient roughly *where to look.*

Similarly, in Christian psychotherapy, only when the source of the anxiety or depression is known is it permissible to do *directive* Christian counselling. For example, if the patient acknowledges that he is scared of the thought of death and that this really is the 'bottom line' of his problems, then the counsellor can mention the advantages of Christian belief and the fact that Christ has conquered death.

Alternatively, if he feels depressed because he had a row with one of his parents, who then collapsed and died a couple of weeks later without time for the argument to be made up, then the counsellor can talk about what sort of difference it made as far as God was concerned, and encourage the person to ask for forgiveness from God, if forgiveness is needed.

But the counsellor shouldn't do any directive counselling until he's gone through the non-directive part and found what the real problem is. In other words, when the patient says, "I'm frightened", the consellor *shouldn't* say, "But Jesus has conquered all fear. Just believe and you'll be all right." Instead he should be asking, "Why are you frightened?" – and once the patient has got to the cause of his fear (fear of death, fear of failure, fear of punishment), the counsellor can go on to talk about the Christian reponse.

It is, of course, quite permissible at any stage to tell a depressed person about Jesus – but *it shouldn't be used as a part of the psychotherapy itself*. It isn't right to say, "Just believe and all your problems will disappear." What you *can* say is, "If you choose to follow Christ then all *true* guilt will disappear – but it won't get rid of false guilt, and to deal with this we may have to do some mental digging." Diagnosis first, treatment later. Do it the other way round and you'll end up in a mess.

How to Help – Properly This Time!

The best way you can help a depressed friend is by being available. Someone to phone, someone who is available (twenty-four hours a day if necessary) provides him with a 'safety net'. A two a.m. call may not be necessary, but in case of problems the net is there, and more importantly, *felt* to be there. The presence, the availability, just the existence of a friend like this provides a tremendous degree of comfort to the depressed person, as it demonstrates in physical terms how much he is cared for, accepted, loved, as he is, warts and all. It is not difficult for the depressed person to go on to realise that if individual Christians can love him that much, how much more will God do the same.

Tied in with the helper's commitment to make himself available is the prayer support he can provide. It is comforting for the depressed person to know that, by dialling a few numbers, he can reach somebody to pray for him or with him.

But make no mistake, being available to this degree is a huge commitment. Patience is essential, because, by the nature of his illness, the depressed person is likely to go over the same ground time and time again, needing the same reassurance that was given a day, a week or a month ago.

Unconditional friendship is the key, as is loyalty. The real friends are the ones who can accept the depressed person as he is – on good days, bad days, sad days, frightened days and angry days. Friends like this don't put on pressure in any way, but allow the sufferer to be himself, however horrid that may be. As one of my depressed friends said, "It's a relief not to put on a disguise."

Encourage Honesty

Talking of disguises, encourage your depressed friend to be honest, and to tell God of any anger or resentment that he feels. At first most people feel that it is some way wrong, ungrateful or blasphemous to behave like this, but it really isn't and God doesn't mind: in fact He would far rather that a depressed person be honest with Him. The sufferer feels that way, in any case, and at the very least might as well own up to it, get it out in the open and start to learn to deal with it. He needn't worry that God will get angry with him – He won't! The Lord can handle feelings of anger and resentment quite easily, and will be glad that the depressed person is at last starting to admit to those feelings he has so far tried to keep covered up.

It helps to remind the depressed person again and again that his feelings are not necessarily related to reality. (See the chapter on Emotions.) Anger and terror often come from within, from previous hurts and memories, rather than being a true reflection of external reality.

Treat Depression as a Real Disease

One of the problems of depression is that there is nothing external to show for the illness – it's not as if a person has a plaster cast round her leg or needs injections. Because no physical infirmity is apparent to the outsider, the depressed person all too easily feels, "I'm not really ill anyway, it's just my stupid fault I'm like this", and "Other people will think I'm shamming." But she *is* ill – as much as if she had a broken leg, or needed insulin injections. Although it isn't always a good idea to let depressed people wallow in their infirmities, sometimes it helps to tell an individual to imagine that she really does have a large bandage wrapped round her head, just to remind her that she really is *physically* unwell. The more she realises that she has a *disease* and that it is not her fault, the easier will she find it to come to terms with being depressed.

Understand the Difference between Guilt and Guilt Feelings

Guilt feelings surface time and again in depression. Do make sure you understand the difference between true guilt and guilt feelings (see Chapter 22), so that you can more sensitively help the sufferer to understand that depression is an illness, not something they've deserved. Remember that if there is a sin in depression it's connected with not accepting forgiveness, rather than not asking for it. Encourage the prayer, "Lord, help me to accept the forgiveness You offer."

Be a Constant, Loving Friend

It's important to realise that improvement happens in stages, and that the level of depression goes both up and down. As a helper you've got to be prepared to cope with the days when things are getting worse, despite all efforts to the contrary. Just being there, being a friend, being available, being supportive, is the best thing that you can ever do at this time. Loyal, unconditional friendship is the best medicine that you can possibly provide, with the depressed person feeling that at least he can trust you. (He doesn't trust himself any more and any little bit of stability in the outside world is a great help.) The real curse in depression is that not only do you lose confidence in the outside world, you also lose confidence in yourself, and the knowledge that somebody else actually has confidence in you and cares about you can have electrifying results!

Helpers help when they touch: as we discovered in Chapter 19, our society is not very good at this! But even when working within society's conventions, you can express a lot of support and comfort for someone who is depressed through the simple action of touching him. The hand on the arm, the arm round the shoulder (and for those who are more close a kiss and cuddle) all speak much more loudly than words.

Above all, the thing that really helps the depressed person is that *you* accept them as they are.

Help like this is called love – not the namby-pamby, prissy sort, but deep, rugged, strong, caring, turn-the-other-cheek love: the kind that accepts and forgives, but equally the kind that won't be manipulated. The more that you can display this kind of love to your friend, the more he or she will feel cared for, supported, accepted and acceptable.

25

HELP FROM FAMILY
AND FRIENDS

Depression doesn't just affect the sufferer. We all live in families, we all have friends, we all have workmates and colleagues, and all are likely to suffer from the knock-on effects of our problems. When you're depressed you aren't able to relate to other people as well as you once did – your loss of energy reduces your ability to work; you may get suspicious or even downright paranoid about the motives of other people; you may indulge in continuous self-deprecation in front of others, or become irritable, flying off the handle at the slightest provocation. These difficulties occur both at work and at home.

Within the family the most common problems are caused by lack of energy, lack of concentration, irritability, and lack of sexual drive, all compounded by a poor sleeping pattern.

It is important that the other members of the family realise what is happening, so they can understand how to help you get better. Just recognising the problem is half the battle. Once children and husband realise that the increasing confusion and untidiness of the home, the forgetfulness, and the increasing arguments and flow of criticism emanating from Mum are due not to their own faults but to her illness, they will be better equipped to cope with what is happening, and especially to ignore *unfair* criticism directed at them. They will also be more sensitive to her problems and needs.

Until the family realises that one of its members is depressed they tend to think that the whole world is falling apart! They may well feel guilty about it, even if it's not their fault. However, they mustn't make the mistake of blaming everything on the one person who is ill as a result of family stresses – perhaps the husband has had an affair, there are money troubles, or the children are very rebellious; and it is important not to make the depressed person a scapegoat for problems which really emanate from others in the family.

Any member of the family can get depressed. Firstly, let's look at what happens when it's the wife/mother who is the victim.

THE DEPRESSED WIFE

What are the effects of her depression? There will be difficulties in every single role that she takes in the family. Her symptoms will interfere with her behaviour as wife (both as helpmeet and lover), as housewife, and as parent.

As a Helpmeet

One of the joys of marriage is the way in which each partner can pour out his or her troubles to the other, share them, laugh over the funny things that have happened, plan things, enjoy life together, and generally share everything, whether it be good or bad. Hence, when one member of the partnership is depressed it puts a great strain on the other. A depressed wife can no longer share the emotional burden of her husband's problems – she hasn't the energy. The knock-on effects on the husband are *appalling*. He comes home from work with worries on his mind (particularly if his job is in management or one of the professions) – and there's no one to share them with.

Not only does he lose the benefits of a helpmeet, but (if he has never experienced a depression himself) he finds out very rapidly that all his attempts at helping his wife end up in miserable failure, which he sees, incorrectly, as his wife's fault, because she isn't doing what he suggests. (In fact, he's probably been suggesting the wrong course of action, so no wonder it doesn't work.) Then he feels that the problem is becoming insoluble, because of her contrariness and unhelpfulness. Under these circumstances it's very difficult for him to sympathise with his wife's worries and complaints, when he feels at heart that she's being difficult.

His wife, in the meantime, thinks her husband is a selfish, uncaring brat (which he isn't) because he doesn't understand her (which is true). She then adds to the general misery by relating all her problems to him in detail.

The husband is thus left with a large burden. He comes home full of problems, to find that his wife requires him to listen to *her* problems in great detail and extremely repetitively, but has no time for any of *his* difficulties. He can't off-load his own worries and has to take on board a whole lot of his wife's. There can easily come a time when the stresses of being at work are less than the stresses at home, so the husband finds good reasons to come home later and later. Unfortunately, this only exacerbates the situation because the wife will (correctly) complain that her husband doesn't come home to support her or help with the family.

Her husband may have struggled on valiantly for a long time trying to improve the situation without much success; how can he give support if he's run out of ideas and, more pertinently, run out of energy?

The cure is for the husband more fully to understand depression:

then he can help his wife more appropriately and effectively. If the husband has never been through a depression himself, then almost certainly he won't know what one is like and as a result won't be able to help his wife all that effectively. But once he understands what is going on in his wife's mind, and sees that he has to change his way of trying to help her, he will then be able to give more appropriate assistance.

Once things start to improve (because he is using the right methods) he will be encouraged; and will no longer perceive the family as a threat – so he won't fear coming home.

The husband of a depressed wife needs to have a lot of patience. He also needs *a lot* of support, because if his wife is severely depressed he will be trying to do his job, run the family, and cope with the emotional stress of his depressed wife. It will help immensely if friends can take some of the load off him. This is true not only at the physical level (the cooking, the cleaning, the shopping) but also at an emotional level; he needs people to replace some of the 'helpmeet role' that his wife can no longer fulfil; he needs friends with whom he can talk through and off-load worries about his work, his finances, his Christian problems, his wife, his family. However, it's probably safest to do this with someone of the same sex – he must be careful not to get overinvolved emotionally with any woman who is helping him. It is all too easy for overinvolvement to occur without any prior intention: the more you unburden yourself, the more people know your innermost secrets and problems, the closer you become. This is good provided the relationship stays on a platonic level, but if it becomes more than this, beware.

The loss of his 'helpmeet' is one of the most difficult things that can happen to a married person, and can be the source of much emotional disruption. His wife needs to know just how important she is as a helpmeet, and how much it matters that she continue this role for her husband, if at all possible. The more she can do this, the more easily will he be able to shoulder the additional responsibilities thrust upon him. Trying to help your wife through a depression is difficult enough – trying to fight it when she's lost all interest in you and all sense of partnership with you is a thankless task indeed.

As a Lover

Depression often takes away the sexual drive. This only adds to the problem of the husband, whose sexual drive may well be just as much if not greater than before, particularly because of the emotional stress he is under. Not only may he find that his wife is unable to function as a helpmeet and a source of emotional support, he also finds that sexual comfort is progressively being denied him. At first he may be patient, but as his wife's problem extends through weeks and months he may become frustrated – frustrated in his ability to help his wife, frustrated in his need for a helpmeet, and frustrated in his emotional need for endearment and physical love.

It's not just the husband who gets frustrated. Sexual intimacy is very helpful in relieving the effects of depression. It's a comforting, relaxing activity, and to be told physically that you are loved speaks much louder than being told the same thing verbally.

A depressed person's capacity for enjoyment is often greatly reduced, and this applies in the sexual area as well: you may be just too tired to be bothered. However, once she's actually embarked on a session of lovemaking, she may find halfway through that she actually quite enjoys it.

However, when a depression goes deep, the sexual drive may be all but turned off – sometimes to be replaced by a revulsion for everything sexual. This may represent a loathing for anyone fool enough to like such a worm as you, or sheer anger, directed outwards at the nearest vulnerable person (the 'kick-the-cat' syndrome), or inturned anger with oneself, denying oneself the right to any pleasure out of sheer self-annoyance. (Remember in this how closely anger and depression are related, and how depression is often inturned anger – see Chapter 15.)

The danger in this situation is that the wife will rebuff her husband's advances. He now feels rejected on all fronts – she hasn't the energy to run the house and family properly, so he has to do more; she won't share his problems; she unloads her own problems onto him incessantly; he can't stand the problems and tensions at home and has nowhere to go to relax, and what's more, his wife is turning frigid. What is he most likely to do under the circumstances? Answer – have an affair – or at least he's likely to if he's not careful. An affair, needless to say, won't help the general situation – but is at least understandable, under the circumstances. We enter marriage feeling that we have a helpmeet and a supporter in whom we can confide, with whom we can give and take physical and emotional comfort and with whom we share *everything*. If these benefits suddenly disappear we find ourselves having to live as single people, yet with the married responsibilities of a famiily whose demands are even greater than normal. Under these circumstances the stress on the non-depressed partner has to be experienced to be believed.

As we discussed in the chapter about sexuality, lovemaking is a God-given experience central to marriage and intended for the joy and mutual comfort of both partners. The emotional peace and satisfaction from making love extend far beyond the immediate physical activity. Because it is so central to marriage, it is very important that lovemaking should continue as much as possible through a depressive illness. It's important for the depressed partner – and it's necessary for the non-depressed one! Even if you don't feel much like making love, may I encourage you to do it, even if only as a duty – towards yourself and towards your partner.

Isn't it an abomination that something as sacred as the act of intercourse should be reduced to a mere duty? Isn't is awful that one partner should impose him/herself on the other? Well, actually it isn't. Remember the time when you took your marriage vows? Why did you take them? The bride and groom look lovingly at each other and all they want to do is to be alone with one another – "To have and to hold, for richer for poorer, for better for worse." They don't *need* those vows at the moment because they *want* to be with each other. So why make the vows? Simple – they are there for the times when each partner no longer *wants* with quite the same intensity. In other words, the vows are there not for the times when you love each other madly, but for the times when things aren't so rosy. Therefore if lovemaking is a great big bore for the person who is depressed, my advice is quite simple – do it because you promised to when you got married. Even if you haven't really got the energy to make the effort, at the very least respond to your partner's attention, because in this way, you will give him physical and emotional comfort, which he needs, and can't obtain in any other way.

Even if you are depressed, do try to respond to the emotional and sexual needs of your partner. *You* will benefit because you'll feel happier and more relaxed afterwards, even if summoning up the energy beforehand was rather difficult. *You* will benefit because you won't feel guilty afterwards for depriving him of something he needs and wants. And *your marriage* will benefit, firstly, through the increased intimacy and togetherness lovemaking brings (at a difficult time), and also because your husband is unlikely to find emotional and sexual comfort elsewhere if you are able to provide it yourself.

There is such an emotional 'letting go' during and after intercourse that a lot of hitherto inexpressible feelings may be able to surface. Therefore if your depressed wife cries after making love don't feel that there is anything wrong – it is because her deep-seated emotions have at last been able to surface, assisted by the nearness and the comfort of being in the arms of the one she loves. Lovemaking is deep and tender and a great healer. You promised to do it when you got married. In times of stress you neglect it at your peril.

The Depressed Husband

When it's the husband who is depressed, rather than the wife, then all the previous advice applies, with just one or two changes in emphasis.

Firstly, the depressed father doesn't have quite such a deleterious effect on the family as does a depressed mother. The depressed man is much more likely to have problems at work: with the wife to keep family life together, a depressed husband is less likely to affect the family.

However, if the husband is in a creative job (such as being a writer, or an artist), or is in leadership or management, his depression will strike at the very root of his ability to carry out his job properly. Concentration, study, inventiveness, creativity – all these tend to go out of the window if you're depressed.

If your depression is having a really bad effect on your ability to do your job, then go to your doctor: a sick note may well be appropriate. (At least if it's the husband who is depressed, he can get time off work – not possible when it's the wife who's depressed and yet still trying to run a family with small children.) Being off work for a time takes at least some strain off your shoulders, and the load will be a little lighter.

On the other hand, most men have a degree of 'macho' image, and their self-confidence takes a knock when off work with 'something namby-pamby like depression'. Living with this stigma, either from workmates or (worse) from yourself, may be even harder than trying to go to work.

Having a depressed husband undermines the wife: because the husband is often the leader in the household, she may find taking up the reins of leadership both strange and difficult. She may need to get help over handling family finances, filling in the income tax returns, and so on, if her husband was the one who always did it in the past. In addition she may need friends to give extra emotional support over decision-making if she finds herself in charge of the family, with a husband who can no longer take decisions because of his illness.

Handling a depressed man is not easy: the 'macho' image takes a huge tumble when depression strikes, and it needs a particular strength of purpose and tact to encourage without appearing to be patronising, and thus injuring that already-dented pride even more. Encourage him; if necessary, take decisions for him without worrying him to try to make them himself.

You will find that it's the male 'driving force' that you miss most – so it will be up to you to organise that trip to the cinema or the skating rink; or even just to get the family to church on time.

As we discussed earlier, sexual intimacy is important too – you'll probably have to take the lead here as well, which is not easy for most women: but do it, because you love him, and because it will help him keep his self-respect. (If you don't, he'll think, "Not only am I depressed, but my wife doesn't want me, either...")

Self-respect is important to most men, and it is this that goes first in depression: by loving him, respecting him (even if he is depressed and can't take decisions), and honouring him, you will help preserve his self-esteem and give him the best platform from which to recover.

DEALING WITH THE CHILDREN

Depression often hits women with young families. Children are very demanding and the mother often feels guilt-ridden because she is not fulfilling as many of the maternal functions as she would like, because she is running out of energy. Add to that the broken nights, perhaps another pregnancy, the difficulties of coping with a husband who may be in the early stages of his career and therefore working long hours, studying, or away from a home a lot, and the end result is a great deal of strain on the wife. Children are demanding enough when you are happy, full of beans and don't have anything else to do. When you're desperately trying to cope, with minimal energy and lots of calls upon your time, then a little child tugging at your apron strings saying, "Mummy, come and play", "Mummy, look, I've painted the lounge", or "Mummy, I've wet myself again" – these can cause a total breakdown of your ability to cope. Under stresses like these mothers can break down, cry, get angry with the children unnecessarily and inappropriately, or in extreme circumstances abuse them physically or verbally.

Children have an uncanny way of saying the truth in an unbelievably brutal fashion:

"Why does Mummy cry so much?"

"*Our* Mummy never takes us out – all she does is sit in the chair drinking tea."

"Mummy, why doesn't Daddy come home any more?"

These and a thousand other comments slice the depressed mother into little pieces, daily. Not only does she feel depressed, she feels a *bad mother,* and being a bad mother is something our society views with particular horror. In contrast, the adverts on the telly all portray wonderfully happy, smiling Mums with wonderfully happy, smiling families (which is enough to make *non*-depressed people spit, I can tell you, but is even worse for a depressed parent!) Then, because she feels she's a bad mother, she gets more depressed, and being more depressed becomes even less capable of giving time and energy to her children.... and so the spiral goes round and round.

The cure is twofold. Firstly, acquire a good supply of friends with small children. The important criteria are that the friends must know that you are depressed, not criticise you for it, and accept you as a human being. Get these mothers to take your children off your hands on a semi-regular basis. If necessary, pay a baby-minder to do it, but it "feels" better on a voluntary basis – it doesn't feel quite so clinical.

Now you know that your children will be well looked after. You will be a 'good' Mum for making sure that they get surrounded by fun and laughter, even if it is somewhere else. This starts to give you hope. It also gives you time to rest and to summon up your energy for the remainder of the activities of the day. It has the additional advantage that if you are trying to summon up your meagre supply of energy in order to clean the house, then you don't have the awfully depressing effects of a small child undoing all your tidying as fast as you do it.

If you haven't got a good supply of friends like this, then find a child minder or a baby-sitter who can be trusted – get one who is specifically paid to go out with the children to the park or play football, or go fishing with bent pins and worms. After this you can hold your head up high, knowing that your children are not being deprived of their childhood through the exhaustion of your illness.

The next thing to do is to take the children into your confidence. *Tell* them that you are not well. (Unless they're teenagers, don't mention the word 'depression'. They're likely to misquote you.) Tell them your illness makes you feel very tired and short-tempered. If the children are small, say that it's rather like they feel when they're in bed with a bad cold, only you don't have to blow your nose and, what's worse, you have to get up and do a lot of work.

If they are older tell them that your illness means that you haven't got any energy, and you feel as tired when you *get up* as they do when they *go to bed* after a *really* hard day's play.

If they're teenagers tell them that you are depressed, that it is an illness and that it is nothing to be ashamed of, but that you need to be treated rather gently, because you've lost most of your energy, most of your concentration, and unfortunately with it, nearly all of your patience. Apologise to them in advance for the times when they will get shouted at unnecessarily, or when things that they would like you to have done have been forgotten, or for the times when you just can't summon up the energy to do what they would like you to do.

And then tell them how much you love them, and how sad it makes you when you can't do what you would like to do with them, and for them.

Children are remarkably honest and fair and if you level with them, they will often be surprisingly helpful in return. Do emphasise to them, whatever their age, that although progress perhaps will seem to be slow, ultimately Mummy will get better, and that *they* can help you to get better more quickly by being patient and understanding.

Once the great secret is out.... you'll feel happier: happier for not having to 'keep it away from the children'. (Silly idea that – they knew there was something wrong all along: the fact that no one would acknowledge it meant that it must be something really horrible, like Mummy was dying....) Now they know what it is, they'll understand a bit; they'll be more on your side; and they know you love them. Honesty within the family is often the very best policy, even – *especially* – in the most difficult circumstances.

THE DEPRESSED CHILD

Often it's a child who's ill: usually a teenager. It's important to involve your GP at an early stage: there are some types of depression that respond well to help from child guidance. It's ever so easy to slip into an incorrect habit within the family, and sometimes the caring but impartial observations of an outsider can show you quickly and clearly why things are going wrong, and what you can do about it. If your GP suggests child guidance, don't take it as an affront: no one thinks you aren't trying! – but you may be trying in the wrong way.

This happened with one of our sons – when he was about ten he started stealing money from around the house, and was obviously very unhappy. We went with some trepidation to the child guidance clinic, hoping no one would see us. (I am, after all, a doctor. I'm supposed to know about these things... only you can't when it's your own family.)

Within two hours we had the answer. We'd fallen into one of the classic traps: because his behaviour had been so bad, we had got into the rut of only paying attention to him to correct him when he was misbehaving, and letting sleeping dogs lie when he wasn't – so, quite inadvertently, we were paying attention to him only when he was bad. Sounds daft, looking back – but it was easy to slip into at the time.

Once we had been helped to see what we were doing, the rest was plain sailing. We gave more attention at the good times, and our son's behaviour changed almost overnight.

It's not always as easy as this, though, and depression can hit teenagers in particular quite hard. The best advice I can give is fivefold:

1. Get professional advice, and use any medicines suggested.
2. Don't forget that illegal drug-taking can cause depression.
3. Love him/her unconditionally.
4. Provide an emotionally stable home that your child can come back to.
5. Show your love through touching.

Don't give up. You may need to be patient, and it's heart-rending to see your once-happy child (all those pictures of him at the seaside when he was seven) sitting in the corner staring glassy-eyed at the wall. But it will go eventually – just give it time (a lot of it – years even). Don't try and argue him out of it – it won't help. Give him emotional security, and if the depression is accompanied by religious doubts and questioning, *be honest* about your answers. As I've said many times, God honours honest doubters! The process of growing up/testing one's faith/maturing is a very difficult one, and it takes time.

Above all, love your child unconditionally, quietly, though you mustn't patronise or go over the top, especially in public. Guide where you can, gently; encourage whenever you can without patronising; pray *for* him; and pray *with* him if he wants you to.

THE DEPRESSED GRANDPARENT

Depression can hit the elderly, too. The causes are much the same as in younger people – you might think that the fear of death could be a factor, but surprisingly, this is seldom the case. Most old people don't fear death – the zest for living ebbs quietly away, and even non-Christians don't find the thought of dying that disconcerting. (How different from the young man or woman!)

On the other hand, depression in older people can often be much more difficult to treat successfully. I suspect this is because the emotional resilience of the brain is reduced as a result of the ageing process. We all start to lose brain cells from the age of about twenty-one, and there comes a point when we haven't got too many to spare. So our minds become more rigid, less adaptable. This process is accelerated in some of the ageing diseases such as Alzheimer's. Life also gets even more confusing when you can't hear or see as well as you used to: the isolation that comes from impaired sight or hearing can be the final event that tips an older person into a depression.

With or without Alzheimer's disease, depresssion in old people can often be extremely resistant to treatment. This is one group of people in whom electro-convulsive therapy (ECT) often has a part to play, and I've seen it work wonders in otherwise resistant cases.

Depression in the elderly is often compounded by forgetfulness and apathy. Their short-term memory is often poor, though long-term memory (of childhood events) can still remain crisp and fresh. So an older lady will be able to remember what she was wearing on the day of King George V's coronation – yet forget she's left the kettle on the gas only five minutes ago.

Caring, sympathetic, understanding love is required. Granny isn't necessarily being difficult when she forgets she's left the kettle on – her brain may well be working at the very edge of its capacity, just remembering how to live and eat.

On the other hand, some old people manipulate extensively: so be on your guard! Think of Steptoe in the TV series *Steptoe and Son,* who would always manage to be ill just at the right time to frustrate his son's independence! If in doubt, seek professional advice – the impartial observer can often pick up things you are too near to see properly.

More than in any other group of people with depression, depression in the elderly can be difficult to diagnose and difficult to treat. Therefore, it is all the more important in this group to seek medical advice early on.

EXERCISE

1. There is a super book called *Building Your Mate's Self-Esteem* which should be an obligatory wedding-day gift. Written by Dennis and Barbara Rainey, and published by Word, it's quite the best thing I've ever read on supporting one another, in both good times and bad. Get it, read it, and put it into practice! (This applies whether it's you, or your spouse, or neither, who is depressed.)

2. If you're the one who's depressed, getting help from your family and friends is good, but it can be a bit one-way, and the trouble with depression is that it can easily turn into self-centredness. So *you* can start helping *others*!

   Make a list of your particular attributes and the things you feel called to. Now make a list of the pressing needs in your immediate neighbourhood and/or church. How far do your talents fit a need? Now go and do something about it!

26

WHAT THE CHURCH
SHOULDN'T DO
(AND SOMETIMES DOES)

In theory the church should be well equipped to deal with depressed people: after all, it is the earthly representative of God, so presumably it should possess some of His insights into the problem! The church also has available to it the power of prayer to that same God, who can change the situation. So shouldn't membership of the church guarantee immunity from depression? And won't the church always be right when commenting on the spiritual standing of those with depression?

Unfortunately, no. Churches are made up of fallible humans who don't always listen properly to what God has said. Wherever there is a church, then to a greater or lesser extent there will be mistakes, misunderstandings, and misapplications of Christian truths. We are all human, we are all fallible and as a result the earthly church can never be perfect.

Nor do Christians necessarily exert enough earthly wisdom, either. Sometimes it's because mankind doesn't know enough (such as what causes multiple sclerosis) – but sometimes it's because we haven't listened to, and learned from, the answers. (The best-known, if somewhat ancient, example of this was when the church of the day persecuted Galileo for saying that Jupiter had moons.)

In other words, Christians' knowledge of the world, at either a physical or a spiritual level, may be deficient. And if you don't understand how things fit together, how can you advise in cases of difficulty?

We've already looked at the secular mistakes helpers fall into (see Chapter 24). Christians can make all these as well! But there are also specifically spiritual mistakes that churches and individual Christians make.

All gaffes, whether secular or spiritual, imply a lack of understanding of the mechanism of depression, and it is vital that the church understands the condition well enough not to make mistakes like this. As with the secular gaffes, not everyone makes all the mistakes all the time! So if the cap fits..... Otherwise, make a mental note and move on.

DENOMINATIONAL PROBLEMS

Most differences between the denominations involve different methods of church government, differing types of church services and differing emphases on specific doctrines. Strangely enough, as far as depression is concerned, there are few problems that relate to denomination.

The only exception is that some churches or sects (usually very small) tend to behave as though they had a complete and absolute monopoly of the truth. *Any* church that thinks in a dictatorially dogmatic way is pathological, suspect at both religious and psychological levels, and in its ability to help/hinder depressed people. We'll come onto this subject later.

EVANGELICAL AND LIBERAL CHURCHES

Although there is no great difference between the *denominations* in their ability to help those with psychological problems, there *are* considerable differences between churches according to whether they are evangelical or liberal.

Let's start by defining these terms, because they're important. The evangelical church believes that God sent His Son, Jesus Christ, to die in our place in order to atone for our sins. Evangelical churches take the Bible at face value, treat it as the inspired word of God, and believe that, properly interpreted, the Bible provides the only reliable guide to godly Christian living.

The more liberal wing of the church tends to dissect the Bible; it sees it as a collection of various people's ideas about God. These ideas matured as mankind matured. Liberals conclude that the Bible contains human (rather than revealed) wisdom about God; that as we understand God better we can discard earlier, less subtle concepts; and that much of what happened in the way of 'miracles' in the Bible was merely an unschooled approach to perfectly natural phenomena.

The more extreme liberal churches have tried to 'demythologise' the Bible by taking out the supernatural. They also find it difficult to come to terms with the idea of a God of love who is also a judge, and therefore reduce the importance of the atonement and the need for conversion. This leaves the liberal churches with little to do in the way of practical religion other than meditation, worship, and social work.

Depression and the Liberal Church

Many liberal churches have dispensed with the idea of judgement, the Devil and hell, and look positively at all aspects of human behaviour, usually non-judgementally. Because of their beliefs, liberal churches have one advantage and one great disadvantage in dealing with depression.

The advantage is that in practising from the start a loving, uncritical, non-judgemental approach towards *everyone,* they are quite prepared to accept a depressed person as a fully paid-up member both of the human race and of the church. Liberal churches are likely to be sympathetic, understanding, caring, supportive, and kind.

The disadvantage of the liberal approach is that if you no longer believe in the supernatural, the laying on of hands, healing, conversion, and the atonement, then you miss out a great deal which can assist in the recovery from depression – in fact, you've ruled out all supernatural help.

Because they don't believe in judgement or hell, many liberal churches don't believe in conversion either; but this misses out a large chunk of Christian experience and source of spiritual power. The depressed *non*-Christian who is converted – in Biblical terms 'born again' – often undergoes striking changes. The very phrase 'born again' implies a new beginning – the old has been left behind. This is of immense psychological advantage at an earthly level, never mind the spiritual implications!

Often the psychological state of non-Christians undergoes a complete change after conversion: many of the old worries disappear. For example, it is common to find that addicts lose their desire for drugs: this is partly because the original reason for using them (to numb the emptiness of their existence) has vanished now they have a reason for living and a hope of everlasting life. Additionally, there may be a directly supernatural input, reducing an addict's interest in drug-taking.

Therefore, the liberal's denial of the existence of conversion, and his refusal to believe in the supernatural power of God in being able to change people *now,* means that a lot of the guts have been torn out of his Christian beliefs. Within the more liberal wing of the church the depressed person will get a lot of sympathy and acceptance, but the only power to change is of human origin. The thought that *God could actually heal him* is missed out – a big price to pay.

Depression and the Evangelical Church

I believe strongly that the evangelical wing of the church represents the nearest thing we have on earth to what God wants Christianity to be. However, no one and no church is completely perfect and we all make mistakes over doctrine, beliefs and actions. We also make mistakes over how we *apply* doctrine. The problem of the evangelical church is therefore not so much whether it has the right doctrine, but whether it is *applying* it correctly, and *expressing* it properly, sensitively, and lovingly.

The *true* evangelical church will adopt the attitudes that Jesus had towards people who were weak and poor in spirit – it will comfort them, help in their conversion (where appropriate), build them up, and be the channel for supernatural power through prayer, the laying on of hands and the application of the gifts of healing.

On the other hand, the evangelical church makes mistakes – sometimes big ones. I want to look at some of the incorrect attitudes the evangelical church can hold, and in particular discuss those areas where the 'evangelical approach' can slide into unbiblical ways of handling depression. Please understand that it's not the evangelical position itself that is at fault, but that there are traps that evangelicals can fall into if they don't think carefully.

DOCTRINE, FAITH AND DOUBT

The evangelical church has a rightful emphasis on correct doctrine, and in particular the importance of the Bible as the revealed word of God. However, correct doctrine isn't everything, as we'll see shortly. Equally, correct doctrine isn't something that comes immediately on conversion, but quietly assembles itself over the years.

It is important to understand that Christians can differ widely on doctrine, be wrong, and yet still be Christians. This happened in the Bible – where Paul, who had never seen Jesus, (except in a vision on the Damascus road) went to Jerusalem to challenge Peter, who had been the constant companion of Jesus for three years, and whom Jesus had appointed the head of the church. Paul said Peter was wrong in his attitude which required Gentile converts to adopt Jewish customs. Paul won! Peter was clearly acting inconsistently, and needed to be corrected.

The moral is – even the best Christians, the most holy, those nearest to Jesus, can get it wrong sometimes! And it is important for *all* Christians to remember this, in humility.

However, doctrine is also something that weak people hide behind when they feel threatened. 'Purity of doctrine' is a sacred cow in some churches, and the more extreme and isolated the sect, the more 'doctrine-ism' is likely to be a problem: you know the sort – the ones who insist that all members are premillenialists / *must* be baptised by immersion/ *must* speak in tongues, and so on.

The weaker the church, the less it can stand any thought of

doctrinal opposition, and the more any individual's beliefs are likely to be questioned judgementally.[1]

In turn, this leads to a 'them and us' situation, in which everyone who agrees with your particular stand is 'OK' and all the rest are 'not OK'. This is all very well if you are dealing with massive differences – such as those who believe in God and those who don't; but a 'them and us' situation is not helpful where the doctrinal differences are slight. Unfortunately, many people who lay heavy emphasis on doctrinal purity seem to have a psychological need to put down others who don't agree *exactly* with them.

This is of direct relevance to depressed Christians. If you're depressed, you're probably going through a very difficult patch spiritually.

"Where is God?"

"Why has He left me? "

"Why won't He take this depression away from me?"

"Is there a God......?"

And as we have discovered, some depressions centre round a spiritually orientated knotty problem, such as whether God is there, how a loving God can send people to hell, and so on. It's a testing time, not just for the Christian as a person, but also for his beliefs, and sorting out just what he believes may be the key to getting rid of his depression.

The 'testing' Christian like this may, quite rightly, be checking out his faith to make sure that it is watertight. Along the way he may ask himself a lot of very pertinent questions, and for a time may find it difficult to agree with the 'accepted' Christian answers until he is *sure* they are right.

Testing one's faith like this is good: 'organised doubting' is quite different from heresy or 'falling away'. The Christian doing the testing will end up with a stronger faith as a result – but for a time seems to be a doubter.

Under testing conditions like this, the very worst that the church can do is to say, "Because your faith is faltering, we don't think you're a proper Christian. You're in a condition of sin. *Repent!*" Yet this happens, all too frequently.

In times of trial – and believe me, depression *is* a time of trial – the last thing you want is someone criticising from on high. Often,

---

[1] Incidentally, I believe strongly in the importance of both baptism and the gifts of the Spirit, but I would never dream of saying that Anglicans can't get to heaven, or that you're not a Christian until you speak in tongues. It's the emphasis and balance that counts. And the love.

though, the person who is criticising your shaky faith has never had a depression in his life; he won't understand what you're going through, and will misinterpret your feelings.

Unfortunately, when you're depressed it's all too easy to believe that anyone who criticises you is correct, and that you are the one in the wrong. So you start to feel that he is right, and your faith really is at fault. Maybe it really *is* your fault you're depressed – which makes you feel even worse. (And what's more, you know you can't do anything about it.)

Strangely, Jesus never worried excessively about doctrine, though it is obvious He thought it important. He was always encouraging and congratulating people for whatever faith they had, rather than criticising them destructively for their lack of it.

However, there was one group of people who thought they'd got all the answers – the Pharisees, doctrinally pure and a million miles away from God. Jesus wasn't very pleased with their performance, was He? Yet they were *meticulous* about their observance of the law. The Pharisees read the Scriptures avidly, and many knew whole books of it by heart. It didn't do them much good! They had assimilated the law itself without understanding its meaning: that God is just, righteous *and loving*.

Because the evangelical church lays (rightful) emphasis on correct doctrine, it is all too easy for us to slip into the Pharisees' mistake of 'all doctrine and no love' (rather like the definition of a crocodile – 'all teeth and no smile'....!) A church like this is an unlovely caricature of what the true church is all about.

Of course it is important to study the Bible. *Of course* it is right to learn the correct doctrines, to pray, to give to the poor – the Pharisees did all of this, and look where it got them. The similarities between the two positions (evangelical and Pharisaical) mean that it is all too easy to slide from the one to the other. In other words, the easiest sin for us in the evangelical church to fall into is that of becoming Pharisees, and all evangelical churches (and individual Christians) should be on their guard to make sure this doesn't happen.

The reason the Pharisees were in a mess was because they had sacrificed love on the altar of doctrine. It's so easy to do! "If I speak with the tongues of angels, but have no love ...," wrote Paul. It was obviously a problem at the time of the early church, and has often been so since.

Too doctrinally orientated a church can actually prove a stumbling-block to the depressed Christian. We discovered in the chapter on Conscience that the strong Christian has a *less* tender conscience, whilst those weak in the faith may have a 'strong' conscience. In many ways this parallels the attitude of the church to doctrine. 'Strong' doctrine may mean 'weak in love'. Doctrine *is* important – but not more than love.

Is this relevant to depressed Christians? Not half! There is nothing more guaranteed to depress an already depressed Christian even further, than being taken to task for lack of faith, or made to feel unchristian and beyond the pale for expressing doubts. I have known depressed Christians to be unable to go into church because of the criticism they get from the pulpit about "those who don't believe".

Jesus never behaved like this: He *always* commended people for whatever faith they showed (whilst encouraging them to display even more). He *never* squashed a genuine doubter or enquirer. Look at His reaction to the rich young ruler, who genuinely asked, "What must I do to be saved? I've done everything the law lays down." Jesus didn't say, "You know-all hypocrite." He looked at him and *loved* him – *because He knew the man was asking honestly*.

Doctrine *is* important – but sympathy, understanding and love are even greater. Paradoxically, the church that is prepared to accept a depressed Christian's doubts without criticising him will find ultimately that his Christian faith ends up greater, and his doctrine more firmly based, through being tried and tested.

"If you're depressed there must be something wrong with your faith."

It was once aptly remarked that the Christian church is the only army to shoot its own wounded. When we see someone who is having a period of Christian struggle because his faith is being tested, it is all too easy to jump to the conclusion that he must be a very poor Christian because he should be triumphant over all situations.

When we say this we judge our fellow Christian. How do we know that *our* faith would survive under the sort of problems that he has had? Can we be sure that under sustained pressure from a series of personal and family tragedies we wouldn't have cursed God a long time ago? We give VC's to people who run the gauntlet of enemy bullets – but we don't seem to respect emotionally wounded Christian warriors in quite the same way.

The church can fall down badly when it confronts doubt and depression – twin problems which may *or may not* be related to each other. It is all too easy to say to someone going through a depression, "If you're having a depression then there must be something wrong with your faith. You ought to pray more. Or maybe your depression is because you have sinned, so you ought to repent more."

It is all too easy to assume that a depressed Christian is lacking in faith, that the hand of God is against him because of something that he has done, or that he ought to exercise more faith and get spiritually healed. It's exactly the trap that Job's comforters fell into. They assumed Job was directly responsible for the disasters that were happening to him. He wasn't: *God* was testing him.

And just as Job's 'comforters' proved to be anything but, Christians who treat depressed Christians in this way are guilty of exactly the same faults. Their conclusions are untrue, although it is easy to fall into the trap of using them. There is nothing more depressing to an already depressed Christian than being gunned down with hostile verses coming from a critical Christian who has never had a depression in his life, and who hasn't the wisdom nor the subtlety to see that he is hurting a man or woman for whom Christ died. Those who say such things are guilty of the sin of judgement, and a judging attitude hurts and destroys the depressed Christian as nothing else can. It stifles whatever Christian growth there is, and kicks away any meagre emotional integrity his tattered personality still possesses. It's the holier-than-thou attitude of the Pharisees *and it isn't what Jesus would do.*

"It's a sin to be depressed."

No, it's not. Like cancer, depression is the *result* of sin but in a general sense. Had sin not entered the world we wouldn't have depression, and we wouldn't have breast cancer either.

Yes, there are occasions when depression in Christians is related directly to a specific sin – but these are few and far between, and as we have discussed earlier (Chapter 4), depressions like this are related to a specific sin that the Christian is not prepared to give up – like the refusal to end an adulterous relationship.

"You need to seek forgiveness."

Yes – but for what? Just for being depressed? As we've discovered, being depressed is not sinful in itself, but is the *result* (often totally indirect) of sin. For most depressed people, then, there is nothing for which to ask forgiveness directly. You can't confess something that isn't there.

However, there are sins that tend to trail in the wake of depression, and these need addressing. Firstly, it's easy to get self-absorbed in depression, and talk about nothing but yourself and how dreadful you feel. In the right environment, and at the right time, this can be therapeutic – but it can also be just wallowing in self-pity, which is wrong.

Secondly, although sufferers from depression often ask for forgiveness, their real problem is often whether they will *accept* it. I suppose that a refusal to accept forgiveness might be counted as a sin – but the sufferer has such a poor opinion of himself that he can't believe that God would stoop so low as to forgive a worm like him.

Remember – no matter how low you go or feel, God always wants to pick you up and forgive you. You cannot go so low that you are unredeemable! If you ask for forgiveness He will *always* respond, whether you *feel* forgiven or not. (See the chapter on Guilt for a more detailed explanation.)

DOUBT AND GUILT

The great antidote to guilt is love, but it's not always easy to be aware of the depth of love God has for you. Like a mountain shrouded in a fog, just because you can't see it doesn't mean it's not there!

Someone who is so depressed that they feel God has got no time for them and doesn't love them may have their faith and fears lifted by a very personal and intimate experience of God – such as messages from Him during speaking in tongues. It is surprising how often a word of encouragement coming directly from God seems to lift people's spirits. I remember particularly going to a Christian concert feeling really very low, angry and irritated, for no particular reason. During the concert there was a message in tongues for the congregation as a whole, talking about God inhabiting the praises of His people and of His being *pleased* with the praises of His people. The sense of encouragement was tremendous, and all the irritations and sadness and tiredness dropped away.

As I've said elsewhere, when God challenges you, you feel encouraged by the way He does it. It then becomes an easy privilege to change your behaviour, not a tiresome duty. God is an encourager, not a discourager.

In my experience God seldom works by condemnation, especially not of believing Christians: if He does, it's only as a last resort to stop a Christian going off the rails in a big way. If you look at how Jesus related to those who came to Him, He was always courteous, always considerate and always loving – even to those who were sinful.

My experience is that whenever you hear the big voice of condemnation, then you're listening to the Devil. When God condemns He does so extremely quietly in a still, small voice that says, "Please don't do that – it hurts Me, and it hurts you. I don't like it. Please stop." No loud fanfares, no sense of overwhelming guilt, just a sense that there is something here that ought to be changed – so you go out and change it. And then you feel better afterwards – as though it's been a privilege to get rid of a sin.

Now contrast this with the way in which some preachers try to lay guilt upon their congregation – the so-called 'worm theology'. The theory goes that the more broken you are, the better a Christian you are. The 'logic' runs as follows: "I am more broken than you, therefore I am more humble than you, therefore I am a better Christian than you. And therefore I have the right to tell you where to get off (in love, and in the name of Jesus, of course, just to make it sound holy)." It's really inverted pride and snobbery – back to the Pharisees again.

How many times do you go into a church service feeling small – and come out feeling smaller? If so, you've been under the spell of worm theology. It is beguiling, because on the surface it seems very 'Christian' but in reality its father is the Devil. It depends upon legalism, and is completely opposed to the real intentions of Jesus, who would never, *ever*, 'break bruised reeds'. Beware the Christian who tries to push you down emotionally – the one who is truly speaking the words of God is almost always the one who seeks to build you up. You should be going out of church feeling twelve feet taller than when you came in.

If you've been to church and have really met with God then you will not come out smaller, ever. You may come out humble – but being humble means that you are aware of just how much God loves you, how much God is prepared to do things for you and how much God treasures you. Although it makes you feel very humble that such a great being as God would be prepared to do that for you, it doesn't squash you in the process. On the contrary, it makes you feel truly humble and about fifty feet tall!

God does sometimes challenge individual Christians during services – in much the same way as in Revelation he challenged the church at Laodicea to stop being lukewarm. However, challenges like this are directed towards people who can and should start to do something about it; whereas God in His infinite wisdom, patience and mercy understands the exhaustion of your depression and is not going to challenge you if you do not as yet have the energy, strength, or resilience to deal with it. He is certainly not going to get out the big stick and wave it at you. Nor is He likely to issue challenge upon challenge, criticism upon criticism, condemnation upon condemnation, *especially* if you're broken, bruised and battered. However, if you're being challenged repeatedly over a *specific* problem then it may well be God who is doing it – if, on the other hand, you just come out of church feeling lousy and criticised from all sides, then it is almost certainly not from God!

There are certain occasions when God does 'turn up the volume' and starts to make you feel guilty. But in my experience this is related to one reason and one reason only – a *specific* sin which is not being addressed by the particular Christian. It can be anything – from a refusal to heal the breach with another Christian, to the continuation of an adulterous liaison or a failure to go where God is *clearly* leading. But in all cases it is a *specific* condemnation, and quite unlike the general feeling of 'being under a cloud of condemnation' that so many depressed people have.

CONDEMNATION FROM THE BIBLE

Because the evangelical church treats the Bible as the inspired word of God, some Christians assume that they can conduct arguments by using any verse of Scripture that contains words that describe the current situation. This assumes that the verses are applicable to the situation, which unfortunately is not always the case. For example, how many people apply "Your good deeds are as filthy rags" without understanding that this is a verse for the *non*-Christian?

This is important for the depressed Christian. Dealing with depression requires subtlety and understanding: what at first sight appears obvious turns out to be anything but. Therefore quoting a verse 'at' the depressed person will only be of relevance if it really applies.

For example, " 'The fruit of the Spirit is love, joy and peace.' Brother, you're not very peaceful; so you're not filled with the Spirit, are you?" (Therefore it's your fault you're depressed. QED. Case proved. Judgement given. Wash hands of problem.) Only it doesn't help the depressed Christian, and it isn't correct, because although the words are true, they are not the whole truth and they are not being *applied* correctly. It's not even a whole verse that's been quoted.

The quotation is part of a passage which compares our sinful nature, which leads to "sexual immorality, impurity and debauchery ... witchcraft... drunkenness [and] orgies" with the fruit of the Spirit which leads to "love, joy, peace, *patience,* kindness, goodness, *faithfulness*, gentleness and self-control."[1]

It looks a bit different, doesn't it, now it's quoted more fully and in context? Depressed Christians often have to be very patient, and may well be exercising faith beyond measure in continuing to be a Christian in the middle of an extremely trying situation. You can't just extract the convenient and more memorable bits about love, joy

---

[1]Galatians 5: 19-21, 22-23 (NIV, my italics).

and peace and use them in isolation. (Come to think of it, if you *did* you'd come to the conclusion that when Jesus was in Gethsemane, He was no longer showing the fruit of the Spirit – where was *His* joy and peace? We are told that He began to be greatly troubled, and that sweat began to fall from His forehead like drops of blood. Peace? Joy? Only afterwards.)

Yes, the fruit of the Spirit *does* include love, joy and peace – but when? *After the fruit has ripened,* not during the pruning process. Fruit takes a season to ripen, and it can't be rushed.

Hermeneutics is the study of how we extract information from the Bible and apply it. One of its most important principles is that a verse must be seen *in context*. For a start, which part of the Bible does it come from: Old Testament or New Testament? Is it part of the history (to be taken literally) or part of the poetry (to be understood more symbolically)? To whom is the verse applied in the Bible, believers or unbelievers?

The answers make a lot of difference. Although you may think you have proved a point by quoting verses of the Bible, if you are quoting out of context you are misapplying the word of God, and will get nowhere.

The moral for everybody (but especially the depressed Christian) is: just because somebody quotes bits of the Bible at you, don't necessarily accept that it applies to you, because the truth of the matter depends not just upon whether the words are from the Bible, *but whether they are correctly applied*. And they may not be.

Equally, it is not always easy to remember whether you have quoted a verse fully, or in its proper context: for this reason (and *especially* with depressed Christians) I personally prefer not to quote verses in isolation. I would far rather recount the *essence* of a whole chunk of Scripture. In this way you can get a much broader perspective of the Biblical approach to your particular situation.

"Look at the Biblical promises, and be happy." "Have faith."

If only life were that easy! And if only people who said things like this realised that just *living* with depression is for some a matter of the greatest faith imaginable, never mind living triumphantly. To appreciate the Biblical promises, and to be able to put them into practice 'in cold blood', you have to be emotionally well-balanced – something that the depressed Christian is not, because his emotions are all over the place. Depression is *such* a numbing experience that sometimes you're hard put to feel any positive emotion at all, throughout the whole day. It is enough that the depressed person is still clinging onto his faith.

"Doesn't the Bible say, 'I can do everything through him who gives me strength.'?" *(Philippians 4:13)*

– which means you should be able to stop yourself being depressed, doesn't it?..... Doesn't it?

Try this experiment. Pray, then attempt to juggle five eggs, preferably raw, in public!

OK, so why doesn't it work? Simple. Although I could do anything *that God wanted me to do* through Christ who strengthens me, there are lots of things God chooses *not* to ask me to do, and if I tried to do them I would probably find that Christ (who is in me) wouldn't let me, because it isn't the way He wants me to go!

What the passage *actually* means is that in those tests and trials that God wants me to face, God will give me strength to tackle them – quite a different matter from being given an ability to carry out the action directly. I don't doubt that in an emergency God might give supernatural assistance with the juggling, but He doesn't usually choose to work like this! Instead He gets *us* to carry out the *actions* – while giving us supernatural *strength to keep going* while we do it/ practise it / learn it (whatever 'it' is), perhaps for months or even years. The supernatural gift is of the strength to keep going until the battle is won – very relevant if you're depressed and a Christian!

"You ought to pray for healing."

If by 'praying for healing' we really mean 'ask for forgiveness', then say so. (It's probably not appropriate, anyway, but at least let's be honest.) And why pray for healing? Do you say this to a Christian with a broken leg and expect him to throw away his plaster cast immediately? If not, then kindly don't apply sanctimonious ideas to a situation you obviously don't understand.

Having said that, there are occasions when depression *is* alleviated through prayer, by the laying on of hands, or by simple conversion. In any case, if a depression is related to the individual's search for the meaning of life, or to his sense of guilt, then conversion, or a deepening of his faith, will undoubtedly alleviate the psychological problems that caused the depression in the first place.

Yes, of course the depressed Christian should pray for healing, and others with him: but onlookers shouldn't think that depression is something which will lift 'just like that'. It's much more complex and deep than most non-depressed people could ever imagine: praying for healing is a good option, but not necessarily what God wants to happen – *so if the depression doesn't go, don't blame the victim for his lack of faith.*

There's a whole chapter of this book devoted to spiritual healing in the positive sense – but if you look at the chapter on The Spiritual Gymnasium you will also see just why God might not want to perform an instant miracle on you.

THE 'EVANGELICAL LEADER'

One final point should be made about the evangelical church (and in fact about all leaders in all churches). There is a subtype of the 'evangelical person' which consists of a hearty, extrovert, well-balanced, outgoing Christian, converted at an early age, mature in the faith, wise, a good speaker, a good evangelist, and generally a 'giant-sized' person. People like this are often good church leaders, and the church generally (and rightly) looks up to them for wisdom and guidance. Unfortunately, this personality type tends not to include those who are more prone to depression, and because they do not have first-hand experience of depression, they are not always the best people to approach for counsel, guidance and help when you are depressed: *their* exercises in the spiritual gymnasium will have involved different trials and problems, but *not* usually depression, so they are not always able to react sensitively to such problems.

Now here comes the difficulty – because people like this are often leaders within the church their voice is often heard from the pulpit. We all talk and preach about what affects ourselves emotionally – especially those lessons we have learned at first hand, because these are the most vivid. People with these character traits are more likely to have problems regarding the need for holiness, humility or dedication. What tends to happen, therefore, is that speakers end up preaching to people of *other character types* about answers to *their own* type of problems. For example, if you are aware of your own lack of dedication then you may feel called upon to encourage everyone to be dedicated. If you are aware of your tendency to become big-headed, you will preach about humility.

Unfortunately, to the person who has got precious little sense of self-esteem, sermons about humility feel like a bucket of cold water thrown at them. People who are depressed have enough trouble with their self-esteem without others trying to get them to be more humble! Do remember therefore, when you are listening to a sermon, that the preacher may well be preaching to himself or for people of a similar character type, and therefore the criticism, exhortation and cajolement *may not apply to you at all*. It is all too easy to think that, because a subject has been mentioned as part of a sermon, it necessarily applies to you (and that God's got it in for you again!)   It may not ... and He hasn't!

The moral for preachers is – be aware that not everybody has the same emotional attitudes and problems as you do.   There is a psychological truism that says *we criticise in others those traits we can't tolerate in ourselves*. This is the real significance of the text, "Judge not, that ye be not judged." Criticising others for what we do ourselves gets no one very far.

★   ★   ★

As I said at the beginning of this chapter – if the cap fits, wear it. Otherwise ignore it. If I've described some of the things that happen in your church, then I've also told you a few of the answers.

The ultimate answer to all these problems is *love*. "Perfect love casts out fear."   If a church concentrates on showing love, encouragement and support to the depressed Christian, and leaves the criticisms behind, it will help more than anything else.

There are other specific positive things that the church can do. We'll consider these in the next chapter.

27

WHAT THE CHURCH
SHOULD DO

So what should the church be doing for those of its congregation who are depressed? The answers, in principle, are very simple and very easy.

1. The church should be providing a **loving, warm, under-standing, compassionate aura of friendship and acceptance.** If God has accepted an individual as a Christian and as one of His friends, then how can the church possibly exert judgement over that person and say that he is not truly a Christian?

2. The church should be providing **a totally uplifting sense of support** for the person who is in distress, whether physical or mental, refusing to criticise them for their state (because that could be the sin of judging others). It's surprising, isn't it, how we say that we should not be judgemental, and then, on the pretext of keeping doctrine pure and with the intention of 'challenging' others, proceed to drag through the mud other groups of people on the assumption that *we* are entitled to judge them in that fashion because *they* are in error.

3. The church needs to remind itself constantly that **a negative approach to life is not Christian** – Christ didn't come to say "Don't do this" and "Don't do that" – instead He came to say, that it would be better to do things differently. "My yoke is easy, and my burden is well-balanced." The people He condemned were always those who were not prepared to listen at all – and it's surprising how frequently He congratulated people on very modest amounts of faith. We have to remember that, and in the light of this remember to measure the success of preachers by their ability to uplift and encourage rather than their ability to lay a blanket of condemnation on everybody.

4. The church needs to make sure that **it looks after the large number of depressed people it will have within its community.** Someone who is depressed finds it easy to misapply Bible verses to himself and experience condemnation where there is none, (or at least none implied for *him*). It is so important on these occasions to help depressed and insecure people to appropriate to themselves the underlying meaning of the whole passage rather than to go into detail over little bits of it.

For example, consider the story of how King Saul was finally abandoned by God because he offered sacrifices that only the priests could make. The depressive's first reaction is to apply this to himself – "God abandoned Saul because Saul was disobedient – I've been disobedient, so God will abandon me." Therefore it's important that teachers and preachers remind their congregation of the background to those verses – that it was completely against the Mosaic law for anyone other than a priest to offer sacrifices to God. To do so was a deliberate contravention of the law, made worse because it was the King doing it, and doing it publicly to boot. In fact, Saul was really saying, "God, I don't care anything for your rules and regulations, I am great enough to offer a sacrifice to you." It was a deliberate, public act of rebellion – a real two-fingered salute to God. No wonder God got cross!

The preacher has to compare this with the attitude that David had. David did some heinous things, of which the best-known was his murder by proxy of Bathsheba's husband after he had committed adultery with Bathsheba and made her pregnant. But David had the grace to be truly repentant when he was told about his sin. The real difference between Saul and David is that their underlying approach was quite different. David was truly repentant, but Saul was only superficially sorry – mainly upset about the difficulty his sins had caused *to himself*, rather than to God.

This difference is seldom brought out in sermons. There tends to be a concentration on the fact of sin and its punishment by God. The difference between Biblical characters who are condemned and those who are forgiven depends not upon what they did, but where they were in overall relation to God – 'where their heart was' if you like. Translated into modern terms, it means God is prepared to be infinitely patient with His people, whom He will also forgive infinitely.

As I've said earlier, it's not what we *believe* that saves us, nor what we *do,* but what we *are* that counts. And, in the famous "By faith we are saved" quotation, notice that the little word 'by' could better be translated as 'through'. It's not our faith that saves us directly. It's *because* of our faith that God saves us. And He looks on what we are, not what we say we are. The difference between Saul and David was in the overall direction of their lives, not in a catalogue of individual sins.

This should be the heart of the church's response to sin. However, if the Christian, and especially the depressed Christian, goes away with the feeling of condemnation (and we can all be made to feel guilty about something in our lives) then he ends up a fearful Christian, more aware of his sins than he is of his Redeemer. God wants you to forget your sins – remember the illustration of God wanting to throw your sins into a deep sea and then putting up a sign saying 'No Fishing'! If we want to be like Jesus, we'd better do what He does, forget sins once they've been confessed and forgiven, and stop referring to them over and over again.

5. The great antidote to being a Pharisee (a nit-picker) is to **be a Barnabas – an encourager.** How nice it is to have an encourager in the church – one who sees when you do things well and congratulates you, one who notices when things are going better for you and encourages you to continue. By comparison, think of the person who notices when things are going wrong for you and delights in needling you about it.

6. The church also needs the wisdom to **be sympathetic and empathetic** to those who are depressed. It needs, collectively and individually, to say, "There but for the grace of God go I," and to realise that it is given to certain people to undergo a depression, because God feels it is right for this to happen to them. Anybody who is tested in this way should be applauded and encouraged as being one of the chosen for whom God has got great plans, but whom He first needs to refine through the traumas of depression before they are able to be of increased use to Him. We applaud, support, pray for and encourage those who are going through missionary training. Even more should we be supporting those who are undergoing God's training in the spiritual gymnasium of emotional upheaval: they need *more* support because, whereas in a college for prospective missionaries there is an atmosphere of optimism and enthusiasm, the very reverse applies to those graduating in the spiritual gymnasium of depression. If the church thinks of those who are depressed as being soldiers in training, then a completely different attitude will prevail, an attitude which will shift from discouragement to encouragement.

The helpfulness of encouragement cannot be overemphasised. We encourage by our attitude more than by what we say. If we say on the one hand, "God be with you," but are not then prepared to lend a listening ear, or help in physical ways such as by preparing food, taking the children off a depressed parent's hands for an afternoon, or spending time listening to tales of woe, then we are not being truly Christian, however 'holy' our words may be. As James says in his epistle, "you demonstrate your faith by what you do."

How Do We Encourage?

a. **We encourage by what we say.** I have lost count of the number of times I have needed to repeat to a depressed person the

270 A Practical Workbook for the Depressed Christian

message that God loves them. This message may have to be repeated and repeated until it sinks in.

We also encourage (greatly) by praising people for what they've done, blessing them for who they are, and telling them what they mean to us.

b. **We encourage by what we do** – by getting alongside the person; by not being afraid to be the friend of a depressed person, and what's more to be *seen* as their friend. We encourage by what we do to help them when they've run out of energy: simple things like preparing a meal for them, or calling with an invitation to go out swimming, or by simply washing up for them when they haven't got the energy to be bothered but are troubled because they've got a kitchen full of dirty dishes. Finally, we encourage by who we are – their friend. All the good words, all the verses of Scripture, all the prayers, all the laying on of hands, all will be as nothing if we are unable to put our faith into practice and encourage others in this way.

c. **We encourage by pulling along with somebody,** by dwelling on the positives, not the negatives (and not too much on the uncertainties either), by confirming that they are in the centre of God's will whatever is happening to them, by treating failings and doubts graciously and by not criticising them inappropriately nor scoring points off them.

It has been said that the *average* boy leaving school feels sub-standard: the Devil would have Christians feel that way forever. It can take a lot of effort to make people realise that they really are treasured by God, and to make them walk tall as a result. In practical terms the church has to encourage its members to get into the habit of praising and thanking people for what they do and what they are.

However, there is one great problem connected with Christian approval and understanding. The message of the Bible is that holiness is the target for every individual Christian. Holiness implies one hundred per cent perfection, and it is easy therefore to put people under a cloud in thinking that they have to attain perfection on their own. Perfection essentially comes from God and through God, so the individual doesn't have to struggle to attain it in quite the same way that he might at first imagine. Unfortunately, the more sensitive you are, the more you will see how far you fall short of what you should be. It is vital that the church learns to encourage people towards perfection, rather than discourage them by pointing out how far from perfection they are. It's merely two attitudes to the same problem, but the one is critical and the other is encouraging. This in many ways is the real bite in the statement, "Don't judge as otherwise you may be judged in your turn." When we judge other people we pull them down and tear them to bits. We may think we are encouraging them by pointing out their faults, but ultimately we are destroying them if we do it in an unhelpful way. There is a time and a place for Christians to correct and admonish one another but the manner of doing it is crucial: the right way is infrequently and gently. Only use as much verbal force as absolutely necessary to get the message across.

d. Finally, we have to **treat doubts graciously.** Jesus never worried about the amount of doubt an individual person had (except gently to imply that there was room for a lot more faith) and He never crushed anybody who had problems. Instead He always encouraged those who were genuinely seeking the truth. The prophecy about Him in Isaiah was that "he will not break bruised reeds", and this applies to everyone. My experience, as someone who has spent a *long* time doubting God and worrying about His existence, is that (as one of my friends so neatly put it) God is big enough to take it! He really doesn't worry about the fact that you may, as a Christian, come to doubt His existence. If you *are* doubting His existence as part of seeking for the truth, then He will not let you down and He will not allow your faith to vanish. Therefore, don't be afraid of the truth; don't be afraid that you will somehow lose your faith through trying to make sure that it matches up to intellectual and scientific truths. If God is a God of truth then the truth ultimately will set you free. My experience is that the more that you understand of truth in whatever context, whether it be theological, scientific, or any other form (including the personal truth about yourself), the nearer you will ultimately get to God, because the more you understand His universe, the more you will understand the mind of the Being that created it. God never disowned a genuine doubter whose doubt was part of the process of searching out and testing his own faith.

By contrast the person who is proud in his faith, especially when that faith is rather shaky, can be a right pain in the neck, and very dishonouring to God. I don't believe for one minute that people who say, "Don't question, just have faith" are saying what God wants them to say: this is naive Christianity. It may help babies, but it doesn't help adults. It is therefore vital for the church to distinguish very carefully between heresy and searching for the truth. Remember, faith is not a matter of what you *believe,* nor what you *do* – it's what you *are* that counts. Faith is not a matter of sticking one's theological brain in the sand and then reciting the creed. Faith is not about lying to oneself in persuading oneself to repeat, "I believe". Real faith often says (recurrently), "O God, I don't know. I don't understand. I don't even know if I'm sure you're there." And in my experience God respects this attitude, and answers this prayer of faith. After all, as the Bible says, faith is about things we *can't* see and *can't* hear, otherwise it wouldn't be faith. On the other hand, the man who's got it all worked out, who knows exactly what he believes (because he never dares question it) is exerting no faith at all. He is merely being complacently ignorant, and a pain in the neck to others, on whom he will have a totally dampening effect.

When the Bible tells us not to judge our fellow Christians it specifically implies that we accept them. Christ died for them; Christ therefore accepted them. We are not to judge their beliefs, just as we would be wrong to criticise another man's servant. *We* don't know their background, their traumas. It is not for us to judge and say, "You're not a Christian." It is up to us to encourage, and perhaps (lovingly and caringly) point out other ways of looking at things. *But it is not up to the church to judge from on high.*

There may be times when we have *gently* to point out a specific sin that may be souring everything else up. If you are having an affair, then the guilt this engenders will be quite enough to give you a depression. On the other hand, to say "Stop" isn't enough, because there are reasons why you're having an affair – it's obviously meeting some deep unfulfilled needs in you. So we have to go back another stage and encourage you to explore the reasons why the affair became a fact, and tackle those needs, at the same time as gently disentangling your emotions and your affair.

Refusing to judge doesn't mean the church acquiesces in sin – far from it. A refusal to *judge* is not the same as a refusal to maintain certain standards, merely a reflection of how we go about encouraging people to keep to those standards. Judging always implies, "I'm better than you, and I'm going to tell you what I'd do in your place and you'll see that it could be *much* better." How do *I* know that, given *your* problems, I wouldn't have collapsed emotionally long ago?

In the long run, it's not so much a matter of what the church says, but the manner in which it says it. The church can be very firm over the boundaries between good and evil, without in any way becoming destructive to its own members in the process. In any case, Christians benefit more from encouragement than from a big stick – give a man a vision of God and he *won't* want to sin; he'll *want* to get nearer to God; he'll realise how great and wonderful God is, and how petty by comparison are the alternatives.

In short, the church's function as far as all Christians are concerned (whether depressed or not) is to lift them up so they get nearer to God and bathe in the knowledge of His Presence, His love, His truth, His patience and His infinite care.

★   ★   ★

In this chapter I've dealt with the 'earthly' church problems: in other words, how the church uses Biblical and human wisdom to create an environment in which the depressed person can begin to flower. We haven't even started considering supernatural gifts! – the power of prayer; healing; the laying on of hands; the use of spiritual gifts. We'll come on to these in the next chapter.

EXERCISE

Although it's not a sin to be depressed, depression can still involve sin, in some cases. Three of the most common faults are:

- wallowing in self-pity
- refusing to *accept* forgiveness
- refusing to tackle your depression head-on.

But note – these are quite different from the 'sins' that unthinking churches sometimes accuse depressed Christians of committing.

In dealing with depression it is important to distinguish carefully between those areas of your life which are not properly sorted out and those areas which may be directly sinful. It's very easy to muddle these up, and very dangerous too. If the church treats as sinful something which is merely not sorted out (delayed development), it will magnify the problem, and through making the sufferer unnecessarily guilty, make his or her burden twice the size. On the other hand, it is just as bad to treat that which is sinful as though it were delayed emotional development. If the church does this, it encourages the Christian to wallow in his depression, basking in the attention others give him as a result.

So – *treating unsorted-out areas as sinful makes the depression worse; and treating things which are sinful as if they were unsorted-out causes the sufferer to wallow in his misery, and get stuck.* It's vital to make sure we know which is which.

Remember what Christ said at the pool of Siloam? Sick people were waiting by the pool, because when an angel stirred up the waters, the first one to get in the water was healed. One cripple had been there fourteen years. Jesus said, in effect, "You've been here fourteen years – how come you never got in first?" In other words, *"Are you sure you want to get healed* – or are you *enjoying* your ill-health?"

Depressed Christians can get like this. There's all the difference in the world between, on the one hand, explaining why you feel so rotten, and unburdening yourself in the process; and on the other hand, enjoying the attention you get from recounting your woes to all and sundry for the fiftieth time.

How do you tell the difference? It's not easy. It's probably a good rule of thumb to divulge the details of your inner misery only to a small group of friends; if you find yourself doing it time and again to many different people you are probably wallowing in self-pity rather than trying to find a solution.

One of the giveaway phrases is "Yes, but..." After asking for help, and being given advice, the sufferer counters with, "Yes, but....." The person who uses "Yes...but" all the time is trying to prove that no one has an answer for her problems, that she's in a mess and isn't it really awful. ("And I have no intention of changing and I'm just loving all this attention I get because of my plight...." is her *real* message.) Her secondary message is, "Because no one can provide an answer for my problems, then it's not *my* fault if I can't get better – so I'm not going to try." Her problem is not that there isn't an answer, but that she's got a vested interest in being ill. It's easier to wallow in sympathy and stay stuck where she is. Changing herself might be painful.

If you catch yourself saying, "Yes, but" more than twice in a row you're probably wallowing: you're not prepared to try to change; you like it where you are. You're sinning. So shut up, listen to the advice others have for you (especially those who are wise and/or well versed in psychological things)....and put their advice into practice, straight away, noiselessly!

It may help prayerfully to consider (in the company of close and astute Christian friends) which areas of your life are unsorted-out and which are sinful; it will crystallise your thoughts to do this.

Once you have a list of (a) things to sort out, and (b) sins to change, you can begin to work out what you should be doing in very practical terms. We'll deal with this in greater detail in the final exercise in the book.

28

SPIRITUAL HEALING

Where does spiritual healing fit into all this? What is it? Shouldn't all Christians aim to be spiritually healed, thus bypassing ordinary medical processes? Isn't it a sin to trust in medicines when the Bible gives so many examples of divine healing? And if a Christian is depressed, isn't this a sign of his lack of faith in not seeking or not receiving healing?

The answers are not simple. For a start, what we often refer to as 'divine healing' covers a group of events ranging from the purely psychological (but divinely inspired) to the frankly miraculous. Additionally, we need to be aware that God *chooses* whether or not to heal, so we can't lay down rules about it. Nor does healing relate to the degree of faith we possess – after all, St Paul asked three times for God to heal him and God said "No"; so if that happened to St Paul....

Divine healing can be split into three main groups: diagnostic healing, enabling healing and direct healing. These groups are not mutually exclusive, and there may be considerable overlap.

Enabling healing is where the sufferer is made better because he is enabled to understand more about God. This enabling can be through conversion; or through putting into practice the principles of Christian living until he has adopted a more thoroughly Christian outlook. Sometimes it's that leap of understanding whereby the pieces of a specific spiritual puzzle fall neatly into place. Often a deeper appreciation of some great spiritual truth (such as "God really loves *me*") can be enough to provide *real* answers to all those problems richocheting round the brain. On other occasions it may be a deeper understanding of a spiritually orientated problem, such as the problem of pain.

Whatever the trigger, there is no longer a short circuit of mental energy which was previously attempting to deal with all those unsolved problems. Mental energy is now available in abundance, and the depression lifts.

Yes, it is spiritual healing, but mostly working through a very physical mechanism. If, as happened to one of my friends, God gives a specific word of encouragement through the ministry of tongues in another Christian, then the most incredible sense of personal relationship with God develops afterwards – a sense of "Gosh, He's taken all the trouble to speak to *me* personally. Wow!" Good for the flagging spirit! A good dose of the presence of God in the here and now puts paid to an awful lot of doubt and distress about what has happened in the past – not least because you know immediately that if God is going to have this relationship and reaction to you *now*, then it implies that He has dealt with and sorted out your past, and accepts you as you are, whatever may have happened earlier.

A deepening of your spiritual awareness (through study, prayer, and putting your Christian faith into practice) will help to remove many of the emotional stresses and strains that were previously bubbling underneath the surface. The strains are alleviated simply because now you understand better how things fit together. If you become more actively aware just how much God does care for you and looks after you, then persistent problems – such as whether He will forgive your adultery that took place fifteen years ago – have already been answered. They no longer pose a threat, they are no longer a problem, they have been solved.

Diagnostic healing is more directly supernatural. Here a Christian is led to understand the cause of someone else's problems through the direct intervention of the Holy Spirit. God supernaturally reveals to him what is the linchpin of the matter. For example, a Christian may be counselling someone, listening to him pouring out his troubles. Then, for no reason connected with what is being talked about, he feels strongly that he ought to ask, "And how does Anne fit into all this?" "Who told you about her?" the other replies – and then out comes a whole layer of problems/guilts/anxieties/worries that have so far been untouched.

Sometimes a 'word of knowledge' like this triggers off repentance for some dark and hidden problem that the subject hasn't dared tell anyone. But don't think that this means that it always relates to sin in the sufferer – far from it. The mind has a way of causing us to forget things that are really too traumatic to remember: one of the ways of revealing these 'forgotten' (yet still subconsciously active) memories is through the influence of the Holy Spirit. It's not a matter of opening a known door, but of unlocking a hidden door you never dreamed was there.

The sorts of hurts that are revealed in this way include things such as memories of seeing a particularly unpleasant car crash; of being abused as a child; of failure in front of others; of how we reacted to the death of a grandmother, and so on. You might think that events like this would be engraved on the mind and recalled as if they had happened yesterday. Far from it: with subjects that are emotionally traumatic the mind does a good job of walling off these memories. However, it doesn't do it completely, and when ripples from those memories jolt our *sub*-conscious we feel uneasy, without consciously knowing why.

Hence the usefulness of the spiritual 'gift of knowledge' in which a Christian is told directly where to probe. Again, the healing process is mainly 'natural', as those deep-seated hurts come flooding up into the conscious mind, where they can be dealt with: but it's finding the right trigger spot that's the wonderful supernatural bit!

Allied to this 'diagnostic trigger' is the ability of the Holy Spirit to delve deep down into our subconscious memories and heal them directly. How does this fit in with 'orthodox' psychiatry and medicine? With psychiatric treatment we can identify the source of the problem – for example, the person who is afraid of the dark because as a child she was locked up in the coal cellar as a punishment. Once this fact has been recognised and understood, it is quite possible that her fear of the dark will greatly diminish simply because she knows why she has it, and where it comes from. On the other hand, the accumulation of anxiety, tension, and emotion has still to be dissipated (emotions acquired over the years since the beginnings of her phobia). Sometimes these will dissipate with the passage of time, helped through consciously realising its origins, but sometimes God uses a more active approach. This is another area of spiritual healing – the removal of accumulated emotional debris.

Psychiatry can show what is causing the problem, and how not to exacerbate the situation further; but the healing it gives is sometimes slow, particularly as regards dissipating past hurts. On the other hand, spiritual healing removes these stored-up effects directly. To put it another way, psychiatry tells you how not to scratch the spot that is causing the pain, thus giving it time to heal, whereas spiritual healing heals the wound directly by removing the pus.

So should a Christian seek both psychiatric and spiritual healing? I have a Christian friend who, as a pastor, has great spiritual gifts, especially in relation to psychiatry and healing. His line is always, "Pray first, use the doctor second." On the other hand, as a doctor, I tend to put things the other way round! Of course the two approaches are not mutually exclusive. (There is nothing wrong with praying for healing, then going to the doctor to receive it, for example!)

It is helpful to think of both psychiatric and spiritual healing as going on in parallel (normally with the psychiatrist's knowledge). The psychiatrist can uncover problems that need to be faced, and perhaps also prescribe physical treatments; at the same time the Christian can take these problems to God and let His power deal with them.

There can be problems of conflict of interest: psychiatrists are not always sympathetic towards Christianity, nor do Christians necessarily respect psychiatry. Mutual tolerance, understanding and respect is essential on *both* sides. (And it should go without saying that you should never stop taking medicines (especially *suddenly*) without first seeking advice from your doctor.)

As in all things, it's a matter of doing what seems most appropriate at the time. In some cases an orthodox psychiatric approach may be appropriate. With a course of tranquillisers or antidepressants and/ or counselling, in a few months the natural healing processes within the body can put an end to the matter.

On the other hand, when we are dealing with deep-seated problems that have been present for years, decades, or even a whole lifetime, it is likely that much more than this is going to be required. Fear at a very deep and intense level can be present, and is not always alleviated by psychiatric treatment. Seeking direct spiritual healing may be very appropriate on these occasions, where the Holy Spirit can focus onto, and heal, specific problems.

The formal Biblical way of healing is by the 'laying on of hands' with prayer, sometimes accompanied by anointing with oil. However, this is not the only way: for example, healing coming as a result of conversion may well not be associated with any of these physical activities.

Talking of conversion, isn't depression a sin? Doesn't it demonstrate your lack of faith? Not at all. Some of the strongest, most godly characters in the Bible went through depressions and emotional torments, totally unrelated to any sin – Elijah and Job, for a start. So it is quite possible to be fully God-directed and God-orientated, yet still be depressed. As we've discovered earlier (see the chapter on Guilt), if there *is* a sin in depression it lies in not *accepting* forgiveness, rather than not seeking it.

On the other hand, there may be a need to forgive or to accept forgiveness; there may be deep-seated guilt about areas of your life that you *feel* you haven't really repented of, and you may well benefit through knowing that you are both acceptable to and blessed by God *whilst still in the middle of your problems*. This deep seated repentance / forgiveness / acceptance / blessing can be a vital force in the inner healing of the wounded Christian's spirit.

Can I elaborate on repentance in this deep form? I have said earlier that many Christians take a very superficial view of depression and say, "It's because you haven't repented enough." These two sorts of repentance are not the same. The repentance involved in spiritual healing may well be where, in the presence of somebody who is laying hands upon you, you reiterate a confession that you have already made. It is, if you like, the formal sealing of the confession / repentance / forgiveness triangle – rather akin to the signing of the register at a wedding: it formally records that the event has been carried out and there can be no arguments about it thereafter. Please *do not* imagine that if you are depressed then you have to repent more, or better. The repentance involved in spiritual healing may well be only a reiteration of what has already gone before, with the proviso that sometimes, during the course of spiritual healing, God may give either you or the one laying hands upon you further insights, and may draw your attention to aspects of your life which you have never previously thought about in relation to your depression. Just as with the marriage service and the signing of the register, so the laying on of hands can be usefully accompanied by a statement of repentance for and renunciation of past sins, followed by a formal declaration of forgiveness. This 'ceremony' (if you like) of wiping the slate clean allows you to know more completely that all that you have confessed really has been taken care of by God.

On the other hand, there may be more to it. There may be hidden reasons why in the past you have not truly been able to *accept* forgiveness: during the laying on of hands this bond may be broken, and healing experienced.

Sometimes the effects of spiritual healing are spectacular: lives changed virtually overnight. On the other hand, the effects may just as easily be slow growing, like yeast. Don't feel obliged to 'feel' different immediately after the laying on of hands – if you don't *feel* any better then be honest and say so. You don't bring any credit upon God nor upon yourself by pretending that things are any different, if they aren't. If you don't *feel* any change don't give up – your healing may be gradual, not instantaneous: a gradual awakening of your mind to a new way of thinking.

Sometimes a physical cure doesn't come. (Note that healing isn't necessarily a cure, though a cure is healing.) Don't forget that Paul prayed three times for his 'thorn in the flesh' to be removed and yet God declined to do it. God presumably had His reasons. The fact that you have requested spiritual healing means that you have been obedient to God and that any problems remaining are there because God knows that you will ultimately be better with them than without them.

Isn't this a bit hardhearted of God? No, it isn't. God has promised that everything that happens to us is ultimately for the best – unfortunately we can't see into the future as He can, so we don't know what He's got in mind for us, and we can't appreciate at this moment why our painful situation is really 'the best'. But remember this: dealing with our depression gives us insights we might otherwise never have; it refines us, sorts us out, makes us knuckle down to learning things we might otherwise be too terrified to approach. In some ways, it's the spiritual equivalent of being thrown in at the deep end – a very quick way to learn that, yes, we really can swim! (See the chapter on The Spiritual Gymnasium for further discussion of this subject.)

God has chosen to work mainly within the laws of science, and He usually works by getting His subjects (Christians) to exercise their God-given talents and ability to get on with the job. This is the basis on which Christian doctors work for most of their lives.   In psychiatry, healing frequently comes when the individual finds answers to his own problems; if we were to be healed miraculously, we'd never go through this learning process, and we'd end up the poorer. It is often better for us to sort out our problems logically. If we do, we can then communicate our new-found understanding to others – which in turn may help them. If, on the other hand, solutions appear supernaturally, it leaves us nothing with which to help others.

My own personal experience of depression has encompassed several different areas of healing. During the long initial depressive episode I felt as if nothing miraculous were happening, and I couldn't understand why God wanted me to undergo it. However, I now know that I learned a great deal of sensitivity through it, and looking back I can see how important it was in my spiritual and psychological development.

Then, much later, I underwent spiritual healing of the 'lancing of the boil' type, in which all the hurts and problems of the years, which had been accumulating deep inside, were let out – and I cried, and cried and cried, tears that I never dreamed I had. And during that period all the things I couldn't cry about at the time I first experienced them (such as my daughter's illness) welled up into my consciousness, and were dissipated.

So healing for me has come in several different forms, over a long period of time. Don't be disappointed if divine healing doesn't immediately happen to you, because that means God wants *you* to sort out your problems. It may be better for you: you'll learn things on the way. It requires hard work to do it yourself – a miracle might be the lazy way out.

29

CREATIVITY AND SENSITIVITY

One of the most significant things I've ever read came from Edith Schaeffer, and it has become one of the guiding lights in my life. To paraphrase her: "God made man in His own image. God is a creator. Man, being made in His image, must also be a creator. Therefore we become less human, and less than God wants us to be, if we fail to be creative. We fulfil our humanity partly through being creative."

When you think about the implications of this it hits you like a thunderbolt. We *measure* human beings by what they create – in fact one of the tests in anthropology for whether a particular skeleton is human or not is whether there is any evidence of tool-making. Given the chance, humans create things. And by 'create' I don't mean writing symphonies or painting masterpieces, I mean that they express themselves in what they do. It can be in the arrangement of a bowl of flowers, or the decor of your room, the pictures that you choose to put above your bed, the things you collect, the way you customise your car. Even your signature is a unique statement of yourself (and graphologists will tell you just how much can be inferred about you from it).

Creativity is the opposite of anonymity. If the only way that you can distinguish your house or flat from others is by the number on the door, because your house looks identical to the other hundred and fifty on the estate, then you become less of a person, more of a number, more anonymous. The antidote to this is to stamp your personality on that house through what you do with it – the way you decorate it, the things you put in it, the mat on the door. (One of my friends has a mat which reads, "Oh no, not you again!")

Creativity has two distinct aspects: creativity that is for *us;* and creativity as a way of communication with *others.*

Creativity is not just 'making something out of nothing'. 'Our creativity' is *'our'* just as much as *'creativity'.* Just as our personality comes across in our signature, so our basic feelings and emotions come across in what we create. Obviously this reaches its highest peaks in the works of the great masters of art, literature and music, but this should not stop each and every person thinking of what they do as being a representation of what they think and what they are. You create in the way you lay the table; that vase of flowers you arranged; that piece of music you chose to put on; those tropical fish so lovingly selected and cared for.

When you do create, you notice firstly how satisfying it is, secondly, how much of yourself you feel is in your creation, and thirdly, how much healing of your inner emotional hurts can occur through your being creative. Surprisingly, you don't necessarily have to set out to express that particular emotion in order for healing to occur. If you are angry, but decide to carve a meticulously beautiful figurine or do some delicate fretwork, then your anger may get transmuted through your effort into the intricacy of your creation, and may be dissipated as a result. Alternatively, if you feel very sad it may paradoxically be quite possible for you to create very happy music or paintings. Tchaikovsky did this in writing *The Nutcracker Suite,* which contains some of the most joyful music ever created, even though it was written during a time of black despair for him. On the other hand it may be appropriate to vent your emotion in exactly the form in which you feel it – one has only got to listen to Mahler's symphonies to feel the angst he felt and which he expresses so well.

Don't be put off because I'm referring to great or well-known art. *Your* creativity is for you, and should be an expression (whatever the standard of its execution) of yourself and your personality – whether happy or sad, peaceful or troubled.

On the other hand, if you want to communicate your thoughts to others using art forms, you need to have a certain amount of technique – sheer self-expression is not the only answer. It is very easy to think one is being creative by 'just doing things' without any formal background or training – and one has only got to look at the 'art' that is produced by children to realise that although that art may mean a lot to them as individuals, nevertheless it does not necessarily convey to others quite what they had intended! Total 'free expression' is not always the same as being creative, because being creative actually requires a certain amount of discipline within which to work. The composer Stravinsky once stated this very perceptively. "I find I have a lot more freedom when I am writing for a small orchestra then for a big one." Too much choice can sometimes be daunting. Have you ever tried to choose a pattern for the curtains? It's all very well when you have a choice of nine alternatives, but once you get into a fabric shop with perhaps two thousand different patterns available, then you begin to get overwhelmed.

Small is Beautiful Too

Things do not have to be big nor 'art' to be creative, and sometimes the things which are small and executed in a relatively circumscribed area can be just as creative as something which is apparently more artistic. The fact that you're not being very original doesn't necessarily matter either. So a thousand people before you, or a hundred thousand people, have painted a still life with a vase and flowers. Never mind – the fact that it is not as original as Picasso's *Guernica* or as valuable as Van Gogh's *Sunflowers* doesn't mean that it isn't of immense importance to you as a creator – so don't be put off! Creation is initially for you alone and will help you to establish your own identity, to express your personality, and to dissipate those intense emotions that you find it hard to come to terms with, or difficult to express purely verbally.

The more that you can create and appreciate others' creations, the more sensitive to them you will become – particularly at an emotional level. Now an increase in sensitivity is a very good thing as far as men and women are concerned. Because we spend so little time thinking about our real emotional needs, we are often very insensitive to the real emotional needs of others. Anything that helps to increase your sensitivity to the unspoken problems and the unsaid feelings of others cannot be bad! The more that you are able to appreciate the creations of others, the better you will come to terms with your own emotions, and with their emotions also.

One of the side effects of trying to be creative is that you notice the outside world more: you become more aware of its natural beauty. You also start to admire and appreciate the beauty that other people have created, and the technique that they have acquired, whether it be as a composer, a painter, a gardener, a writer, a cook or whatever. Being more aware like this makes you a more truly sensitive person.

Let me repeat that the concept of creativity is not limited just to the creation of new works of art. The performing arts are involved – playing music that others have written, or being an actor or actress, or a dancer. (In passing, what a shame that the church has missed out on the use of dance in worship. We are told in the Old Testament that David danced before the Ark of the Lord with all his might and this was obviously an acceptable form of praise as far as God was concerned. Dancing involves *you,* your logic and your emotions, your body, your mind, your soul and your spirit. The person who is dancing feels that he is giving the whole of himself and I am sure that this cannot be a bad thing. Again, because it is non-logical and involves the use of our *bodies* (shock, horror) it has been frowned upon by certain sections of the church, but I do not think that it is right that this should have happened. Incidentally I speak as a complete and utter non-dancer in the 'performing' sense.)

Nor does creation have to involve 'art'. You create when you make models or establish a collection of wild flowers. You create in your job, wherever you have the opportunity to put something of yourself into it: for example, as a receptionist, you can create a warm encouraging atmosphere with which clients are greeted. You create in engineering when you design a structure that does something more efficiently or more smoothly than it has been done before. You can create entirely non-physically – for example in *good* administration, where the administrator is seeking to make the works for which he is responsible run as efficiently and easily as possible. You can create in how you cook: even if it's meat and two veg, the fact that you have put some parsley on top of the potatoes makes it look just that bit different, that much more special.

It's often the little touches that do it. At breakfast in a hotel, one of my young sons said that he would like two poached eggs on toast – and then rather mischievously said, "Could I have a rasher of bacon underneath to make it look like a face?" Well, it came like that – only the cook had also put a little piece of tomato in between to make a nose, and I am sure that the joy with which she did it was matched only by the joy of my two sons on seeing the finished product! It's the little touches that make for creativity, not just the big canvases or big symphonies. It's the way that you dress, the things that you collect, the plants that you choose for the garden; it's where you go for your holidays; it's what you do with your time; it's what you have as a hobby. In short, anything and everything that you do that is an expression of your own individuality is part of being creative, and you will find that there are immense benefits awaiting you once you learn to tap into the creative aspects of your personality.

It is no coincidence that art and music therapy feature prominently in progressive psychiatric hospitals – they enable unspoken feelings and emotions to be vented. How do you convey the intensity of the grief you feel? In words? "I am very sad"? "I am very, very sad"? "I am extremely sad"? Is it not much more appropriate to put on a record of Samuel Barber's *Adagio for Strings* (try it, in the version for string orchestra – I bet you can't listen to it without shedding a tear or two). Then you can say, "I feel like *that*." Emotions by definition are not expressible in words. We must learn to express our deepest emotions in non-verbal ways, or we won't express them properly, and if we don't learn to express our emotions properly they go inwards and eat away at us. In contrast, by using our emotions and by being creative we are able to become more complete, more mature, and nearer to our original state of being 'made in God's image'.

EXERCISE

If you haven't already got one, get a hobby – preferably something in which you put something of yourself. It doesn't have to be grand or arty, but try to make it very personal to you: researching your family tree; collecting stamps on a particular topic that interests you; taking up pottery; playing a musical instrument; learning to play a new sport. The more creative it is, the better; the more you can put something of yourself into it, the more fulfilling you will find it – eventually. Don't expect the benefits immediately – this is something that takes a little time but is very helpful in the end.

30

MATURITY

Why talk about maturity in a book which is essentially about depression? If you've worked systematically through this book, you'll realise how often depression is related to hiccups in the maturing of the individual person, usually brought about because a particular problem has not been solved. What is more, your subconscious *knows* that the problem hasn't been solved – but doesn't know what to do about it. By learning how to become mature, to seek out the ways of wisdom, and to put them into practice in both a Christian and a secular manner, you will find that the problems and conflicts resolve, and as a result your depression disappears. The obverse is also true – once a person has been through a depression he is *much* more mature and usually realises himself how he has matured through his crisis.

For many people adolescence is *the* major time when they get a depression. The problems of growing up, separating from parents, forging a new life, career and life style, dealing with sexuality, courting and all the associated stresses and strains are often more than enough to push you into a depression. Life can be very confusing. As children we saw things in terms of black and white, and the goodies always won. In adult life there are a lot more shades of grey: things are not as clear-cut in the real world, and coming to terms with this requires a great upheaval in emphasis and goals.

Maturity comes by getting through these adolescent crises and finding solutions to the problems that they pose. The converse is also true. Many of our 'problems' are really childhood difficulties that we failed to resolve when we were young, such as coping with the problem of how Mummy still loves you when she punishes you; or perhaps how to make your own decisions about your own life and destiny whilst not actually letting go of the apron strings (or not yet anyway).

When you become mature you are able to look at life in a less aggressive, more mellow way, understanding a little more of why and how the world works as it does, what to get worked up about, and what not to worry about. As the prayer goes, "Lord, grant me the serenity to accept the things that I cannot change, the courage to change the things I can, *and the wisdom to know the difference.*" Because people who are not fully mature get hung up about the wrong things, or get worked up about things out of proportion to their significance, they can get themselves into emotional crises, which in turn can lead to depression.

Acquiring a mature outlook on life does not apply only to adolescents. If there are problems from an earlier part of your life that you should have faced but never managed to, then your maturity will be inhibited until you find answers to the questions that have been bugging you. These questions can be very wide-ranging:

- "How do I learn to like myself when I fail so often?"
- "Is there a God?"
- "If so, what does He think of me?"
- "What do I think of myself?"
- "How will I manage on my own without my parents?"
- "How will I be as a parent in my own right?"
- "Can I do a job properly?"
- "What do I do when I don't match up to what my boss wants me to do?"
- "How do I cope with being a child (to my parents), a husband (to my wife), and a father (to my children) all at one and the same time?"
- "How do I cope with anger / grief / joy?"
- "What is the right thing to do in problems of a tricky or moral nature, such as abortion / homosexuality / war?"
- "Are there absolute answers?"
- "How do I match up the world (where things are often in shades of grey) with the Christian gospel (which often seems so black and white)?"

Getting to grips with these and a thousand other problems is the basis for the gradual development of maturity.

You can also define maturity in terms of law − a question of knowing what is most important and which law takes pre-eminence. And here we have the problem of reconciling apparently conflicting laws, such as the law of love (preventing war) and the need to fight to protect innocent victims.

We come therefore to the problem of *Christian* maturity. What is it? If we know what we are aiming for, and what road we can use to get there, then we will more clearly see what we ought to be doing in any given situation.

Maturity involves knowledge, wisdom, and sensitivity. You may have a lot of knowledge about the Bible, but you need wisdom to know which piece of the Bible to apply to any given situation, and sensitivity to apply it lovingly and appropriately.

Wisdom is derived through knowledge, but is not the same as knowledge. Wisdom is all about understanding the basis of what is happening. For example, what is the next number in this sequence?

1   1   2   3   5   8   13

The answer is 21. It's not an easy sequence to remember, but once you work out that each number is formed by adding the two previous numbers together, then you don't need to see the examples nor learn the list of numbers – you can apply your new law to whatever string of numbers you've got and you know that the next one will be correct. In other words, knowing the underlying law simplifies things – provided it *is* the correct law!

The Bible is exactly like this. Having passages on a particular subject spread throughout the Bible is rather like seeing the numbers in a sequence. Once you understand the basic law that governs *all* those verses, then you are well on the way to acquiring Christian wisdom in that subject. But note, it was the complete sequence of numbers which told us what the underlying law is. If you were to take the central sequence of numbers, i.e.

2   3   5   8

you might derive a law which said (erroneously) that the difference between each number and the next one goes up by one each time – so the difference between 2 and 3 is 1, between 3 and 5 is 2, between 5 and 8 is 3. If you only worked on those four numbers you would incorrectly assume that the next number in the sequence was 12. Again, this is rather like somebody who is trying to find the Christian approach to a particular problem, but bases his understanding of the situation only on a selected number of quotes from the Bible. On the basis of inadequate information he has inferred an inadequate law. Therefore *the first lesson in acquiring a mature understanding of Christian behaviour is to have a thorough knowledge of the whole of the Bible, not just selected fragments of it.*

The second principle of wisdom is to understand that *there is a hierarchy of laws* – as C.S. Lewis aptly put it, "If you fail to obey the law of prudence you may well find yourself obeying the law of gravity." This hierarchy applies particularly in the non-physical and spiritual worlds: at appropriate times certain laws are superseded by others. It is perhaps easier to see this in reverse – to see what an immature person does when he tries to treat all laws as equal. The classic example of this is the schoolboy who is told that no one is to leave the dormitory after ten o'clock at night. On a subsequent occasion he is told that if the fire-bell rings everybody is immediately to stop what they're doing and assemble in the playground. He puts his hand up. "Sir, sir", he says craftily, "you told us that we weren't to leave the dormitory after ten o'clock at night." A typical schoolboy comment, and one that shows why a schoolboy is a schoolboy and not a man! He has a greater interest in trying to show up ambiguities in supposedly equal laws than in understanding the necessity for one law to override another.

The third principle of wisdom is that *the nearer you are to the truth, the simpler the law*. In the physical world, things seem to boil down to very simple and eloquent solutions. We are, for example, all made up of various combinations of ninety-two naturally occurring elements, and these elements are made up of protons, electrons and neutrons (plus one or two other particles); and as if this were not simple enough, it may well be that all these subatomic particles are in fact made up of just one building block (like a giant Lego model!). We have also found that there is a relationship between energy and matter which is a very simple one (the famous $E=mc^2$ equation of Einstein's theory of relativity). So it seems that the whole of the universe may be made out of one basic particle which itself is interchangeable with energy. Just think of it – the *whole* of the universe made of just one particle repeated in various forms throughout. Staggeringly simple. Physically, the ultimate law – how amazingly, elegantly simple, yet how varied in all its applications!

Scientists usually know that they are on the right track when the results come out in a simple fashion like this. You may know that the planets appear to move very slowly against the background of the stars, sometimes being in one constellation, sometimes being in another. Plot out the path that a planet takes against the stars over the course of two or three months and you will find that it is the most odd loop-shape. The ancients thought that the sun, the moon and all the stars went round the earth, and spent ages trying to work out a system of cogs on the 'heavenly dome' that could account for such a bizarre motion. Now we know that the earth goes round the sun, and the path that each planet traces out against the night sky is very simply explained by the path of two planets, (ourselves and the planet we're looking at) moving round the sun at differing speeds.

So in the scientific world we find that as we understand things better, the laws governing them seem to get simpler.

If this is true in the physical world, then why not in the spiritual world? We can see this in action. The Lord's Prayer has 69 words, the Ten Commandments 296, and the European Commission's Report on the Import of Duck Eggs 27,251! The better the law, the simpler it gets. You can go even simpler than the Lord's Prayer – Thomas Aquinas said, "Love God and do as you like" (seven words), which of course implies that if you love God, then what you want to do will be what He wants you to do; "Love your neighbour as yourself" (five words); "God is love" (three words), or even just "Love". It gets simpler and simpler as you go on like this, but deeper and more profound. Unfortunately, as the phrases get simpler you have to define more precisely the meaning of the words you use, and this is where things can get more complex – you have to understand what you mean by an apparently simple phrase such as "God is love".

This is again where law comes in. Think of the problems of a Borneo tribesman on being introduced to a car and a road and being told to 'drive safely'. That simple phrase will mean absolutely nothing to him. On the other hand, if you teach him that you drive on the correct side of the road, that in built-up areas you're not supposed to go above the speed limit, when to give way to other road-users, and so on, then he will start to get an idea of what you mean when you subsequently say, "Drive safely."

But note that to 'drive safely' doesn't mean that you have to obey the minutiae of all the laws. Ambulance drivers and firemen drive safely – totally ignoring speed limits and red lights and often going onto the right-hand side of the road! Yet they *do* drive safely, because they understand at a deeper level that 'drive safely' implies that they should be aware of all the little restrictions they have had to obey in the past, and know exactly when *not* to apply them because there is a bigger and more overriding principle at stake – somebody's life is in danger. This is the hierarchy of laws coming into action again – which law is the greater, and which laws are to be ignored because of the application of the greater law.

This is precisely analogous to the Christian situation. We have a lot of ceremonial rules and regulations in the Old Testament that were given to teach the Jews the basics of faith and godly living. Now that Christ has come, a lot of those laws are no longer appropriate. Christ has fulfilled them (not swept them away), but in fulfilling those laws He has also implied (like 'drive safely') that there are now a lot of laws which are no longer appropriate and therefore no longer applicable – such as the ceremonial laws about circumcision, animal sacrifice, and ritual cleanliness. He has come and in His death created a greater law of cleanliness, forgiveness, and holiness which supersedes the others.

Areas like the application of Biblical laws can be where Christians get into difficulties. If you don't understand the heirarchy of laws, or if your concepts of the laws themselves are wrong because you have only derived them from a part of the Bible, then you will not necessarily do the 'correct' Christian thing because you will be applying the laws incorrectly.

For example, consider the person who doesn't understand the underlying balance necessary between the principles of forgiveness, love, and justice, especially in relation to the way in which God acts. Apply these attributes incorrectly, and you end up with a concept of a God who is vengeful at the times when it would seem appropriate to be loving, and unjust because He would appear to be too forgiving. On the other hand, sort out your understanding of the laws (and, by implication, how and where to apply them) and suddenly everything drops into place, and peace, order, love and justice are seen magnificently displayed in the person and nature of God.

Maturity covers all areas of our personality. It is not just our logic which has to mature – our emotions must be mature as well. We must know what to do, but we must also have the right emotions to accompany it. The person who is logically mature but emotionally icy cold (the 'Sherlock Holmes' type) is not a mature person overall. Unfortunately our society tends to value logic and denigrate emotion, so the 'Sherlock Holmes' image is one that a lot of people would like to have. It is, however, not real maturity. Getting the emotions right is not easy, particularly in the sort of society we currently have where emotions are somewhat frowned on. (In fact, our society is more bothered about emotional*ism,* which is probably a good thing to frown on, but in doing so we go overboard and get rid of true *emotion* at the same time, which is not helpful.) Please see the chapter on Emotions and their healing for a further discussion of this subject.

All of our personality has to be mature – logic, emotions, spirit. It is no use having mature logic and emotions if spiritually we are babies – this is the condition of many of our so-called 'wise' men (in earthly terms) and it is this unbalanced type of 'wisdom' that the Bible condemns. The truly wise person is mature in knowledge, logic, emotion *and* spirit.

In practical terms, maturity is about having the wisdom and the sense not to get involved in things that you can't change. This doesn't mean being resigned to one's fate, but applying common sense and realising that there is no point in expending energy trying to change something which inherently cannot be changed. We are, after all, living in an imperfect world, and it is always going to remain imperfect. Even as Christians there is no way that we will be able to create heaven on earth, and it is potentially dangerous to think that we could do so: we are inevitably going to be frustrated. Instead we should accept patiently those things that, at a human level, we cannot change, or don't have the time or energy to change.

It is also important to know what to get involved in, rather than thinking that you should do absolutely everything that comes into your field of view. The mature person will know where he is going and what he is aiming for. In particular the mature person knows when to say "No". But he doesn't just say "No" to things which are wrong, he says "No" to things which are inappropriate. If, under God, it isn't right for him to get involved, in what may be a thoroughly worthy cause, he will say "No" to it, even though it may be the weekly prayer meeting / an evangelistic rally / preaching / witnessing. If he hasn't got the time for it, or if he knows that this particular type of work is not really within his ambit, he is the wiser for not trying to do it. Instead he can concentrate on those areas to which he really is called. Nor will he feel guilty about saying "No", because he has worked out where he is going, and why.

Conversely, the immature Christian may well waste his efforts running round chasing his tail. All he generates is heat, light, and hot air. In the long term, the value of his work may be far less than he imagines, even though he may well be involved in many 'good' aspects of church life. 'Jack of all trades and master of none' is just as applicable in the Christian sphere as in the secular, and sadly there are many in church circles to whom this applies.

In maturing you will sort out many of the underlying problems driving your depression onward. Being more mature means that you become a more 'directed' person, of more use to God because you spend your time concentrating on what He wants you to do, acquiring those attributes and talents that He wants you to have. Through studying the Bible thoroughly you will more accurately understand what the Christian response should be in a given situation. Finally, as you become fully mature logically, emotionally and spiritually your conscience will also mature (see the chapter on Conscience to find out why). As a result it will be less 'tender', more appropriate, and more Christian, and having a mature conscience in turn reduces your level of unnecessary anxiety.

EXERCISE

Maturity isn't something you can gain by doing a specific exercise! It's a lot of things – knowledge, wisdom, attitude, spirituality. On the other hand, it *is* possible to help yourself along the road to maturity through learning things at a deeper level – not to acquire mere knowledge, but to obtain understanding, which is a different thing altogether.

To show the sort of thing I mean, try doing a series of Bible studies around a specific subject. You'll need a Bible, of course, and a suitable concordance (don't forget that you need the same version of concordance as the translation you use.) It may help to have a more general guide, such as *The Lion Handbook to the Bible,* or *The Illustrated Bible Dictionary.*

Instead of just reading a passage from the Bible, try chasing an idea through its pages, from start to finish. Take a theme and look up all the major references to it: then see if you can find additional occasions when the subject is referred to, but not named (for example, the Incarnation is seldom referred to as such).

Try one or more of these subjects to study in this way:

- The concept of being 'chosen'
- Covenants
- Brothers
- The land (of Israel)
- The tabernacle
- Heaven

No clues on how to begin? Let's take 'Brothers':

- Cain and Abel
- Isaac and Ishmael (half-brothers)
- Jacob and Esau (dissimilar twins)
- Joseph and his brothers, whose offspring formed the tribes of Israel
- James the brother of Jesus
- The early church as a brotherhood
- Jesus as a brother

When you've gone a little way into the subject, you'll find your ideas have changed, widened, matured. You'll begin to see the subject in a broader perspective – across the whole sweep of the Bible, as an *idea* rather than a physical thing. Then, because you understand the meaning of the concept that much better, you will be the better equipped to apply it to answer the questions: "Who is my brother?" "What does 'being a brother' mean?"

Maturity, especially Christian maturity, is this approach, applied widely.

31

RESOLUTION

The natural pattern of a depression is for it to resolve spontaneously over a number of months. Assisted or unassisted, recovery is not smooth: it's a series of ups and downs, better one minute, not so good the next.

Many people have minor depressive episodes which eventually resolve spontaneously and for which they need no medication or psychotherapy; for others the problem is much deeper, more intense and emotionally very painful.

The effect of treatment with medicines is not to stop the depression, but to alleviate the symptoms whilst the body is going through this spontaneous healing process. Except for depressions which are caused by an underlying biochemical or hormonal defect, medicines don't get rid of depression; they merely cover up the symptoms.

Reducing the effects of depression can be a good or a bad thing, depending upon the circumstances. Even if your depression is going to resolve spontaneously, it may be helpful to alleviate the *symptoms* by using medicines. However, in some circumstances this can actually be counterproductive – it may be better for you to find the cause of your depression and deal with it, for if the symptoms are covered up you will have no internal stimulus to get to grips with the underlying problem.

How do you know whether delving into your personal problems will help? I suggest you leave it up to your doctor to decide – he will be able to assess whether you have the sort of depression which is best helped by this type of approach.

In general, if your depression doesn't seem to be getting better, or is accompanied by distressing and intense emotions or recurring insoluble thoughts, then psychotherapy may be helpful. Under these circumstances medication alone may be insufficient to effect a permanent cure, and it may be appropriate for you to delve a little more into the mental causes of your depression.

Because depression is such a long and intensely uncomfortable illness, it is common for sufferers to seek help from any available source. However, there are dangers in this. Firstly, you may not want to face the thing that is *really* troubling you (such as your relationship with your parents) and may go off hunting for acceptable alternatives, such as hormonal imbalances. This doesn't help because you will never truly get better if you don't get to grips with your real problems, but instead try to address imaginary problems, or problems that you have only to a minor degree. You think it unlikely that people would behave like this and not attack the *real* source of their difficulties? Don't believe it – GPs' surgeries are full of people like this who will seek any possible alternative to addressing their real problem.

The second and more insidious danger in seeking help from any source is that it is easy to read a book, listen to a sermon or read an article, and think to yourself, "Ah yes, this is the answer – I must do this and all will be well." So you try it – and nothing much happens (because it wasn't an appropriate thing to do in the first place). So you try the next thing ... and the next thing ... and the next. Disillusionment follows.

People who are depressed do have a tendency to think that comments and advice (and criticism) are 'for them'. This is one of the reasons why depressed people find it difficult to listen to sermons, because they pick out any condemnatory aspect and think that this is 'God speaking to them'. It takes some time, and a certain degree of Christian maturity, to realise that while something may be true, it may not necessarily be true *for you, at this time*.

If you feel 'challenged', the acid test is to ask *if other people think that it is an appropriate verse for you*. You would be surprised how often something which seems emotionally very relevant appears as anything but to an impartial observer. If in doubt, ask your friends (those who are close enough to talk to about such things). You may get a surprise!

Therefore, learn to be very discriminatory about the things that you apply to yourself. Use your logic circuits! A sense of balance is necessary to put things into perspective: depressed people often lose this balanced attitude, which is why it helps to have a confidant(e), a mentor, or a therapist who can tell you when you're getting things out of proportion.

*   *   *

Recovery from a depression takes place in a non-uniform manner. It is not like walking up a valley onto the hillside, but more like climbing a high mountain peak: you start at the bottom, and go up to where you think the peak is, only to find as you come to the top that the real peak is much further on, *across another valley*. The trouble is that when you start to go down into that second valley you feel that you are descending to where you started, not realising that the new valley bottom is considerably higher than the original valley bottom where you began!

So why is this important? Simple. Once you start to come out of a depression and feel a bit better, the thought of going back into the original depressed state is, quite frankly, terrifying. When you progress beyond that first little peak and realise that you are on the way down *again,* then the natural reaction is sheer panic. You feel immediately that you are going back to where you were before, and that there will be no ultimate solution of your distress.

At this stage it is important to realise what is happening. These oscillations are quite natural and quite normal in the recovery from depression. *Everybody* gets them, and the trick is to remind yourself constantly that you *are* getting better and that you *are* getting nearer to that peak, even if you have first to go down to get there. Remind yourself that the new valley you have come to is, even at its worst point, way above your original starting point, and recognise too that this new valley will eventually flatten out – then you will start to go up again on the far side.

The fear of going downhill is colossal, overwhelmingly frightening, and, unless you have experienced it yourself, quite unbelievable. Sometimes you can be so terrified at the thought of going downhill that you would rather stay where you are, partly better, than descend again into the depths in order to get down into that valley and climb up the other side to full recovery. You can get scared to move from your current position in case you feel worse, despite the possibility of ultimately getting better.

It is important to ensure that you *do* keep moving onwards and that you are well supported emotionally at those times when you have to go down into the valley; the same applies when you consciously choose to go down into the valley to face things which make you feel worse, whilst attempting to sort them out.

Therefore, don't be fearful when you find yourself going downhill for a time. It doesn't mean you are going back to where you started. Instead, remember that this is part of the natural process of the disease, that you will eventually bottom out and start to come up again. If you think of your depression over a long enough timescale, the day-to-day ups and downs will seem less worrisome than they do at the time you experience them. So instead of looking for progress from day to day, or from week to week, measure it from month to month or even from quarter to quarter.

It is easy to get disillusioned because you cannot see any great and obvious change. But just because you can't see the change doesn't mean that it isn't happening – as a quick glance in the mirror at the crow's-feet or the balding head will remind you! You never actually saw any of these things starting, nor observed the hair falling out in handfuls, but you can see the difference in your looks by comparison with the picture of yourself taken two years ago! The changes are very definite – but too small to be perceived from day to day.

Your depression will get better in exactly the same way. Don't measure your current state of health by how you were this time last week. Compare it instead with how you were six months ago. Once you do this, things take on a different perspective and you may well be able to see with a thrill that in the intervening months you've actually sorted out a lot of the problems that underlie your depression.

One of the prime causes of unease in depression is to live entirely on how you *feel*: as we've seen in the chapter on Emotions, it is important to experience fully the emotions that are appropriate to the events of that day, rather than to dwell upon emotions that come to you from your past. Therefore, concentrate on the emotions that you should be experiencing from the day's events, and ignore as far as possible those emotions that are coming to you from the past.

★   ★   ★

The actual manner of healing takes lots of different forms and depends upon the exact source of your depression. If you have one distinct cause for your depression – such as your relationship with your boss, or a hormonal imbalance – then finding this out and rectifying it may result in a swift resolution of your problems.

However, for most people depression is a complex affair with many interlinked causes; so it usually takes a lot of time and patience to get free from it. A few general rules are appropriate:

1. Look after yourself, both physically and mentally. Don't get overstressed. Have enough time for recreation.

2. Find a suitable Christian friend you can unburden to.

3. Reappraise your life style to see if you are doing too much, or doing the wrong things.

4. Try to deal with today's problems today, and consciously avoid worrying about the future, or grieving over the past.

5. If there are obvious causes for your current depression, attack them head-on, where this is possible.

6. Express your emotions: and use your day-to-day emotions properly, whilst at the same time delving down into those emotions coming at you from the past, to work out just where they come from and what they mean.

7. Learn to deal properly with feelings of anger.

8. You may need to learn different ways of responding to problems generated by other people. You may have to be more decisive, and avoid being pushed around quite so much.

9. Above all, learn that God loves you so much that even if you were the only person who had ever wanted to become a Christian, Christ would still have come and died for you alone. You are very acceptable in His sight – and don't you forget it!

Don't worry! (Potentially trite advice, I know, but I want you to take it on board and consciously choose to think of other things when you are tempted either to worry about what could happen, or to ruminate on what has happened in the past.) Concentrate on getting your life sorted out piece by piece and eventually the whole lot will fit together. All that matters is that you continually make progress (judged on a six-monthly basis). Keep at it! You'll get there in the end.

★   ★   ★

Finally, a word about ... bravery. (What has bravery got to do with it, I hear you ask?) The braver you are, the quicker your depression will go. Apart from the 'biochemical' causes, depression consists of old, unsolved problems which have come back to haunt you. They are painful because they are unsolved and because you *know* they are unresolved. It is easier to retreat from the task of solving them, because to face them is painful. If you retreat from solving them, the immediate pain goes, but then you're stuck – you can't move forward because your problems will hinder and upset you, yet your present situation is less than desirable.

It's rather like being on a desert island, desperately wanting to cross to the mainland, but being aware that the water in between is shark-infested. As long as you stay on the island you are safe (but in the wrong place). Only by risking a fight with the sharks can you get across to where you want to be.

Whichever analogy you pick – going down into a valley, or crossing shark-infested waters – it is still a matter of bravery before you get to your goal. You have to face your problems. If you don't, you'll stay on the island, or halfway up that mountain, without ever getting to the top.

And it does take bravery, too. It takes bravery to solve those problems which were so hot to handle that you buried them in your subconscious. It takes bravery *really* to face up to what you are, warts and all. It takes bravery to find that what you thought you were doing for noble reasons turns out to be not so noble after all (but be encouraged – it also works the other way round!).

It takes bravery to recognise that perhaps the reason you married your husband was because you needed a replacement father; it takes bravery to recognise that you turn the other cheek because at heart you're a coward; it takes bravery to admit that you've got homosexual tendencies; it takes bravery to admit your faults; it takes bravery to delve deep into your innermost secrets and fears and the skeletons in the cupboard, haul them out and have a good long look at them – but it's necessary, because you'll never get better properly without it.

One word of advice – it's better to be brave in company. If you are going to face your fears, make sure you are as well supported as you can be. Don't pick the week when your closest confidant(e) is on holiday to attack your biggest problems or your deepest fears. Being brave is exhausting (and exhilarating). A supply of friends is helpful, and knowing that your friends are praying for you at this time is also a great help.

Only when you eventually do decide to get off your desert island (but *only* then) do you find, as the sharks come up to you, that they actually have no teeth ... but you can't work that out on the island: you have to come up close and stare them in the face. And as you get nearer the mainland, you'll look back and see to your surprise that the sharks were only minnows – you were looking at them through a magnifying glass, so they were out of proportion to their real significance. Thus it is with psychological problems – huge before you come to them, minute once you've dealt with them. So be brave, be patient, be realistic. Getting better is hard work, and sometimes a long slog, but worth it in the end, not just because you *are* better, but because of what you learn on the way.

And above all, at all times, remember that, whatever He may want you to change in the future:

> *God loves you, as you are,* ***now.***

EXERCISE

Are you feeling better yet? Don't worry if you're not! Depression may take weeks or months to lift – I hope you didn't think you'd get better immediately you'd finished reading this book!

There are lots of things to say at this point. Most important is this: now you know that your depression isn't as a result of God turning His face away from you, you can at last begin to go forward, knowing He is with you. *But this doesn't mean life is suddenly going to be all sweetness and light.* You have to learn a lot of very important lessons, and, as with exams, learning the work beforehand takes *time*. You may have a lot to learn and a lot to unlearn, and you may need to adopt a whole new set of attitudes. It won't happen overnight – there's too much of it.

So don't expect miracles (what an odd thing to say in a Christian book!). Getting out of your depression requires a long hard slog on your part: a miracle cure wouldn't equip you for the future as would getting on and doing the work yourself. (The real miracle is how patiently God will wait, guiding and correcting us until we have made the changes that are appropriate.)

There are several parallel exercises that will help you at the moment.

Firstly, now that you've worked through the book and understand some of the reasons why you might be depressed, make a list of your own problems; and against each entry, put what you think might be an answer. You might have:

1. I often feel a failure in the eyes of God.

   I must remind myself daily that God loves and accepts me as I am, whatever I may *feel* about the matter.

2. My father left when I was six, so I find it difficult to trust God as a Father.

   I must consciously learn from other 'father figures' how real fatherhood implies constant, unremitting care.

3. I feel other people don't trust me.

   This is a feeling: when I ask others about it they say it's not true. I must remind myself frequently that this is a *feeling*, nothing more. If I behave as though others trust me, it will give them more confidence in me, and ultimately give me more confidence in what they *really* feel about me.

4. I have a lot of problems over whether science disproves God.

   I must be brave and read up on this. There are lots of good Christian books I could get stuck into.

5. Given the opportunity, I tend to tell everyone about my problems, to gain sympathy.

   This is sinful, and I must learn to stop it.

....and so on. Your diary may contain completely different things – it doesn't matter what is in it so long as it's relevant to *your* problems. It may be a good idea to discuss the problems and possible solutions with close Christian friends – they may have ideas and insights you'd not thought of.

*   *   *

You do need to be brave. Depressions often come when we are stuck at a particular point in our emotional development and haven't the courage to go on. *Face your problems*. It's the quickest way to get rid of them. God loves you, as you are, now – but He also wants you to develop fully into the person He designed you to be, so get cracking on it!

– Appendix 1 –
'ALTERNATIVE' MEDICINE

If you are a devotee of science fiction you will doubtless have heard of Arthur C. Clarke, inventor of the communication satellite, and author of the film and book *2001*. His third law runs as follows:

> "Any significant increase in science or technology is indistinguishable from witchcraft."

This is one of the most perceptive comments on science and religion that I have ever heard. Think of the effect of flying machines on primitive tribesmen and you'll get the point.

Christians have often run away from science, especially science they do not understand, and proclaimed it as being of the Devil. It was on this count that Galileo was arraigned before the Inquisition. Doubtless the first users of electricity were considered to be in league with the Devil when they produced flashes and blue sparks and caused frogs' legs to twitch.

It is very dangerous to dismiss as unchristian anything that is inexplicable on current scientific theory. Until a short time ago it was aerodynamically 'proved' that bumble bees were incapable of flight. This unfortunately does not seem to have been communicated to the bumble bees because they still kept buzzing around fertilising the flowers, but the 'facts' were there for all to see – until a slightly more astute engineer realised that the calculations for the bumble bee had failed to take into account the forward movement of their wings: once this was included the theory made sense, everything dropped neatly into place and bumble bees were allowed to fly again!

It is very, very dangerous for Christians immediately to condemn those aspects of science and medicine which they do not understand, (and which perhaps *nobody* understands). For example, consider acupuncture, which is an ancient Chinese system of medicine. In China it was originally backed up by *theory* which can best be described as scientific rubbish. On the other hand, some of the *practical* aspects of acupuncture seem to work. The *theory* stated that there were two non-material forces called the Yin and the Yang which were said to be out of balance in the diseased individual: inserting acupuncture needles at appropriate points in the body was thought to help restore this balance. These concepts of Yin and Yang have completely non-Christian overtones, and because of this some Christians have wondered whether acupuncture is appropriate to use, or whether it is occult.

Although the original theory appears to be completely up the spout, this doesn't necessarily stop the practical side from being scientific. Investigation shows that acupuncture points are often associated with areas of reduced electrical charge in the skin.

We now have a scientific explanation of how acupuncture may work. It's connected with the way in which the body perceives pain, called the 'gate control theory'. There's no need to involve talk of Yin and Yang – sticking needles in various parts of the body can have very physiological effects.

So, on careful investigation, acupuncture seems to include scientific effects that were discovered by the Chinese: unfortunately they put a whole load of unnecessary, quasi-religious theory on top. Scientists and Christians need to recognise that some of its practical aspects may well prove to be valid, even though the original theory certainly isn't.

Equally, we must be on our guard to ensure that *we* don't hijack a perfectly acceptable scientific treatment by placing a lot of extra ideas on top of it. It's easy to do! For example, vitamins are essential in small doses – but there is very little evidence to suggest that megadoses are good (and they can be harmful, depending on the vitamin). Here we have a 'small is good, so more must be better' approach – illogical, untested, inappropriate and, in some circumstances, dangerous.

In other words, as Christians, we must be sure to use our God-given minds critically, and not throw out things which we don't understand, or which don't seem to fit into our current scientific understanding. Equally, we must be wary of unproven techniques, especially those with possible occult connections.

*   *   *

'Alternative' medicine is very fashionable today, and is often allied with a 'back to nature' reaction against the heavily scientific and technological orientation of our society. Because they do not use drugs or medicines, these alternative therapists have a particular appeal for those who do not like the idea of 'poisoning' themselves with medications. As a medical practitioner who has spent some time looking into the claims of various complementary medical approaches, I think it is fair to say that they can be divided into three groups.

The first group consists of **methods of treatment that are valid pragmatically but have not yet found favour with the medical**

establishment, mainly because the relevant scientific tests have not yet been carried out to prove that these treatments do work. This is not as daft a problem as it sounds – for example, it is virtually impossible to test homoeopathy according to existing scientific principles because homoeopathy is specifically tailored to each patient, and it's not easy to devise a proper scientific test-bed to take into account these variations.

Treatments in this group may well not be accepted by 'orthodox' doctors, because although there may be practical evidence that this approach works, there is no theory behind it. Some people are scared to accept a treatment for which there is no current scientific rationale.

In other words, this group consists of valid treatments whose manner of action is not yet worked out. I would include in this group osteopathy, chiropractic, and probably both homoeopathy and acupuncture. (It is interesting that twenty years ago acupuncture was thought of as being 'fringe', but it is now becoming more and more acceptable as orthodox medicine, though it must be said that a sizeable group of Christians have considerable anxieties about the wisdom of getting involved with it.)

The second group consists of **treatments which have no effect in themselves and whose response depends upon the degree of attention given to the patient** – technically this is called the placebo response. In other words, the patient gets better because of the *attention* given to him or her, not because of the *treatment*.

Thirdly, there are **types of treatment linked with the occult,** which should be avoided like the plague. I would include in this group meditative yoga and transcendental meditation (TM), both of which have a background of eastern and mystic religions, and both of which include meditative techniques involving 'emptying the mind'. (The *relaxation* techniques in some varieties of yoga may be all right but the *meditative* techniques are not.) Note that there are many different varieties of yoga, which vary in their depth of occultic involvement. In some forms of meditation the subject uses a 'mantra' which is a word given by the teacher, to be repeated over and over again in order to induce a state of relaxation and altered consciousness. This mantra often turns out to be the name of a Hindu god.

From the Christian point of view, meditation and relaxation intended to induce altered states of consciousness (as in transcendental meditation and yoga) should be avoided. They involve a conscious emptying of the mind, in a way which those who have undergone it suggest is unchristian. It is quite true that many of the more *basic* yoga techniques are broadly similar to medical relaxation, and hence may be helpful, but nevertheless there is danger in starting off on a course of action, the end of which is not quite clear. Therefore it is probably better to stick to orthodox medical relaxation techniques rather than getting involved in yoga.

Hypnosis is a different problem – in hypnosis an altered state of consciousness is achieved by techniques akin to relaxation, and then ideas are deposited in the mind when it is in a particularly receptive state. These memories are then replayed by the mind at times of stress. For instance, someone who is trying to stop smoking may be told under hypnosis that when he next sees a cigarette he will feel it is distasteful, and that he will not want to smoke it. When next offered a cigarette he may feel revulsion for it, and hence find giving up smoking much easier.

Despite the apparent simplicity of this technique, it does involve altered states of consciousness and many Christians with experience of the occult advise that hypnotherapy should be avoided.

There are various sorts of relaxation and meditation that a Christian *can* use. Purely medical relaxational techniques are very valid and helpful, especially in those who are overstressed. Consciously relaxing the body, breathing evenly and so on, can be a very good thing. Similarly meditation, when one concentrates quietly on some specific aspect of God or of the Christian life, can be a very edifying technique. Christian meditation involves *filling* the mind (with things of the Spirit) rather than *emptying* it.

*   *   *

It should go without saying that anything to do with 'faith healing', other than that which is done in a specifically Christian context, should be avoided at all costs. Any faith healing where there is the laying on of hands *without* the invocation of the power of God, Jesus or the Holy Spirit falls into this category, and is likely to be occult.

*   *   *

How many of these techniques have relevance in depression? Probably very few. The danger is that people stumble into yoga, transcendental meditation or similar practices imagining that the techniques they use are beneficial. They are not, and involvement in any of these subjects should be avoided.

On the other hand, purely *medical* relaxation techniques and *Christian* meditation are both acceptable and appropriate for those who are stressed or tense.

– Appendix 2 –
POSSESSION AND OPPRESSION

Demonic possession is mentioned in the Bible as the cause of many ills. Jesus Himself cast out a number of devils, notably in Legion (Mark 5:9 and Luke 8:30). However, the Bible mentions disease and possession as being two distinct and separate things: Jesus both cast out demons, and also healed people who were 'sick of a fever', with 'diverse diseases', who 'had an issue of blood', and skin diseases (possibly leprosy), and in none of these cases does the Bible raise any question of demonic involvement. So how far is demonic involvement relevant to modern-day depression?

There is no doubt in my mind that, clinically, demonic possession occurs today, but it is quite distinct from other psychological conditions. It is *not that common,* and the symptoms and signs are quite different from those of depression. However, it is not helpful for a depressed person to think too much about this subject, because when you are depressed, your ability to assess yourself is shot to bits, and it is all too easy to imagine that various symptoms of demonic possession might apply to you.

Therefore I'm not going to tell you what the symptoms and signs of demonic possession are! However, if you are mentally unwell and in the past have had *considerable* involvement with the occult (such as ouija boards, tarot cards, and seances) then it may be appropriate for you to get help. (This also applies if the involvement with the occult was not by yourself, but by a close relative, such as parents or grandparents.) Having a medium for a grandmother really can cause problems of oppression and possession for, say, the grandchildren.

How do you get help and advice? You could tell your minister and ask his advice. But this is unlikely to be of help if your minister is very liberal – he may not even recognise the existence of the occult! In this case you might like to write to:

The Evangelical Alliance
186 Kennington Park Road,
London SE11 4BT

who will be able to put you in touch with someone in your area who will be able to advise and help you, as appropriate.

– Appendix 3 –
FOOD ALLERGIES

Food allergies can sometimes cause depression, anxiety and other mental phenomena. Diagnosing food allergy is not simple, mainly because it doesn't behave as you might expect.

Any of the following symptoms may point to the possibility of a food allergy: migraine, asthma, eczema, irritable bowel syndrome (colitis), Crohn's disease, ulcerative colitis, hayfever, or hives. If there is a personal and /or family history of any of these illnesses, then there is an increased chance that your depression might be food-related.

Patients with food sensitivity often find their symptoms vary in intensity from day to day. They are often non-specifically unwell / fuddled, and may have prominent bags or dark rings under their eyes; they may have a long-standing inability to lose or gain weight, or have marked changes in weight. They often eat certain foods repetitively.

Diagnosis is simple in theory, but difficult in practice. Firstly, skin tests are *unreliable*. Secondly, because we eat so many foods repetitively, you can't just eat a food and watch for a reaction: you must omit a food for five days and see if your symptoms improve, and then recur when you reintroduce that food.

The best way to organise this is to omit all your usual foods for about five days: to avoid discomfort from hunger you can eat as much as you want from a limited range of foods that you don't usually eat – often my recommendation is turkey and rice (and *nothing* else – sea salt can be used for flavouring, but not spices nor gravy thickeners). The only drink is water. Don't use toothpaste – salt will do instead. If you are allergic to a particular food then during the first day or so of the elimination diet your symptoms are likely to get *worse* (surprisingly, to the layman) and then improve gradually, until by about day five you are feeling much better than usual. Then you reintroduce foods one at a time: if your symptoms return after eating a particular foodstuff, it shows it's one of the culprits.

Sounds simple, doesn't it! It is in most cases, but there are lots of little traps.

Two *don'ts*:

- DON'T do food allergy testing without first consulting your doctor, especially if you have asthma, intermittent swelling of the lips or tongue, or any serious diseases such as diabetes or heart problems, or if you are pregnant.

- DON'T reintroduce large quantities of food at a time, *particularly if you are suffering from hives or asthma, and especially in children with these problems.* If in doubt, talk to your GP.

If you do identify a food sensitivity you may have to avoid the particular food for some time – probably a number of years, if not for the rest of your life. Make sure that you don't eat the food by mistake, as things pop up in unexpected places – there's wheat in mustard and processed meats, cornflour in toothpaste, and milk solids in many tablets.

★   ★   ★

I can't possibly do justice to such a complex subject in a few paragraphs. There is a good book about food allergies called *Not All in the Mind* by Dr. Richard Mackarness, published in paperback by Pan. It's well worth getting, and will fill in all the details.